Leadership Style and Soviet Foreign Policy

LEADERSHIP STYLE AND SOVIET FOREIGN POLICY

Stalin, Khrushchev, Brezhnev, Gorbachev

James M. Goldgeier

The Johns Hopkins University Press
Baltimore and London

© 1994 *The Johns Hopkins University Press*
All rights reserved
Printed in the United States of America on acid-free paper

03 02 01 00 99 98 97 96 95 94   5 4 3 2 1

The Johns Hopkins University Press
2715 North Charles Street
Baltimore, Maryland 21218-4319
The Johns Hopkins Press Ltd., London

ISBN 0-8018-4866-0

Library of Congress Cataloging-in-Publication Data will be
found at the end of this book.

A catalog record for this book is available
from the British Library.

Contents

Preface

When a world leader is confronted with a difficult foreign policy decision, there are a multitude of questions he must ask himself. What is the balance of forces and interests? What are my domestic political constraints? Which advisers should I trust? When has the country faced a similar threat or opportunity?

These are the questions that concern most discourses about foreign policy. But there is one fundamental question that decision makers ask themselves that typical analyses usually ignore: What strategies and tactics have worked for me before in similar situations? World leaders have a history, and that history is shaped to a great extent by their experiences at home during their rise to power. Most modern world leaders, after all, come to power trained not as diplomats but as politicians. And their experience as politicians has taught them lessons about how to deal with friends and foes that they carry with them into the international arena.

This important connection between key domestic political experiences and foreign policy decision making can be seen in the behavior of the four key Soviet leaders of the Cold War period—Joseph Stalin, Nikita Khrushchev, Leonid Brezhnev, and Mikhail Gorbachev. To understand their behavior toward the United States in the most vital foreign policy events of the Cold War, we must examine the strategies and tactics they used in their domestic political bargaining. And an analysis of their foreign policy shows that while those strategies were successful in one political environment, they often backfired in the international arena.

The foreign policy events examined here were among the most important in each leader's relations with the United States. Joseph Stalin's blockade of the Western zones of Berlin helped start the Cold War in the transition period following World War II. The showdown between John F. Kennedy and Nikita Khrushchev over missiles in Cuba was the most dangerous of the Cold War confrontations. The 1973 war in the Middle East was the major conflict between Richard Nixon and Leonid Brezhnev in the early detente period. And the negotiations over German unification between Mikhail Gorbachev and his Western counterparts signaled that the Cold War was finally over. In each case the stakes were great, uncertainties mounted, and leaders had to make decisions quickly. Each of these events was of the utmost importance to the Soviet Union, so the leaders were heavily involved in the details, and the strategy each one chose was central to the outcome.

The conflict over the fate of Berlin erupted in 1948 because as the Western Powers and the Soviet Union vied for power in Central Europe, Berlin's governance was at the heart of the question of who would control Germany. When the Soviet Union imposed the blockade on June 23–24, 1948, all the powers involved believed that the inhabitants of West Berlin could survive for only a month or two in those conditions. Although the airlift conducted by the West proved to be a viable strategy for almost a year, neither side could afford to allow the stalemate to go on forever, given the drain on resources. The United States seriously considered using force to break the blockade, especially since the airlift had been intended as a short-term measure. As Stalin's position worsened during the summer, he engaged in talks with the Western ambassadors. Those talks provide an excellent opportunity to study Stalin's style of political bargaining, since he and his foreign minister met a number of times with the ambassadors in an attempt to win concessions on the future status of the Western zones of Germany and Berlin.

Fourteen years later, in Cuba, the United States was faced with a qualitatively new external threat in the Western Hemisphere with the introduction of Soviet nuclear missiles, while Khrushchev was trying to close the recently exposed "missile gap" and to defend his new ally. In those tense October days the United States prepared an air strike to wipe out the Soviet missiles deployed in Cuba, and to the Soviet Union it appeared that the United States was ready to carry out such a strike if the USSR did not respond to other forms of pressure. Kennedy had to act before the deployed missiles became operational, and intelligence estimates impressed him with the need to succeed quickly. Meanwhile, Khrushchev, faced with the threat of an imminent air strike against Cuba, had to decide on a course of action. Khrushchev's bargaining in that encounter included a series of public and private appeals designed to leverage Kennedy's fear of the missiles already deployed in Cuba.

When war broke out in the Middle East in 1973, each superpower sought to protect its main allies in the region. Egypt's early success in the war threatened Israel, and Israel threatened first Syria and later Egypt, especially the latter's Third Army. These threats forced the superpowers to act to halt catastrophes for their allies. The Soviet Union even threatened to intervene unilaterally in the Middle East to protect the Third Army from what would have been certain destruction had the United States not succeeded in pressuring Israel to halt its actions. Brezhnev's bargaining during this war included his letters to Nixon, his meetings with Kissinger, and the Soviet effort to resupply Egypt and Syria.

The most important set of international negotiations in the Gorbachev years surrounded events in the German Democratic Republic that led to the fall of the Berlin Wall and, a year later, to German unification. From November 1989 through July 1990 the Germans and Americans put forth plans for reunification, and the Soviets warned the West not to exploit the situation. Gorbachev floated a number of proposals in these negotiations that were designed to prevent full German membership in the North Atlantic Treaty Organization; after all, the GDR had been the Soviet Union's most important Warsaw Pact ally, and it was the key prize gained by the USSR at the end of World War II.

My examination of each of these four foreign policy events ends with a brief discussion of another major U.S.-Soviet bargaining encounter during the same period. These secondary cases are included because they too involved the Soviet leaders in intense bargaining situations, and thus help to expand the analysis of each leader's style. For Stalin, there is the matter of his role in the wartime conferences at Tehran, Yalta, and Potsdam, in which he achieved his objectives concerning Poland; for Khrushchev, the series of events that led to the building of the Berlin Wall in 1961; for Brezhnev, the intense negotiations between him and the Czechoslovak leadership that culminated in the Soviet invasion of 1968; and finally, for Gorbachev, his encounter with Ronald Reagan at Reykjavík, where the two leaders almost forged an arms control agreement that would have eliminated nuclear weapons.

Many individuals provided advice and criticism in the development of this book, and I am especially grateful to George Breslauer for teaching me so much about Soviet politics and foreign policy and to Alexander George, Ernst Haas, and Kenneth Waltz for introducing me to international relations theory.

A number of institutions gave financial support along the way, including the Institute on Global Conflict and Cooperation, the Institute for the Study of World Politics, and the Berkeley-Stanford Program on Soviet Studies. I am particularly grateful to the Stanford Center for International Security and Arms Control, which provided me with predoctoral and postdoctoral fellowship support.

Several individuals with firsthand knowledge of some of the events examined in this book were generous with their time, and I would like to thank Lucius Battle, Daniel Ellsberg, Raymond Garthoff, Joseph Kingsbury-Smith, Paul Nitze, Boris Surokhov, and Philip Zelikow for providing important insights.

I am grateful to Andrew Rutten and Steve Weber for reading parts of the manuscript. Nora Bensahel and Ann Tappert provided research and insights on Stalin and Gorbachev, respectively. Peter Katzenstein, Jack Snyder, and the anonymous reviewers for the Johns Hopkins University Press gave extensive comments on the entire manuscript. Katzenstein and Snyder have been particularly supportive during the entire review process, and I appreciate their assistance.

I owe a great debt to Richard Ned Lebow, who asked me to submit the manuscript to Johns Hopkins and who offered helpful comments on several draft chapters. I appreciate his invaluable guidance and interest. I also appreciate the assistance of Henry Tom, Gregg Wilhelm, Douglas Armato, Barbara Lamb, and Mary Yates at the press.

Finally, I would like to thank my wife, Kathy. She has watched me develop this project from the beginning and has provided continual encouragement and support during each stage. She also read the entire manuscript and offered brilliant and extensive editorial comments. I cannot thank her enough for all her help and support.

Leadership Style and
Soviet Foreign Policy

The Domestic Roots of Foreign Policy Making

In August 1948 the U.S. ambassador to the Soviet Union, Walter Bedell Smith, as well as the British and French representatives to Moscow, met on several occasions with Soviet leader Joseph Stalin and his foreign minister, Vyacheslav Molotov, in order to negotiate an end to the Berlin blockade. These negotiating sessions would prove extremely frustrating to the Western powers. Twice during that month the ambassadors and Stalin seemed to have a deal within reach, but after each meeting with Stalin in which the Soviet leader offered major concessions, the ambassadors met with Molotov, who took a harder line and frustrated any progress.

The deal that Stalin could have struck in August would have satisfied several of his objectives in Berlin, including giving him a voice in the affairs of the Western zones of the city. Instead, frustrated by the ups and downs of Stalin's "good cop/bad cop" bargaining strategy, the Western powers held firm against him, and by spring 1949, when Stalin was forced to concede, he had received nothing for his efforts and had merely provoked an even tougher Western position against him in Central Europe.

Why would Stalin have thought a good cop/bad cop strategy would be successful? Because it was a strategy that had worked brilliantly for him at home in the 1920s as he outmaneuvered his rivals to succeed Vladimir Lenin as leader of the Soviet Union. And Stalin was not alone in applying to foreign policy those strategies that had been successful in bringing him to power. His successors—Nikita Khrushchev, Leonid Brezhnev, and Mikhail Gorbachev—used their successful domestic political strategies in the international arena, in a way that also led to failure in several major U.S.-Soviet conflicts.

In studying foreign policy decision making, scholars have tended to overlook a key factor that influences the behavior of world leaders. The pattern leaders exhibit in foreign policy stems to a great extent from their "schooling" in domestic politics. This schooling shapes the way they approach any kind of political conflict, and it is particularly important for any leader who has had little prior exposure to international politics.

The Development of Schemas

Success at home shapes the way a leader approaches foreign policy decisions. During his rise to power each of the four major Soviet leaders of the Cold War era developed his own style of political bargaining—as do leaders everywhere. He learned when to confront his opponents, and when to compromise or to concede. He figured out when it was advantageous to stake out a clear position, and when it was better to muddle through. And he carried these lessons with him when he made foreign policy. Unfortunately, international politics can be a very different environment, and previously successful strategies can backfire, as happened to Stalin in 1948.

There are good psychological reasons for using prior experiences and lessons as a guide to policymaking. When individuals respond to new situations, they sort the information they confront by simplifying reality: they match what they see to a familiar category and respond accordingly. Given a limited capacity to process information, people have to take mental shortcuts.[1] Someone on a university admissions committee, for example, will likely analyze an applicant's file by comparing the person either with himself at the same age or with other applicants who have succeeded or failed in previous years.[2]

To sort incoming information, people use "schemas." Schemas are assumptions about how things work. In highly ambiguous settings, human beings need rules of thumb to guide them. As Richard Nisbett and Lee Ross have noted, a variety of different theoretical areas within psychology "all have made essentially the same point—that objects and events in the phenomenal world are almost never approached as if they were sui generis configurations but rather are assimilated into preexisting structures in the mind of the perceiver."[3] While there seems to be no consensus among psychologists about which experiences are most important, how prior cases are "retrieved" by the brain, and how beliefs change, there is good reason to believe that, as Robert Axelrod has stated, the "more important to the person a previous case was, the more accessible it will be as an analogy for a future case."[4]

For leaders such as Stalin, Khrushchev, Brezhnev, and Gorbachev, lessons learned in important domestic political battles were crucial for later decision making in foreign policy. Prior information is much more likely to be retrieved if it is vivid,[5] and what could be more vivid than the crucial battles that brought a leader to power? When Stalin outmaneuvered his rivals in the 1920s, it was a struggle that observers at the time certainly did not expect him to win. His use of the same style of behavior in later interactions with Western adversaries suggests that success in a crucial political realm created a schema for Stalin about political bargaining that he employed later in his foreign policy encounters with the West. The same pattern held true for Khrushchev, Brezhnev, and Gorbachev.

The field of political science is seeing increasing use of psychological theories to explain why leaders act the way they do in making foreign policy. Much of the political science interest in this area was stimulated by Robert Jervis's study of misperception in international politics.[6] Jervis focused on the role of the international events that may shape a decision maker's view of the world, such as the events following the Munich agreement of 1938 or the Japanese attack on Pearl Harbor, which were seen as providing important lessons for postwar American leaders. One recent work has argued that U.S. decision making during the Vietnam war was heavily influenced by the experiences of those decision makers in the Korean War fifteen years earlier.[7] But why simply focus on the role of critical international events in shaping perceptions? As Jervis himself noted, "Especially for a statesman who rises to power through the political processes (as opposed to a career diplomat), domestic politics has supplied both his basic political concepts and the more detailed lessons about what strategies and tactics are appropriate to reach desired goals."[8]

Some scholars have noticed how domestic political experiences may shape later foreign policy decision making. Deborah Larson's rich account of the beliefs of U.S. policymakers about the Soviet Union in the immediate postwar period offers several examples of the role of domestic political experiences in shaping a decision maker's foreign policy strategy. Harry S Truman, for example, who had limited foreign policy experience prior to becoming president, drew heavily on his notion of politics developed during his years in the Missouri political machine of Boss Thomas Pendergast. And according to Larson, Secretary of State James Byrnes, "having no experience in diplomacy . . . relied on analogies from his career as a legislative negotiator in domestic politics. Indeed, before his first foreign ministers' conference, Byrnes confidently told other members of the U.S. delegation that he knew just how to deal with the Russians. 'It's just like the U.S. Senate,' he said. 'You build a post office in their state and they'll build a post office in our state.'"[9]

Drawing on past experiences to guide present conduct is highly rational, especially when leaders are faced with a great deal of ambiguous information that they must sort out and process. As Jervis writes, "In everyday life, in the interpretation of other states' behavior, and in the scientific laboratory, expectations create predispositions that lead actors to notice certain things and to neglect others, to immediately and often unconsciously draw certain inferences from what is noticed, and to find it difficult to consider alternatives. Furthermore . . . this way of perceiving is rational. Intelligent decision-making in any sphere is impossible unless significant amounts of information are assimilated to pre-existing beliefs." [10]

Simply because it is rational, however, does not mean that such a strategy will achieve a successful outcome. The problem for decision makers is that while the past may be a rational guide for the present, it may also be a poor one and lead to failure rather than success. Situations and adversaries may seem comparable when in fact they are not.[11] Strategies and tactics that were successful in domestic politics may not be so successful in foreign policy. In Stalin's case, for example, the bargaining style that had worked for him at home led to terrible failure in the negotiations over Berlin, although this style had also led to great success in the wartime conferences. The wartime conferences may in fact have served as a "confirming event" for Stalin that reinforced his earlier lessons and led to his inability to bargain successfully over the fate of Berlin in the summer of 1948.[12]

Recent psychological research has examined the interaction between top-down processes, like schemas, in which people apply an established framework to a new situation, and data-driven approaches to problem solving, in which people respond to the new information before them by changing their schemas when the situation requires.[13] The results of this research are ambiguous about whether or not people do alter their schemas in the face of conflicting evidence. The same book that argues that people will start looking at the data more closely when a schema is not working also suggests that "well-developed schemas generally resist change and can even persist in the face of disconfirming evidence." [14]

The literature on schemas tells us that human beings, for rational reasons, use mental frameworks developed from earlier experiences to help them understand current situations. Applied to foreign policy decision makers, these theories lead us to consider the international or domestic experiences that shape the way leaders approach the uncertainties of international politics.

Much of the political science research on schemas has assumed that leaders rely heavily on international events, and certainly we often hear decision makers use explicit analogies from previous incidents like Munich or Vietnam in discussing current policy choices. But when studying how leaders bargain, we must remember that, especially in the twentieth century, many world leaders were domestic politicians, not career diplomats. They were in a position to make their country's foreign policy decisions because they succeeded first in their domestic environment by winning the support of key groups in society, either through the ballot box or through other less democratic means.

Which domestic experiences mattered most for the four Soviet leaders of the Cold War period? All four spent time in the schools, possibly in the fields or factories, and then in the local, regional, and national Communist Party organizations (Stalin had the additional experience of being a revolutionary in tsarist Russia). Experiences in all these places likely contributed to each leader's views about life and politics.

But the best place to look for the events that shaped each leader's political bargaining style is his so-called succession period.[15] From Stalin to Gorbachev, the succession period was the time during which top Soviet politicians were vying to succeed a dead or deposed leader. Each period ended when a new leader had consolidated his power by neutralizing his political adversaries—by either killing them, demoting them, or so weakening their base that they posed no threat.

The succession period was often the first time these future leaders acted independently, in the sense that there was no norm being prescribed from above. Until then these leaders had played the role of junior subordinate, and their behavior was so highly circumscribed that they had little chance to develop their own style of political behavior. A study of Mikhail Gorbachev as an up-and-coming politician in the stifling Brezhnev period of the late 1970s, for instance, would turn up little evidence of the groundbreaker who emerged after 1985. For this reason the leaders' success in these pivotal periods, while relatively late in their political lives, can be viewed as their "first independent political success" and the time in which they developed their own distinctive political style. It is this style that formed the foundation for their later international bargaining.[16] Remember that vivid, salient experiences provide schemas for solving later problems. These succession periods were vivid and salient. The rewards and dangers were clear: victory assured the person of the most powerful position in the system, while defeat often meant the end of his political career (or worse, during the Stalin period).

Skeptics may argue that any observed correlation between domestic and international behavior is a spurious one, meaning that the foreign policy behavior that is so similar to the earlier domestic style may not in fact be caused by it; instead, both may be caused by an independent, third factor that we have not addressed, such as a basic personality trait. If spuriousness exists here, then the behavior exhibited by the leaders in the domestic political battles would still predict the later foreign policy behavior, even if it was not necessarily the source. Therefore, the model would still retain its predictive power, though it would suffer a blow to its explanatory capability.

In their study of Woodrow Wilson, for example, Alexander and Juliette George noted that Wilson's battle with Dean Andrew Fleming West over the building of a graduate school at Princeton was similar in many ways to his later battle with Senator Henry Cabot Lodge over the League of Nations. This correlation was spurious, however, because the authors argue that in each case the behavior stemmed from Wilson's "irresistible, never-articulated need to retaliate against the kind of domination he had once endured at the hands of his father." Later they argue that "underlying Wilson's quest for political power and his manner of exercising it was the compelling need to counter the crushing feelings of inadequacy which had been branded into his spirit as a child." [17]

The type of psychobiography that George and George attempt is extremely difficult to do, and the information at their disposal is infinitely greater than the information we have about the early childhood experiences of the Soviet leaders. [18] At the same time, it is difficult to use this type of research to predict specific actions. For example, if we knew that Wilson had an emotional need "to retaliate against the kind of domination he had once endured at the hands of his father," would we then be able to predict how he would conduct his negotiations with the Senate over the league treaty?

Another approach that focuses on personality traits is interpersonal generalization theory, used by Lloyd Etheredge to link elite disagreements over policy options with personality differences. Etheredge argued that people who tended to dominate subordinates were more likely to favor the use of military force, and extroverts were more likely to favor cooperation in U.S.-Soviet relations. [19]

This model, which says that both domestic and foreign policy behavior derive from interpersonal behavior, is problematic for several reasons. First, there may also be a spurious correlation in this approach. Whether or not one dominates subordinates in interpersonal relations may also be a style of behavior that one learns or adopts in one's formative experiences. Both interpersonal relations and foreign policy choices may be correlated, and yet both may derive from some independent third factor, such as whether an individual grew up in a happy or an unhappy home. The way one behaves in interpersonal relations is not necessarily a reflection of basic personality traits.

This first objection is tied to the second, which turns out to be a problem that Etheredge himself noted in setting up his test. He acknowledged that some people manifest different interpersonal behavior, depending on their role and their situation; that is, they may dominate subordinates and yet defer to superiors. He assumed that they would be showing their "true" self in the former case, *and* he assumed that questions concerning the use of force would most likely be about smaller countries. In other words, he compared behavior in structurally similar situations and then argued that the personality evident in the first caused the behavior in the second, even though he implied that had he chosen interpersonal relations with equals or superiors, or debates over the use of force against equals or superiors, the outcome would have been different.[20] Etheredge noted in a footnote, in fact, that "the present personality dimension may predict best to use of force against smaller countries but *relations with autonomously powerful opponents in domestic politics might predict better to relations with the Soviet Union since World War II.*"[21]

A third objection is that while personality surely plays a role in the development of a leader's bargaining style, it seems difficult to argue that one is born a "bluffer" or an "appeaser" or prone to bold commitments. And knowing that a leader with an aggressive personality is more prone to using force in both interpersonal and international relations still leaves much about his behavior unexamined. Perhaps personality does induce a person at critical stages in his or her political career to choose aggressive styles of behavior, but strategies and tactics are *learned*. And when we ask how they are learned, particularly in insulated societies, we come back to the domestic political battles that bring a person to the leadership position.

The political style a leader develops is not completely unrelated to the individual's personality or to the culture in which he or she was raised. Personality undoubtedly plays a role in the bargaining style a leader adopts. Brezhnev, for example, has been described as indecisive, which probably led to his preference for accommodative bargaining strategies. In fact, this combination of individual personality and individual political experience is what causes leaders to have idiosyncratic rather than shared beliefs about correct courses of political action. As Paul Dawson has noted,

The psychological process by which a political belief system is formed occurs in the presence of various elements that are a part of one's psychological context; for example, needs, motivations, and values. These elements of the psychological context are more or less peculiar to individuals and therefore tend to produce relatively idiosyncratic structures of beliefs. Similarly, this psychological process does not occur in a political vacuum. Instead, the result of this process is likely to show the effects of various and diverse encounters with personal political environments. . . . Personal encounters with political environments therefore also are more or less peculiar to individuals and also tend to produce relatively idiosyncratic structures of political beliefs.[22]

We cannot and do not need to know the precise mix of personality and culture and political learning involved in the development of political leaders.

To predict foreign policy styles, what we need to know is who won in key domestic encounters and with what strategies and tactics.

The comparison of political style in the domestic and foreign policy arenas is made using a variant of a structured, focused comparison of case studies.[23] In comparing domestic and foreign policy behavior, we could simply find stories and anecdotes on an ad hoc basis that illustrate an argument. And while excellent studies have been made of the influence of a decision maker's mind-set on his behavior, these studies have not structured and focused the analysis to present a systematic framework for comparing different leaders' bargaining styles.[24]

To be systematic, one strategy would be to apply a formal-model approach to a large number of foreign policy cases in order to test the hypotheses presented. It is difficult to assign values to the kinds of behavior explored here, and the richness of detail that case studies provide allows us to develop and test propositions about the behavior of leaders that cannot be captured by formal models. Formal models of bargaining do exist,[25] but these models only explain and predict *when* a leader will choose to fight or to concede. What they cannot do, because of the inability of numbers to capture the nuances of behavior, is help us understand *how* leaders choose to fight or to concede. And how leaders choose to bargain can have a substantial influence on the outcome of a foreign policy event.

A typology of bargaining strategies and tactics will structure and focus the comparison of domestic and international bargaining. We can then compare bargaining in the different arenas along the same dimensions to show consistencies and variations in each leader's behavior.

A Typology of Bargaining Style: Strategies and Tactics

In any political bargaining, be it domestic or international, there are two basic types of strategy: coercion and accommodation.[26] Coercion is the use of threats, bluffs, warnings, or force to exert pressure on an adversary to accept one's demands, whereas accommodation is the offering of concessions or compromises to satisfy an opponent.

Why choose one or the other? Leaders choose a more coercive strategy when they believe that it is important to stand firm, and when they fear that accommodation to an opponent's position only breeds his contempt. As Pericles stated during the Peloponnesian War, in the face of Spartan demands, "If you give in, you will immediately be confronted with some greater demand, since they will think that you only gave way on this point through fear. But if you take a firm stand you will make it clear to them that they have to treat you properly as equals."[27]

Leaders may choose a more accommodative approach, however, if they believe that compromises or concessions to some of the opponent's demands can lead to a settlement that is mutually satisfactory, and if they fear that coercion is likely to lead to retaliation. In a different example from the Peloponnesian War, Diodotus opposed the use of coercion against the Mytilenians for revolting against Athens: "The right way to deal with free people is this—not to inflict tremendous punishment on them after they have revolted, but to take tremendous care of them before this point is reached, to prevent them from even contemplating the idea of revolt." [28]

Neither approach is "wrong." Each approach has its own logic. The coercive strategist recognizes the danger of looking weak but underestimates the risks of being provocative. The accommodative bargainer understands the risks of provocation but neglects the problem of appearing weak.[29] Whether a given strategy is successful is highly dependent on the situation, the opponent, and the skill used in applying the strategy.

When leaders implement their coercive or accommodative strategies, the key tactical choice they make is whether to make a firm commitment to a course of action, or to preserve their options and avoid commitments. An ability to communicate a credible commitment to a given position is a highly successful bargaining tactic because leaders then have a hard time backing down.[30] The bargainer who commits to an action is saying, for example, "If you do not do X, I will do Y," or "I will give you Z, but no more." If the adversary knows that the decision maker is truly committed to his position, then the adversary is under more pressure to give in to the demand or to accept the concession.

Making a commitment to an action is not cost-free, however, and hence many leaders prefer to preserve their options. One danger of making a commitment to stand firm is that the adversary may do the same. Mutual commitment can lead to a breakdown in negotiations and then to conflict.[31] Another danger is that the adversary may challenge the commitment, and then the leader's reputation for standing firm is placed on the line. Preserving options, on the other hand, enables a decision maker to avoid challenges to his reputation for resolve as well as to prevent mutual commitments, but he is then less able to end the encounter when he wishes, since the adversary can probe alternative possibilities.[32] Deciding whether to make commitments or to preserve options is a major tactical choice that bargainers must make, since they often want both to show resolve and to maintain flexibility.

While making commitments may theoretically be a sound tactic, other studies have shown that leaders in fact rarely make commitments, preferring instead to "straddle." The reason is not the danger of mutual commitment, but rather the concern with future bargaining reputation. Leaders are afraid that if they fail to fulfill a commitment, they will lose credibility for future bargaining encounters, and this fear leads them to avoid making commitments in the first place.[33]

In gauging the level of the commitment the Soviet leaders made in their domestic and international bargaining, it is useful to examine both verbal signals as well as physical actions. A decision maker can move tanks or airplanes to the region of conflict, but he can also signal his willingness to commit to a course of action through diplomatic channels, by sending letters through his emissaries or making televised addresses. These verbal signals can be broken down along three dimensions that are important when a decision maker decides whether or not to make a commitment: the leader's *personal involvement* in sending the signals, the *public or private nature* of the communication, and the *clarity or ambiguity* of the signal.[34] Decision makers whose tactical choice is to make a bold commitment will personally and publicly send a clear signal. If they wish to avoid strong commitments, they may use third parties to send private, ambiguous proposals; in this way they can disavow the message if they receive an unsatisfactory response.

Comparing *actions* in domestic and international bargaining is more difficult than comparing *verbal* tactics, because the means used in domestic and foreign policy can be so different, especially with regard to the use of military force. When leaders take action to signal a commitment, however, it in some way involves the use of resources. At home, for example, a leader can transfer scarce financial resources from one sector to another to signal a commitment to a particular problem, be it education, drugs, or agriculture. In foreign policy, leaders can make three levels of commitment: *low-level* commitments, which involve sending advisers and arms to an area; *medium-level* commitments, which include the use of proxy troops, actions in another area, or troop movements near the area of dispute; and *high-level* commitments, which include the use of force.

A leader's choice of coercive or accommodative strategies and his tactical choice of strong or weak commitments are important because they can influence both the course of negotiations and the terms of their settlement. Each party in a bargaining process uses its strategies and tactics to shape to its advantage the perceptions about capabilities and motivation that the other side holds.[35] In any bargaining situation the parties are concerned with the balance of interests and capabilities because it is easier to induce the other side to concede if one's own side is stronger or more motivated, or both. But *strength* and *motivation* are relative terms, and the values at stake and the capabilities that can be brought to bear are often unclear at the start of negotiations.[36]

Coercive or accommodative strategies can have quite different effects on the outcome of a foreign policy conflict, depending on the nature of the players and the situation. For example, if a leader makes concessions on small points, he may be able to end the encounter by reducing the adversary's costs of retreating. On the other hand, he may raise the adversary's incentive to stand firm by leading him to believe he can hold out for more.[37] Ideally, a decision maker would have a crystal ball with which to gaze into the adversary's mind and would adjust his strategies and tactics to fit the situation and the opponent. But decision makers do not have crystal balls, and hence they draw on prior experiences to guide them.

Because strategies and tactics are important, the relative power capabilities of the parties involved do not necessarily determine who wins and loses.[38] Thucydides wrote that "the strong do what they have the power to do, and the weak accept what they have to accept," but this notion fails to explain why stronger powers often must offer concessions in bargaining in order to achieve acceptable outcomes, and why on occasion they suffer frustration and defeat in contests with highly motivated adversaries.[39] Sometimes, in order to gain final concessions from the other party, a stronger power may need to offer some kind of "carrot" or face-saver. A carrot enables the weaker side to give in without feeling or looking as if it were capitulating. Carrots can be concessions on the issues at stake, offers on another set of concerns, or promises for the future. A face-saver is an offer to reduce the loser's costs after the latter has already decided to concede.[40]

Other Factors in the Development of Foreign Policy Behavior

While Stalin, Khrushchev, Brezhnev, and Gorbachev all used strategies and tactics in the international arena that they had used successfully at home, there were also times when they departed from their usual style. As noted earlier, people may change their schemas when confronted with overwhelming evidence that they should try something different. Factors such as the nature of the international environment or the domestic political needs of a leader may cause a shift in his typical bargaining style.

In searching for explanations for foreign policy behavior, international relations theorists speak about different levels of analysis, including the level of the state (e.g., the type of political system, the nature of bureaucratic politics, ideology, or culture) and the level of the international state system (e.g., the global balance of power), in addition to the individual level of analysis that we use here.[41]

No matter how many levels of possible analysis we may construe, however, there are only two basic answers to the question, Does the individual matter?[42] If we answer no and say the setting induces behavior, then we need not know anything about the person making the decisions, since anyone faced with a particular balance of power, or anyone in a given domestic political situation, or anyone in a particular culture, would act the same way. But if we answer yes, then in order to understand a particular decision, we have to understand the person or persons who made it. Someone else would have made a different choice.

Of course, there is interaction between different levels. The environment or political system or culture might make two or three or four options most likely. But one would still have to know more about the leader to know why he chose option A and not B or C. Or a leader might initially choose one option but then reevaluate and change his strategy because of the influence of the external or domestic environment. Khrushchev, for example, finally abandoned his typical bargaining style of coercive strategies and bold commitments in the Cuban missile crisis when the threat of nuclear war became too great.

One possible factor, then, in explaining the foreign policy bargaining by Soviet leaders is the balance of power. Neorealist theorists of international politics argue that states seeking to survive in an international environment that lacks a central authority to maintain order will balance against opposing powers through either internal means (e.g., arms buildups) or external efforts (e.g., alliances). Knowing the structure of the international system leads to predictions about the general behavior of the states, but theories about balance-of-power politics are not as helpful in studying those states' particular foreign policies. As Kenneth Waltz has noted, "The theory does not tell us why state X made a certain move last Tuesday. To expect it to do so would be like expecting the theory of universal gravitation to explain the wayward path of a falling leaf."[43]

Because of the abstract nature of balance-of-power theory, different strategies are logically consistent with a state's relative position in the international system. The problem, then, with balance-of-power theory for studying particular foreign policy choices is simply its indeterminacy at that level. For example, when one is the weaker party in a given dispute, it is not clear whether it is best to accommodate the superior power and hope for a face-saver, or to bolster one's image, bluff about capabilities, and try to raise the stronger power's incentive to offer concessions. Both strategies are logical, according to balance-of-power theory, but their appropriateness depends on the intentions of the adversary and the nature of the issue.

In a famous example from the Peloponnesian War, the Athenians told the much weaker Melians that given the former's preponderance of power and the latter's presumed interest in staying alive, the Melians should surrender immediately to the Athenian demands. But the Melians did not, both on principle and in the belief that they might prolong the encounter enough to raise the costs of the Athenians' use of force. The Melians argued, "If we surrender, then all our hope is lost at once, whereas, so long as we remain in action, there is still a hope that we may yet stand upright." They based their hope on two outside factors: the gods, who would support the party in the "right," and the Spartans, their allies. The Athenians suggested that the Melians adopt a strategy that was logical according to the Athenian conception of the balance of power; the Melians did not, because they believed that their position was potentially stronger with help from the gods and the Spartans.[44]

While a more structurally based theory may not make specific predictions about foreign policies, it does predict that leaders will choose options that strengthen the state and best assure its survival. If a state is threatened, balance-of-power theory leads us to expect its leaders to address that threat either by increasing capabilities or by finding external assistance, as the Melians hoped to do. If a decision maker chooses an option that jeopardizes the state's survival, then the theory is hard-pressed to explain it. Furthermore, balancing may not always be the surest strategy for survival; in the above case, the Melians might have survived had they bandwagoned with the Athenians instead of seeking external help that did not exist.

One major study of international crises concludes that a major reason for the initiation of those crises is that the balance of power is not clear at the start, but once it clarifies during the course of the interstate bargaining, a resolution of the issues can occur.[45] That argument thus suggests that bargainers shift once the structure clarifies, and a key question is why this shift often takes so long. Why is the adjustment not immediate? The problem with a model focusing solely on the balance of power is that not only are competing strategies equally logical in the face of the same balance, but it often takes bargainers a while to see what the balance actually is.

A second factor in foreign policy calculations might be a leader's current domestic political needs. International politics can be viewed as a two-level game—that is, a game reflecting both the international negotiations and concurrent domestic negotiations. The two levels interact: internal bargaining produces an initial position, and the bargaining that then commences at the international level is conducted with an eye to what is needed to ratify the package internally. Ratification is not necessarily a two-thirds vote in the U.S. Senate; the term refers to any domestic process within which leaders work to implement a decision.[46] A two-level-game approach predicts that we need to understand the domestic political pressures on a decision maker in order to understand his or her position in the international bargaining. Furthermore, it predicts that if the potential settlements satisfactory to both the internal constituents and the external adversary are not overlapping, then no agreement will be reached.

Arguments about the pressures of domestic politics on Soviet leaders blossomed during the Brezhnev period. Since the decision-making process of that period appeared to conform more closely to the collective leadership touted throughout Soviet history, many analysts focused on the competition among top elites, the need for consensus building, and the concern of the leadership with maintaining a possibly fragile coalition of the major actors to explain Soviet foreign policy decisions and actions.[47]

Some coalition theories, for example, suggest that a collective leadership like the Soviet Politburo operates on certain principles, the most important of which is the need to obtain unanimous consent (since the leadership's greatest fear is the breakup of the coalition). When a leadership makes decisions based on the need for unanimous consent, it develops a "lowest common denominator" mentality. Since change benefiting one member of the coalition may harm another, and since all the "major institutional actors have to be minimally satisfied[,] . . . then any change takes place incrementally."[48] One domestic-politics approach applied to Soviet decision making predicted a foreign policy marked by muddling through except when the costs of indecisiveness were politically too severe for the leadership to bear.[49]

A coalition-politics approach looks at the logrolling that leaders engage in to satisfy the major institutional actors in the system. Khrushchev and Brezhnev, for example, had to make concessions to the military and ideological communities that favored Soviet expansion as well as to the economic managers, technocrats, and intelligentsia who favored detente, and thus the two leaders pursued these two contradictory policies simultaneously. Gorbachev, meanwhile, had more latitude to pursue a genuinely cooperative relationship with the United States because the military and the ideologues were no longer as relevant to his domestic political success as they had been in earlier periods.[50]

A coalition-politics model could also conceivably explain consistent behavior in domestic politics and foreign policy across time. Rather than arguing that there were psychological reasons for this consistency, the model would conclude that similar strategies derive from the need to appease the same political groups. But if strategies derive so clearly from domestic requirements, then why did other contenders for the Soviet leadership not choose the same strategies as Stalin, Khrushchev, Brezhnev, and Gorbachev? Surely any potential Soviet leader understood that he needed the support of the major institutional elites. One way of comparing the coalition-politics argument with my own is to look at cases where the domestic constituency changes. A coalition-politics argument would predict a change in strategy, whereas my model predicts that the leader's behavior will remain consistent.

While my model looks at key individual, formative domestic experiences as the source of individual schemas, a third factor in foreign policy making might be *shared* experiences or images. For example, the "operational-code" model suggests that leaders are guided by a set of cultural maxims. For Soviet leaders these maxims derived from factors such as Russian culture, the experience of the Bolsheviks as revolutionaries in tsarist Russia, and the Bolshevik view of the capitalist enemy.[51] An operational-code model is also, then, a framework for understanding the rules of thumb that leaders develop to help them engage in political conflict. But by focusing on culture, history, and ideology, this model predicts consistent behavior from leader to leader and ignores the idiosyncrasies of individuals. In its application to Soviet leaders, this approach also suggests that Bolsheviks followed an "optimizing strategy" instead of merely pursuing a goal that satisfies the elites' lowest common denominator, as the domestic-coalitions model would predict. Optimizers lay out a "set of graduated objectives" and then strive simultaneously for all of them, maximum and minimum.[52]

One approach that is related to the operational-code model focuses more specifically on the decision maker's "image of the adversary." By studying a number of historical cases, Alexander George and Richard Smoke examined different ways in which states have tried to change the status quo. They argued that the primary determinant of the choice of strategy by state A seeking to change the status quo maintained by state B is A's view of B's commitment. Their explanation and prediction is as follows: If A believes that B has no commitment to maintain the status quo, then the former will choose a *fait accompli* strategy in order to change that status quo before the latter has a chance to reconsider his position. If, on the other hand, A is uncertain of his adversary's commitment, he will probe in a limited way in order to clarify the opponent's position. And if A believes that his adversary is committed to defending the status quo, but he thinks that the commitment can be eroded, then he will apply controlled pressure until the commitment collapses.[53] Thus, rather than choose a strategy previously successful in domestic politics, decision makers in this model base their strategy on their image of their opponent and his level of commitment to standing firm.[54]

My model suggests that victory in the key domestic political battles that brought these individuals to the top of their political system created for each a schema for future political conflicts in the international arena. This approach predicts that each leader will act the same way across time in political negotiations, but that each will act differently from the others.

Important competing explanations are based on models of domestic coalitions as well as on operational codes and adversary images. Balance-of-power models make us aware of structural constraints imposed by the international system, but they are too indeterminate to predict specific strategies. Domestic-coalition models look to the key constituencies that leaders must satisfy in order to push policies forward; these models predict consistency as long as the elites remain the same, but as coalitions change, so should strategy and tactics. The operational-code approach argues that products of the same political system share a common framework for approaching political problems and suggests that schemas derive from shared national experiences. The operational-code model predicts that the four leaders would behave similarly to one another as products of a shared political heritage. Finally, the more specific image-of-the-adversary approach developed by George and Smoke focuses on leaders' views of their adversary's commitment, which seem to stem from some combination of the balance of power, the balance of interests, and perceived intentions.

These competing models offer explanations and predictions for foreign policy bargaining that differ from my own. I return to each of them in chapter 7 in order to demonstrate the kinds of behavior they fail to explain as well as to supplement the explanations produced by my model.

TWO

Domestic Bargaining Styles

Joseph Stalin, Nikita Khrushchev, Leonid Brezhnev, and Mikhail Gorbachev defeated their rivals and consolidated their power at the apex of the Soviet leadership in part because of the strategies and tactics they used. They did not, however, employ the same bargaining style. Stalin used his subordinates to undercut his rivals while he pretended to be a conciliator. Stalin avoided commitments, often making ambiguous proposals through third parties before proceeding with his policies. On the other hand, his successor, Khrushchev, was openly coercive and fond of making clear, public statements committing himself to a given position. Brezhnev, meanwhile, was a much more accommodative bargainer than his predecessors, seeking to compromise with major interests in society. Like Stalin, he chose to avoid making commitments to well-defined positions by cloaking his policies in ambiguity. Finally, Gorbachev disposed of his rivals by adopting an openly confrontational style like Khrushchev's, although he did not make commitments to the same extent. Gorbachev and Khrushchev were much more prone than Stalin and Brezhnev to springing surprises to keep their rivals off balance.

Stalin

Stalin developed his domestic bargaining style in the years 1922–29 as he fought with his rivals to succeed Vladimir Lenin, who grew critically ill in 1922 and died in 1924. At the start of this period many observers would have predicted that Lenin's right-hand man, Leon Trotsky, was the likeliest successor. Two of Stalin's other rivals, Lev Kamenev and Grigory Zinoviev, at first joined forces with Stalin, whom they believed posed no threat to them, and by 1925 the three were pushing Trotsky aside. Stalin then joined up with the party's leading young theoretician, Nikolai Bukharin, and turned on Kamenev and Zinoviev. In 1928 he went after Bukharin, whom he defeated the following year.[1] By 1929 Stalin had emerged supreme.

How did he do it? Stalin's strategy was coercive, but he hid his true intentions by pretending to be an accommodator. He would use his subordinates and allies to attack his immediate rivals while he pretended to be a conciliator, a man of moderation.[2] Stalin often used low-level officials to attack his rivals while he looked the other way. For example, at the Fifteenth CPSU Party Congress in December 1927, several junior officials close to Stalin criticized Bukharin while Stalin disassociated himself from their remarks.[3] Trotsky wrote that Stalin used other major figures, such as Zinoviev, Kamenev, and Bukharin, to attack him while Stalin himself "assumed the role of conciliator, the impartial and moderate mediator in the factional struggle."[4] By doing so Stalin was able to deflect attention from his personal role in implementing his coercive policies and make others think he was less of a threat than he was. At home in the 1920s many people thought that Stalin was the moderate even as he plotted to get rid of his rivals in turn; some adversaries in the international system would make the same mistake over the next twenty-five years.

While Stalin honed his political skills in the 1920s, his strategy did include the famous Bolshevik notion of *kto-kogo*, or who will destroy whom.[5] *Kto-kogo* implies that struggles are to the death and are thus zero-sum contests. This concept led to such Stalinist slogans as the "two camps" in international affairs and "He who is not with us is against us."[6] *Kto-kogo* implies that any bargaining is conducted simply as a means of securing an advantageous position for the final battle. This concept helps shed light on the phenomenon of masking coercion with accommodative gestures. Stalin was not accommodative because he intended to implement his concessions; he simply offered concessions in order to prepare for successful coercion. As he stated as early as 1913, "With a diplomat words *must* diverge from acts—what kind of diplomat would he otherwise be? Words are one thing and acts something different. *Good words are masks for bad deeds.* A sincere diplomat would equal dry water, wooden iron."[7]

At Politburo meetings toward the end of Lenin's rule, Stalin, wrote Isaac Deutscher, "was yielding and conciliatory, readily accepting every amendment to the motions he was preparing for the Congress. He almost welcomed every opportunity for making some verbal concession to his critics." Deutscher added that when Stalin joined forces with Kamenev and Zinoviev to prevent Trotsky from succeeding Lenin, "he was at pains to appear as the most moderate, sensible, and conciliatory of the triumvirs. His criticisms of Trotsky were less offensive than Zinoviev's or Kamenev's. Aware that the Party resented the belittlement of Trotsky, he left his partners to go through the crudest forms of mud-slinging, from which their own as well as Trotsky's prestige was bound to suffer."[8]

Stalin was charming to his most bitter opponents, which seemed to work in his favor during the political battles. His personal secretary, Boris Bazhanov, has described how the "troika" entered the first session of the Politburo he attended. Trotsky was already seated; the others came in, Bazhanov said, "obviously having conferred just beforehand. Zinoviev was the first to enter, he didn't look at Trotsky, and Trotsky also pretended that he didn't see him and looked at some papers. Then came Kamenev, exchanging nods with Trotsky as he walked to his seat. Stalin was third. He walked directly toward Trotsky and with a broad sweeping gesture shook hands with him in a friendly manner."[9] Trotsky may not have been fooled, but Stalin came across as less of a threat to him than Kamenev and Zinoviev.

In 1924–25, when Kamenev and Zinoviev made an all-out attack on Trotsky and even called for his arrest,[10] Stalin said publicly that Trotsky's removal from the Politburo was "inconceivable." The Central Committee merely removed Trotsky from his position as war commissar; Stalin said at the Fourteenth Party Congress in 1925, "We [the Central Committee] do not agree with Zinoviev and Kamenev because we know that the politics of severance is fraught with great dangers for the Party and that the method of severance, the method of bloodletting—and they demanded blood—is dangerous and infectious; today we chop off one, tomorrow another, the day after tomorrow a third—then what will we have left in the Party?"[11] The party would find out—only Stalin.

This Congress signaled the split between Stalin and Zinoviev and Kamenev. While Kamenev was attacking Stalin,[12] Stalin was decrying Kamenev and Zinoviev's tactics against Trotsky and Bukharin. Again, Stalin painted himself as the moderate. Standing up for his ally, Bukharin, Stalin argued that Zinoviev and Kamenev had tried to push Bukharin aside as early as 1923, but he, Stalin, had not allowed it.[13]

One by one Stalin was able to rid himself of his key rivals. Since they were more openly confrontational, they bore the brunt of one another's attacks. Each group saw Stalin as helpful, and although they thought they were using him, quite the opposite was occurring. Unlike many of the others, Stalin also avoided making the types of commitments that came back to haunt his opponents.

Stalin sought to preserve his options unless he felt certain of victory; he avoided making premature commitments. In the 1920s he waited in the wings as his rivals battered one another, not coming forward with his own position until he could see which way the wind was blowing. If he had a new position, he put it forward gradually, always in a noncommittal manner at first. If his colleagues accepted his initial position, he made a slightly bolder statement the next time. Stalin avoided letting his own new positions be labeled as innovations; in order to give them legitimacy he framed them instead as policies that Lenin and the Bolsheviks had always followed.[14]

Trotsky argued that in contrast to himself, Stalin avoided committing himself to courses of action. Referring, for example, to Stalin's absence from the Central Committee session on the morning of the October Revolution, Trotsky argued that this behavior was not cowardice: "He was simply politically noncommittal. The cautious schemer preferred to stay on the fence at the crucial moment. He was waiting to see how the insurrection turned out before committing himself to a position."[15] But this helped Stalin considerably. Trotsky, who came to the Bolshevik party later than many of the other leading members, would suffer because he made commitments to positions that in just a few years would become unpopular in the party. Stalin, however, followed the direction the wind was blowing rather than getting out in front.

From his early political life in Georgia Stalin learned to move ahead by avoiding having his name tied to any particular position.[16] N. N. Zhordania, the former head of the Georgian government, noted that by 1906 Stalin had a group of followers, but "he, himself, did not risk his person and always remained in the wings [*v kulisakh*], giving out orders."[17] Thus, some elements of the Stalin bargaining style of the 1920s had their roots in earlier political activity,[18] but he would develop these tactics more fully in the succession period.

In the 1920s Stalin implemented his programs incrementally and avoided commitments. Bazhanov wrote later that he "was extraordinarily careful and indecisive. . . . I many times saw how he hesitated, not deciding and preferring to follow events rather than lead them." Bazhanov argued that in Politburo meetings in the mid-1920s, Stalin would wait to see which way the majority was going, and then he would propose a vote on the measure.[19]

An example was Stalin's development of the theme of socialism in one country, which became the underpinning of the programs of collectivization and industrialization that he would undertake after gaining supremacy in the system. At the time of the revolution and during its immediate aftermath, most of the Bolsheviks believed that the Russian Revolution would be the spark for revolution in the rest of Europe. In fact, they believed that their own revolution could not survive without these other upheavals in the more advanced capitalist countries.

By the early 1920s it was clear that Europe would not be convulsed in revolutionary fervor, and the leaders of the new Soviet Russia turned inward toward reconstruction. Nikolai Bukharin, in early 1924, was the first to speak of socialism in one country and of the need to use markets to build it, but Stalin seized on the notion that one country could survive the hostilities of the capitalist world.[20]

Stalin first presented this theme "almost casually, like a mere debating point, in the 'literary discussion'. . . . He hedged it round with all sorts of reservations and qualifications."[21] For purposes of legitimation, he presented it not as something new, but rather as a continuation of Leninist thought. In December 1924 he argued that Lenin had considered the possibility of a victorious revolution in one country, but, Stalin added, "for a *complete* victory of socialism, for a *complete* guarantee against a restoration of the old order of things, the combined efforts of the proletariat of several countries are indispensable."[22] A year later, at the Fourteenth Party Congress of December 1925, a resolution was passed stating that "in general the victory of socialism (not in the sense of a final victory) is unconditionally possible in one country."[23]

By the Fifteenth Party Conference of October 1926 Stalin was ready for his all-out attack on Trotsky. Stalin dredged up things his rival had said twenty years before on the need to rely on world revolution, and he bent Lenin's words enough that the old master's legacy seemed to be clearly on the side of socialism in one country.[24] The attack was successful, and Stalin seems to have learned that by moving ahead cautiously and by attributing to his rivals positions based on *their* old commitments—or at least his version of them—he could emerge victorious.[25]

Stalin succeeded at home by painting himself as the moderate even as he followed a coercive strategy of attacking his rivals and destroying them politically (and later physically). He saw rhetoric as a way of hiding his true intent and of softening his coercive actions. And he proceeded cautiously with his ideas until he was firmly in power in 1929. His style worked well in defeating his major rivals, who were more openly confrontational and who committed themselves publicly to political positions.

Khrushchev

Khrushchev was successful in the 1950s using a very different bargaining style. After Stalin's death it took Khrushchev four years to rid himself of his most serious rivals, and another two to become clearly dominant. When Stalin died in March 1953, the rest of the Presidium (as the Politburo was called from 1952 to 1966) was most concerned about Georgy Malenkov, who had become chairman of the Council of Ministers (making the dangerous secret police chief Lavrenty Beria his deputy) and first secretary of the party. But the other aspirants joined forces to diminish his power, and within ten days Malenkov had been forced to give up his position as first secretary, which Khrushchev assumed in September. Still, Malenkov kept his position as head of the government and apparently continued to lead the sessions of the Presidium for more than a year after Khrushchev became first secretary.[26] Malenkov was not removed from his position as chairman of the Council of Ministers until January 1955, although he remained on the Presidium for another two years.

In June 1957 seven of the eleven members of the Presidium voted to oust Khrushchev. Arguing that only a Central Committee plenum could deprive him of his position, Khrushchev, with the help of his defense minister, Marshal Georgy Zhukov, brought his supporters on the Central Committee from all over the Soviet Union to the Kremlin and reversed the Presidium decision. Malenkov, former foreign minister Vyacheslav Molotov, and Lazar Kaganovich, along with former Khrushchev supporter Dmitri Shepilov, were then removed from the Presidium. In October Khrushchev demoted Zhukov, his old friend but potentially a strong rival. Then in 1958 Khrushchev finally got rid of Premier Nikolai Bulganin, and the first secretary also assumed the mantle of chairman of the Council of Ministers. By the Twenty-first Party Congress in 1959, Khrushchev was the undisputed boss in the Soviet Union.[27]

He became the undisputed boss by relying heavily on a coercive strategy, but he did not hide behind an accommodative mask as Stalin had done. Khrushchev confronted: he issued warnings, threats and often bluffs, applying continuous verbal pressure against his rivals. As George Breslauer has written, "Khrushchev's strategy was to exploit the atmosphere of crisis after Stalin to make common cause with the masses against intransigent forces within the establishment. He played upon elite fears of the masses by intentionally raising popular expectations, or prematurely publicizing policy proposals, and then argued within the political elite that mass pressure made the acceptance of these proposals a necessity."[28]

An example of this strategy was Khrushchev's use of agricultural policy as he attempted to outflank Malenkov.[29] In September 1953, when Khrushchev became first secretary, Malenkov still apparently led the Presidium. Malenkov had, as late as August 1953, proclaimed that the country's grain problems had been solved, and his proposals for the future amounted to increasing the productivity of lands already under plow so as to increase the supply of potatoes and vegetables.[30] Malenkov was playing safe; he was following Stalin's position that the grain problem had been solved in order to appear as the logical successor to Stalin, much as Stalin had assumed the mantle of the true Leninist.[31]

On September 3 Khrushchev convened a Central Committee plenum session on agriculture and, deviating from Malenkov, would say only that the country was "essentially supplied with bread," not that the problems had been solved. Fortunately for Khrushchev, the 1953 harvest was a poor one, but Malenkov still insisted in November that the "grain problem has been solved in the USSR."[32] In fact, in 1953 the grain output per capita was 25 percent lower than it had been in 1913, and livestock had still not reached prerevolutionary levels.[33] Khrushchev moved ahead.

On January 22, 1954, Khrushchev painted the bleak agricultural picture in his private memorandum, "Ways of Solving the Grain Problem."[34] In this piece Khrushchev came out with his bold proposal to bring thirteen million hectares of new acreage into use in Kazakhstan and western Siberia—the so-called Virgin Lands—as an emergency measure to increase the country's grain supply and livestock. Less than a week later he went public, telling a group of Machine Tractor Station officials that he expected to put this proposal into effect by 1955. The following week, at a meeting with *sovkhoz* (state farm) officials, he called for implementation of his proposal by the end of 1954. Before the February Central Committee plenum had even met to discuss his original proposal, he had spoken with other groups about plowing fifteen million to twenty-five million hectares of new land. And by June Khrushchev had outlined a plan to make thirty million acres of Virgin Lands a permanent part of Soviet agriculture.[35] One scholar has written of the Virgin Lands proposal,

The idea was truly Khrushchevian in both its scope and timing. He risked alienating Molotov and others just when he had to have their support if he was to deal with Malenkov. Again and again in the future he would announce his most controversial policies just when most men would have preferred to play safe. Equally typical of Khrushchev was the size of the project. . . . Seventy thousand workers were needed to man the new state farms that would be set up on the virgin steppe, and in two years they were to produce close to a fifth of the nation's total grain.[36]

Not only was Khrushchev pushing a campaign to send tens of thousands of volunteers to new parts of the country, but he was also asserting greater party control over agriculture at the expense of the ministries, which were under Malenkov. In September 1953 he had proposed that the party secretaries supervise the Machine Tractor Stations, and he closed the *raion* (regional) agencies of the Agricultural Ministry.[37] In other words, Khrushchev was confronting Malenkov head-on, trying to use the agriculture issue to reassert party control over the government.

Khrushchev continued to confront and coerce regardless of the success or failure of the scheme. The Soviet Union had a good harvest in 1954, but a drought in the eastern part of the country led to disaster in 1955. Did

Khrushchev back down? Absolutely not. Despite criticism from Malenkov, Molotov, and Kaganovich, he not only stood firm but urged an increase in the program.[38] Getting out among the people, he blamed local government officials and bureaucrats for the problems and then, of course, demanded greater party control.[39]

Fortunately for Khrushchev, 1956 was a record harvest year, and by March 1957 he was calling for "the most rapid solution of the livestock problem," which led to new proposals to plant corn everywhere to improve feed supplies.[40] These proposals highlight an important problem with the Khrushchev strategy: He continued to apply pressure and sought to gain greater and greater payoffs without thinking through the implications. He planted corn in areas traditionally used for rye and oats, which led to disastrous crop failure. And the Virgin Lands, while productive in the short term, were overused. The amount of fallow land declined sharply; weeds choked the crops; and overplowing led to serious erosion.[41]

Another example of Khrushchev's use of a confrontational strategy was his so-called Secret Speech at the Twentieth Party Congress in 1956 in which he criticized Stalin and his crimes.[42] During a discussion of the Central Committee report prior to the Party Congress, Khrushchev suggested including a section on the cult of personality; Molotov, Kaganovich, Malenkov, and Kliment Voroshilov were successful in their efforts to quash this proposal. After he had delivered his report as first secretary, Khrushchev told his colleagues that they could not prevent him from speaking about the cult of personality as a delegate, and if they sought to stop him, he would go straight to the Congress with a request that they hear him out. Khrushchev's opponents negotiated to have him give a secret speech at the end of the Congress, but the first secretary's strategy of presenting them with an ultimatum had worked.[43] This ultimatum would not be Khrushchev's last.

While Stalin avoided commitments, Khrushchev made them publicly and unambiguously. In discussing agricultural productivity in 1954, for example, he made his claims using the clearest public and personal commitments; he said, for example, "I repeat. Give me the most difficult district. . . . Before all honest people I declare that we will send people—*I'll go myself,* if the CC sends me—and *I will make a signed statement* at this meeting that we will not only fulfill, we will overfulfill, the task posed by the January Plenum."[44] He was getting out in front on this issue in a way Stalin never would have done.

After his agricultural successes of 1956, Khrushchev made speeches in 1957 calling for rapidly overtaking the United States in the production of certain basic foodstuffs.[45] In Leningrad in May, he boldly predicted that by 1958 the USSR would have more milk than the United States, and he said that by 1960–61 the Soviets would have caught up in meat production.

Both goals were highly unrealistic.[46] Of course, to fulfill his public commitments Khrushchev had to push ahead with the campaigns, and it led him to disaster. Furthermore, he ridiculed his more conservative colleagues in public.[47] The May 1957 speech in fact was apparently too much for his rivals, and one month later they tried unsuccessfully to depose him.[48]

Stalin kept his name away from his most far-reaching projects; Khrushchev put his name out front, continually proposing high-risk schemes to solve the country's problems. He too was coercive, but rather than hiding like Stalin behind conciliatory gestures, Khrushchev confronted, blustered, and bullied. Instead of moving incrementally, he took bold steps forward, delighting in the notion of low-cost, high-payoff schemes with which to outmaneuver his rivals, especially in the agricultural sphere. If the schemes succeeded, Khrushchev took all the credit. If they failed, instead of backing off he pushed ahead even further and criticized his rivals for placing obstacles in his way. While his style may have enabled him to succeed, it also led to failure because his opponents could pin the disasters on him. Nonetheless, he refused to play it safe, and in fact the architects of the 1964 coup that deposed him cited his style as his chief shortcoming; they faulted him for "actions based on wishful thinking, boast, and empty words . . . voluntarism . . . and subjectivism."[49]

Brezhnev

After Khrushchev's ouster in 1964, the Presidium members sought to prevent the emergence of a single strong leader. Leonid Brezhnev's top rivals were Aleksandr Shelepin, who had a strong base among the security forces, Nikolai Podgorny, like Brezhnev a member of the Secretariat and Presidium, and Alexei Kosygin, the new chairman of the Council of Ministers.[50] Mikhail Suslov apparently played a critical role in establishing the new leadership and was likely in favor of preserving the collective principle. The new government was known initially as the Brezhnev-Kosygin regime.

By December 1965 Podgorny had been forced out of the Secretariat and into the largely ceremonial post of president. Perhaps more important, the body responsible for checking up on party and state officials, the Party-State Control Committee, was no longer empowered to intervene in party affairs.[51] This institution was the power base of Shelepin, who was gone from the Secretariat less than two years later.[52] At the Twenty-third Congress in February 1966, the Presidium was renamed the Politburo and Brezhnev was called general secretary, a term that had not been used since Stalin held the position.[53] Soviet officials were soon speaking of the "Politburo headed by Brezhnev."[54] While not having the same power as Stalin and Khrushchev, Brezhnev had become the dominant political figure in the Soviet Union, but by using a strategy very different from that used by his predecessors, especially Khrushchev.

Rather than using coercion and confrontation, Brezhnev introduced consensus and accommodation into the top political echelons.[55] He was far more accommodative than either Stalin or Khrushchev, which might seem an odd characterization to those who recall certain harsh policies: his crackdown on dissidents and the invasions of Czechoslovakia and Afghanistan. Brezhnev was accommodative, however, in that he followed a strategy of trying to please his potential (and actual) rivals. Particularly toward the establishment—the party and the state officials whom Khrushchev had confronted—Brezhnev accommodated. He grabbed the political center and assured the elites that they would have the stability they had sought during Khrushchev's tenure.[56] Brezhnev appeased major interests in society: the party, agricultural, and defense elites. He also avoided making the kind of commitments that had proved so disastrous for Khrushchev.

In dealing with the Communist Party, for example, Brezhnev sought immediately to put forward a policy of reconciliation and stability. Stopping the attacks on the party apparatus of the Khrushchev period, Brezhnev at the 1966 CPSU Congress told party members that the leadership had "pride in [the] cadres."[57] In a further concession to the old apparatchiks, he called a halt to the trend of de-Stalinization that Khrushchev had started.[58] Most important to the cadres, the leadership undertook a series of initiatives to assure stability. At the Central Committee plenum in 1964, after Khrushchev's ouster, the leadership agreed to reunite the agricultural and industrial party institutions into one regional party body, then at the Twenty-third Congress the 1961 rules demanding forced turnover in the Central Committee and Presidium were expunged.[59] "Trust in cadres" became the slogan of the Brezhnev era.[60]

Much as Khrushchev had benefited from confronting the Stalinists, Brezhnev succeeded by reaching out to those whom Khrushchev had alienated. Khrushchev had blustered and threatened; Brezhnev gained support by stroking. Nikolai Egorychev, the former Moscow city party chief who was removed by Brezhnev in 1967, has described the Brezhnev approach: "He could always take an oblast secretary, have an informal chat with him, promise help, give him a farewell clap on the shoulder. All of us . . . when the Central Committee General Secretary gives you a friendly clap on the shoulder or calls you in the oblast himself, calmly talks with you—this is pleasing, this evokes sympathy. And to believe that this good, affable guy can be mistaken or can act in an unpartylike way—it's impossible."[61]

Brezhnev's accommodative strategy involved granting to the key constituencies in agriculture and defense the programs they wanted. In the agricultural sphere Khrushchev had put pressure on the elites through his big campaigns and through decentralization; Brezhnev announced a halt to the Khrushchev-style campaigns and to the reorganization of party and state organs at the local level. Furthermore, he announced that pressure from the center would be reduced and higher prices would be paid, especially for livestock.[62]

And whereas Khrushchev had confronted the military, arguing that huge reductions could be carried out in Soviet ground forces, Brezhnev gave them what they wanted. Mistakenly, in 1965 Brezhnev's rival Nikolai Podgorny, like Khrushchev, called for cuts in the military in order to reallocate money for the consumer sector. Not surprisingly, it was Brezhnev's accommodative strategy that gained the military's support.[63]

Brezhnev sought to satisfy all sectors of the defense establishment. Khrushchev had sought an increase in strategic rockets and submarines at the expense of ground forces, surface ships, and bombers. Brezhnev continued to push intercontinental ballistic missile and submarine programs, and he called for increased investment in the areas Khrushchev had cut. In May 1965 Podgorny argued that the Soviet people should not have to endure shortages in material goods in order to "strengthen our defense ability." In contrast, Brezhnev proposed broad, across-the-board increases in Soviet expenditures in conventional and nuclear systems precisely at the expense of the consumer goods sector.[64] After all, in the politics of the times, the military was more important than consumers to a leader's future.

In carrying out his accommodative strategies, Brezhnev sought to avoid commitments. While Stalin had avoided them until he was sure he would win, Brezhnev apparently had difficulty making tough decisions.[65] In his speech on the anniversary of the Bolshevik Revolution in November 1964, for example, Brezhnev spoke a great deal about the problems facing the nation, but he was careful not to propose any specific solutions.[66]

Brezhnev did not claim to be able to solve all problems immediately. He did not, as Khrushchev had done, "pose as the nation's leading agricultural specialist."[67] Where Khrushchev had promised big payoffs from his bold agricultural schemes, Brezhnev spoke in much more modest terms about making progress based on increasing investments and the growth of experience. Other than spending money in the important areas of agriculture and defense, Brezhnev did not make clear, unambiguous commitments. He did not raise expectations about what he would accomplish, as Khrushchev had done; instead he deliberately moderated expectations about what would be achieved.

Furthermore, unlike his predecessor, Brezhnev was careful to keep his name away from projects he was carrying out. Khrushchev had tied his name to proposals in such a way that he would rise or fall on their success or failure. Agriculture was particularly hazardous, given that bad weather alone could destroy a program. Brezhnev, however, was not going to get stuck taking the blame for problems over which he might have little control.[68] He did not make the Khrushchevian commitments to the "full-scale" construction of communism or to overtaking the United States within a few years. The following passage from Brezhnev's remarks on March 27, 1965, reads quite differently from Khrushchev's "I'll go myself" speech cited earlier: "We understand that an upsurge in agriculture is something that is vitally necessary to us for the successful construction of communism. In order to resolve this nationwide task, we must put a firm economic foundation under agriculture. V. I. Lenin regarded this question as one of the most important questions of the Party's economic policy, since it touches upon the very foundation of the Soviet state—the relationship of the working class and the peasantry."[69] Here Brezhnev did not commit to anything more than spending additional money. He used vague, general language and put very little of his personal prestige on the line.

Brezhnev seemed to have learned the right lessons from Khrushchev's failed policies. He was accommodative, trying to assure his constituents and rivals that he could bring much-needed stability to the country and especially to the party. Rather than confront the major interests in society, Brezhnev appeased them. And he avoided the bold, unambiguous, and personal commitments that Khrushchev had made, in part because he was apparently indecisive and in part because he did not want to be blamed for failures. These strategies and tactics worked well, and Brezhnev remained in power until his death in 1982.

Gorbachev

When the Politburo nominated Mikhail Sergeyevich Gorbachev as its general secretary in March 1985, the new leader faced two serious rivals as he moved to consolidate his power: Viktor Grishin, the first secretary in Moscow, and Grigory Romanov, the party chief in Leningrad. Gorbachev moved quickly against Romanov, removing him by July, and in February 1986, just prior to the Twenty-seventh CPSU Party Congress and Gorbachev's first as general secretary, the Politburo expelled Grishin from its numbers.[70]

Gorbachev achieved a dominant position in the leadership between the summer of 1988 and March of 1989. The Nineteenth Party Organizational Conference held in late June 1988 established strong executive powers.[71] A September plenum of the Central Committee demoted conservatives Yegor

Ligachev and Viktor Chebrikov, who were challenging the general secretary; at this time Gorbachev was elected chairman of the Presidium of the Supreme Soviet.[72]

By March 1989 Gorbachev's grip over the central decision-making apparatus was as firm as Khrushchev's had been, and his position would not weaken until the winter of 1990–91. In the spring of 1989, with the election of the new Congress of People's Deputies, Gorbachev became more secure as president of the national legislature, since now, unlike Khrushchev, he could not simply be removed from his position by a vote of the Politburo.[73]

In winning the succession struggle after 1985, Gorbachev adopted a coercive strategy similar to Khrushchev's, appealing to the masses to apply pressure on the other members of the Politburo either to get rid of them or to get them to support his programs of political and economic reform.[74] Brezhnev had assured the party cadres that they would have stability after Khrushchev's ouster, but after the long stagnation of the Brezhnev period, Gorbachev wanted to get the country moving again. To succeed, he had to get rid of the Brezhnev cronies who might stand against him, and this required attacking the party apparatus as Khrushchev had done. While he was wary of making the kind of bold commitments that had backfired on Khrushchev, Gorbachev did three things that were part of Khrushchev's bargaining repertoire: he publicly humiliated his rivals in order to coerce them; he increased the pressure in the face of opposition by raising the ante; and he used ultimata to force his opponents to concede to his positions.

Gorbachev used the media well to humiliate and coerce his most serious rivals. His first trip, two months after becoming general secretary, was to Leningrad. Leningrad was Grigory Romanov's stomping grounds, and while there Gorbachev gave a hard-hitting televised address at Smolnyi, the early Bolshevik headquarters. In this speech he challenged his opponents directly:

It seems that all of us will have to reattune—all of us, I would say from workers to ministers, to secretary of the Party Central Committee, to leaders of the government—all must reattune themselves to the new approaches, to understanding that there is no other way for us. . . . We must of course, must, as it were, give all our cadres the opportunity to understand the demands of the moment and this stage and to adjust. However those who do not intend to adjust and who are an obstacle to solving these new tasks must simply get out of the way—get out of the way, not be a hindrance.[75]

The general secretary added that he had learned from the people that "they will not tolerate abuse, violations of the law, bureaucracy, sponging, drunkenness, thriftlessness, squandering, and other negative phenomena. . . . The Soviet people strongly condemn instances of immodesty, ostentatiousness, and empty talk."[76] In other words, they would not tolerate all the things for which Romanov was famous. The former Leningrad chief resigned from the Politburo the following month. The strategy was working.

Gorbachev did not let up. In June he delivered a broad attack on the ministries for obstructing reform, and he even criticized ministers by name, which had not occurred since Khrushchev's reign. Also in June he traveled to Kiev, home of one of his other opponents and a Brezhnev holdout, Vladimir Shcherbitsky, the party boss of the Ukraine. Gorbachev stated, "If there are good things in the Ukraine, this makes itself felt everywhere. If there are any bad things in the Ukraine, this also makes itself felt everywhere. . . . So, there are many things that interest the Central Committee here in the Ukraine. I will say that they know how to work in the Ukraine. This is true. But it is also true that their work could be better."[77] The new general secretary was clearly not going to accommodate party leaders as Brezhnev had done.

If Gorbachev could not get the support he demanded, he was not afraid of browbeating his opponents. Prior to the Central Committee plenum in late January 1987, Gorbachev met individually with each of the three hundred Central Committee members to get their support for his program. He failed, and then he stood up at the plenum and delivered a speech different from the one he had circulated to them in draft form. Two observers wrote later, "The sheer savagery of his attack on the corruption during the Brezhnev years and his renewed emphasis on political reforms stunned his audience. He criticized 'extremely ugly forms' of corruption in the party organizations of Uzbekistan, Moldavia, Turkmenistan, Kazakhstan, and parts of Russia, including Moscow."[78]

In the period 1985–89 Gorbachev was probably willing to retrench more than Khrushchev had been when the apparat challenged him, but the overall pattern was, like Khrushchev's, to raise the ante on his opponents. Gorbachev started by simply stressing greater economic discipline, moved toward a more serious and (to the elite) threatening program of *perestroika* (economic reform), and then in the face of conservative backlash introduced *glasnost* (openness) and de-Stalinization to coerce his challengers to accept his essentially antiparty program. He may not have taken the risks Khrushchev did, having perhaps learned from Khrushchev's overthrow, but the essence of the strategy was the same.

But while Gorbachev used a coercive strategy, tactically he generally did not make Khrushchevian personal commitments. In this regard Gorbachev himself suggested that he had learned something from Khrushchev: "Politics is the art of the possible. Beyond the limits of the possible begins adventurism. It is for this reason that we appraise our possibilities carefully and soberly and map out our tasks taking this into consideration. Taught by bitter experience, we do not run ahead of ourselves on our chosen path, but take account of the evident realities of our country."[79] In economic affairs Gorbachev introduced proposal after proposal under the general rubric of *perestroika*, searching for one that would work.

Gorbachev's Central Committee report at the Twenty-seventh Party Congress was certainly much more vague than the Khrushchev Virgin Lands proposals or the optimistic scenarios of milk and meat increases announced in May 1957. Gorbachev said that "it is intended" to double resources by the year 2000; "it is intended" to provide every family a separate flat or house. Contrary to specific proposals like Khrushchev's in 1957, Gorbachev noted of his plan that "it is planned to more than double the rate of growth of agricultural production and to ensure a considerable increase in the per capita consumption of meat, milk, vegetables, and fruit."[80]

Gorbachev did on occasion use one form of commitment that was a favorite of Khrushchev's: the ultimatum. On numerous occasions he threatened to quit. Taking advantage of his opponents' inability to come up with an alternative program, at critical moments he essentially told the elite, "If you refuse to play the game my way, I will resign." Since they needed him once he had started the reform processes, their acquiescence to these ultimata increased his power and prestige.[81]

In January 1987, at the Central Committee plenum discussed earlier, Gorbachev threatened to quit if the CC did not support his latest attempts at reform.[82] In the spring of 1988 he called the Politburo together and again threatened his colleagues: "Perestroika cannot stop at the halfway mark. We have to go all the way. I am not willing to continue performing the duties of the General Secretary of the Party unless a clear choice is made in this direction."[83] Gorbachev was still using this tactic after the 1991 coup; he told foes of the union treaty that if they failed to support him, he would resign and leave the country in disarray, and this time he no longer had their support.

So Gorbachev followed Khrushchev's openly confrontational style, but he avoided the kind of personal commitments that might give his opponents an easy target around which to coalesce. He used public pressure to box in his rivals; exposed before their angry constituents, they could do nothing publicly but grudgingly give him their support. And when they dragged their heels, Gorbachev threatened to quit and leave them to find some alternative. But while Gorbachev was bold,[84] he did not commit himself the way Khrushchev had done. He did not make promises he could not keep, and he made more ambiguous proposals in order to blunt his opponents' attacks.

Each of the four leaders attained the top position in the Soviet leadership because his bargaining style worked well in the context in which it was used. After Lenin's death no one could assume his mantle immediately, and the party resented Trotsky for being arrogant enough to believe himself on a par with Lenin. Trotsky's rivals had good reason to believe that he was their greatest threat. While the other would-be successors battered each other trying to prove who was most worthy of succeeding Lenin, Stalin quietly undercut them in the unassuming pose of diligent disciple.

When Stalin died the problems he left behind were so great that glossing over them, as Malenkov did with agriculture, could not generate confidence among the elite that the country's problems would be solved. Staying the course was the wrong strategy, and Khrushchev did not choose it. He made bold new commitments, saying he could solve the country's problems, and he lived or died by his proposals. His style enabled him to gain power, but it also cost him his job when it alienated everyone around him.

When Khrushchev fell from power many people believed that Brezhnev would simply be a transitional leader. But Brezhnev's style proved appropriate to his times. He understood that the party he led wanted stability and moderation after the turmoil of the previous era, and he provided it. That stability may have led to stagnation, but it also enabled Brezhnev to stay in power for eighteen years.

Gorbachev, unlike the other three, was clearly in the driver's seat once he became general secretary, since at first there were no rivals with any real national prominence. But to break the entrenched apparat, he tried to use the pressure from below that had sent Khrushchev's rivals scurrying for cover. It was a high-risk strategy since the elite was well entrenched, and the continual attempts to change the system brought waves of new rivals even as old ones faded into obscurity. The conservatives did finally try to unseat Gorbachev in August 1991, following a strategy similar to that of their predecessors in 1964; and although they failed, the corresponding breakup of the USSR finished Gorbachev's political career.

A coalition-politics model might suggest that the domestic environment of the time led to the unique political style of each leader. One might argue, for example, that Khrushchev's and Gorbachev's strategies reflected the need after Stalin and Konstantin Chernenko to break the power of entrenched institutions, which resulted in a more bold and openly confrontational approach than that adopted by Stalin and Brezhnev.[85] But if the appropriate strategies and tactics for success derived so clearly from the political environment, then all of the pretenders to the throne during a given period should have used the same strategies and tactics—and they did not. Leon Trotsky and Nikolai Bukharin, Georgy Malenkov and Vyacheslav Molotov, Alexei Kosygin and Nikolai Podgorny, and Viktor Grishin and Grigory Romanov had political strategies that backfired or were inappropriate in the political situation in which they were operating. Stalin, Khrushchev, Brezhnev, and Gorbachev emerged on top partly because they were more effective political bargainers, given the constellation of political forces in their own eras.[86] Thus, the requirements of a given period may have led to the *success* of the ultimate winner, but that is because the winner's strategy was most suitable. And since each leader learned that his style was successful in one kind of political conflict, it only makes sense that he would continue to use those same strategies and tactics in the foreign policy arena.

THREE

Stalin and the Berlin Blockade Crisis

The Soviet blockade of the Western zones of Berlin, which began in June 1948 and lasted until May of the following year, created one of the first major U.S.-Soviet crises of the postwar era. The crisis was the final blow to the Grand Alliance of World War II, and it was a major cause of the division of Germany and of Europe that lasted until 1989. During the blockade, Stalin relied on the same strategies and tactics he had used so successfully at home, but this time his efforts ended in a miserable failure for the Soviet Union.

As he had done at home in the 1920s, Stalin applied a primarily coercive strategy but attempted to mask his actions with accommodative gestures. He tied his name only to offers to negotiate. He used his deputies, particularly Soviet foreign minister Vyacheslav Molotov and the supreme Soviet commander in Germany, Marshal Vasily Sokolovsky, to increase the pressure on the Western powers. This good cop/bad cop strategy was particularly apparent in a series of negotiations conducted in August by Stalin, Molotov, and the Western ambassadors. And as he had done in the 1920s, Stalin took his steps in Berlin carefully and gradually, avoiding commitments. He first applied low-level pressure to avoid provoking his adversaries or putting himself in an untenable position. Then, once an initial step had succeeded, Stalin gradually increased the pressure in a way that could be reversed if the adversary's response was too tough. From January to June 1948 the Soviet Union gradually increased its pressure on West Berlin, proceeding from harassment of traffic and communications up to virtually a full surface blockade. Having instituted the blockade, Stalin applied a strategy of gradually increasing pressure *verbally* in order to try to strengthen Soviet claims on Berlin.

This same pattern of veiled coercion can be found in many of Stalin's other foreign policy encounters—including the wartime conferences that established the postwar government in Poland and redrew its borders. That encounter will be examined briefly at the end of this chapter.

The Setting

The crisis in Berlin followed a period of several years when it was becoming increasingly clear that the Allies' common goal of defeating Germany was being replaced by divergent security objectives that were eventually to drive the Soviet Union apart from its wartime partners. The Soviets' goals in Eastern Europe were to establish regimes that were friendly, or at least not hostile, to the USSR, to assure that these countries could not be used as bases for military attack, and to extract resources with which to rebuild the Soviet economy.[1] Stalin hoped to achieve these goals without provoking Britain and the United States into a war with his weaker Soviet Union. In Germany the situation was extremely fluid. Britain, the United States, and the Soviet Union had agreed in the wartime conferences temporarily to divide and occupy Germany among them—France, by war's end, was added as a partner—and to divide Berlin, the former capital, as well; the four powers agreed to carry out the demilitarization and democratization of Germany, to manage the future development of the Ruhr valley, and to exact compensation for wartime losses.

By 1947 events were heading toward a permanent division of Germany into separate Western- and Soviet-controlled halves. In January of that year the British and U.S. zones merged in order to stave off German economic despair. Then, when the foreign ministers of the Big Four met in London in November and December 1947 as part of their regular series of meetings, the conference dissolved amid bitter discord. There were no plans to meet again.[2]

The Western Powers sought in 1948 to improve a deteriorating German economy and to develop a stable political entity in the Western zones. On January 31, 1948, a provisional German government was set up at the federal level to draft a constitution to be voted on by the German people fourteen months later. The Western foreign ministers met in London in March and agreed to establish a federal system of government for their zones of Germany, to allow it to join the Marshall Plan, and to put the Ruhr under international control. The French also agreed to integrate economically with Bizonia, as the joint U.S.-British zone was called.[3]

The major problem that the Western powers faced as they sought to re-build the German economy was currency disorder. The four powers were in charge of printing money, but each printed for its own zone, and the Soviets refused to divulge how much they were printing. So it was impossible to manage the money supply, and inflation was rampant. The Western Powers wanted to institute currency reform for their zones in Germany and in Berlin.

The West suspected that introducing currency reform would bring trouble with the Soviet Union. General Lucius Clay, the military commander of the U.S. zone, had said that if the Soviets were going to try to force the West out of Berlin, they would do so after the West had carried out a separate currency reform; otherwise, worthless old marks from the West might flood the Eastern zone, increasing the money supply there and causing a tremendous shortage of goods. Furthermore, control over currency translated into political control that the USSR would not want to give up.[4]

Stalin apparently did fear that the Western plans would upset his objectives in Europe, since a new West German state might threaten his newly secured East European buffer zone. To pressure the West to postpone a decision about the West German government, the USSR blockaded Berlin. At a minimum, if Stalin could not prevent the creation of West Germany, he might succeed in ousting the Western Powers from Berlin and thus secure the Soviet zone of Germany.

Imposing the Blockade

In his blockade of Berlin Stalin used the same style of bargaining that had worked so well for him in the 1920s. From March to June 1948 he pursued a coercive strategy, gradually increasing the severity of restrictions on traffic into and out of the Western zones of Berlin until the Soviets had blockaded the city on June 24, 1948. While Stalin steadily tightened the noose, he was careful to do so in small steps that could be reversed if the Western response was too threatening. And throughout the period Stalin avoided the limelight. Most of the restrictions were announced by Marshal Sokolovsky or one of his deputies. The only time the West would hear directly from Stalin during this period was when he engaged in a series of personal public exchanges with U.S. presidential candidate Henry Wallace calling for global peace.

In imposing restrictions on Western traffic and communications, Stalin took advantage of the vagueness of the four-power agreements on rights of access. In exchanges with President Franklin Roosevelt in 1944–45, Stalin had agreed in principle that the Western Powers should have complete right of entry into their zones of Berlin for persons and goods, but the technical details for exercising these rights were left for the field commanders. These details were never worked out, and the only written agreement on access rights concerned the air corridor.[5] In a meeting on June 29, 1945, Soviet Marshal Georgy Zhukov and General Clay agreed that British and U.S. forces had the right to use *one* road and *one* rail link to Berlin, but Zhukov warned that even this small concession might have to be changed.

From January to March 1948, consistent with Stalin's gradualist tactics, there were occasional low-level incidents of harassment at the border of the Western and Soviet zones; these consisted primarily of Soviet attempts at inspection. In January the Soviets stopped trains and trucks, charging their occupants with carrying faulty documentation, and they began periodic "repair work" on the canals.[6]

In the 1920s Stalin had taken slightly stronger stands when his initial steps succeeded. In Berlin he followed the same pattern, tightening the screws only after seeing that his latest moves had not provoked a stern Western response. In March Marshal Sokolovsky informed General Clay that the highway to Berlin would be closed for repairs until further notice.[7] At this point, if the Western reaction was too severe, Stalin could reverse his steps with low cost to his prestige.

At the end of March the Soviet Union imposed still more serious restrictions, the so-called baby blockade.[8] The USSR demanded the right to inspect all trains coming into Berlin and required a permit for any train leaving the city.[9] The United States and Great Britain agreed to an inspection of passenger cars but refused to allow inspection of military trains. The Soviet Military Administration controlled the signal system, however, and it could prevent the trains from proceeding.[10]

But Stalin went too far at this time. As the West responded to the new restrictions with what we might call the baby airlift, Soviet fighter aircraft buzzed and harassed U.S. and British planes in the air corridor. These actions resulted in the tragic collision of a British aircraft with one of the Soviet fighters on April 5, which caused several American and British deaths. While unwilling to accept responsibility, the Soviet Union removed the traffic restrictions temporarily, in the face of a strong U.S. and British reaction to the collision.[11]

Stalin's deescalation in response to the Western reaction signaled that there were limits to the level of commitment he was willing to make. He began increasing his pressure again on June 7, however, when the Western Powers publicly announced their decision to proceed with plans to create a West German state. The Soviets stopped rail traffic between Berlin and the West for two days, and they closed the Elbe autobahn bridge for "repairs." On June 16 the Soviet representative left the Allied Kommandatura (the four-power governing body of Berlin), and two days later the Western Powers announced the introduction of currency reform in the Western sectors of Germany, but not in the Western zones of Berlin. That same day all outgoing rail and barge traffic and all incoming passenger rail traffic was stopped by the Soviets, and Western autobahn traffic was subject to Soviet inspection. Thus, at this time, only food and supplies were entering Berlin.[12]

The West did not protest the Soviet actions at this point, believing that the USSR had a legitimate concern in protecting its zone from the impact of currency reform.[13] Thus, having succeeded in increasing his level of commitment without provoking a strong Western reaction, Stalin continued to push ahead. On June 23 the West extended its currency reform to the Western zones of Berlin as the Soviets were introducing a currency reform designed to cover their zone in Germany and *all* of Berlin.[14] Overnight, the Soviet Military Administration announced the following measures: the Berlin-Helmstedt rail traffic would be "suspended" because of "technical disturbances"; all electric power from the Soviet zone into the Western zones of Berlin would be cut; and no food would be allowed to move from the Soviet sector to the Western sectors of Berlin.[15] The city was cut off from the outside world on which it depended for survival.

Soviet actions during the period leading up to the blockade were accompanied by statements that sought to blame the West for the change in the status quo by arguing that the decision to plan for a West German government violated previous four-power agreements, and by claiming that Western access rights to Berlin simply did not exist. In making these statements, the Soviet Union could make its own actions seem natural and justifiable. Each time Soviet actions increased the pressure on the West, the accompanying statements seemed designed to take the edge off.

For example, to emphasize the Soviet position that the West was acting unlawfully, the USSR walked out of the Allied Control Council (the four-power governing body of Germany) on March 20 in response to the Western Powers' decision to proceed with plans for creating a West German government.[16] Sokolovsky stated that because the West had taken secret and separate actions, "the Control Council for all practical purposes has ceased to exist as an organ of supreme power in Germany."[17] This statement was the logical culmination of the constant Soviet refrain from February onward that Western actions were contrary to the four-power agreements on Germany. The Soviets clearly warned on March 20 that they would not accept the London decisions as legal and that the West must bear responsibility for the consequences of its actions.[18]

Soviet officials added that the West had no guaranteed rights of access.

At the time of the baby blockade in early April, Colonel Aleksei Yelizarov, the deputy Soviet kommandant in Berlin, claimed that the Western Powers were pillaging Berlin and removing industrial equipment to the Western zones. Then, three days later Lt. Gen. Mikhail Dratvin, the deputy governor of the Soviet Military Administration, wrote to Maj. Gen. George P. Hays, "I cannot help but consider as a misunderstanding and an error the statement in your letter that there was some sort of agreement concerning free and unrestricted utilization of [access]." [19] Meanwhile, a two-column article from Berlin provided by the Soviet news agency, TASS, stated that when the Western powers liquidated the Control Council mechanism, they then called into question their own right to maintain authority in Berlin.[20] Therefore, Soviet activities were justified.

As Soviet actions became more restrictive, the verbal warnings became increasingly sharp as well. After the introduction of transport restrictions on June 19, Sokolovsky again emphasized that Western actions were contrary to the interests of the German people and to the wartime agreements on four-power control over all of Germany. In his June 19 message to the German people the marshal wrote, "It is generally known that the Soviet Military Administration in Germany, acting in accord with the directions of the German government, always stood for the preservation of political and economic unity in Germany." The Western financial reform, he went on to say, "signifies the completion of the division of Germany." [21]

The pattern of Soviet action in the period leading up to the blockade followed the classic Stalinist style: The USSR gradually increased pressure in order to set a precedent for the adversary's acceptance of each step of the policy. Each action was reversible, and if the Western response was too negative, the pressure could be easily decreased, as occurred after the crash in the air corridor in April. In this case the Soviets, if need be, could simply have "repaired" the "technical difficulties," and the blockade could have been lifted without loss of face.[22] At the same time, Soviet statements were geared toward painting these actions as legitimate and the Soviets as defenders of the status quo. While the Western Powers conceded Soviet needs to protect the Eastern zone, they did not extend this concession to an acceptance of the Soviet attempt to cut off access to the Western zones.

Soviet verbal warnings did have limits. Stalin made no public commitment concerning Berlin. He did not say, for example, "If you do not stop with your plans for a West German state, we will starve the people of Berlin." He also did not personally tie himself to the coercive tactics in any way. His name was associated only with peaceful propaganda: for example, he engaged in a series of public exchanges with U.S. presidential candidate Henry Wallace in May on the need to end the Cold War.[23] Sokolovsky or one of his deputies would announce the imposition of any restrictions.

This pattern persisted in the rhetoric and negotiations from June to September in the aftermath of Stalin's imposition of the full surface blockade of Berlin. The Western Powers circumvented this surface blockade with an airlift whose capabilities to supply the people of West Berlin were initially a surprise to all sides.[24] If Stalin did not want war, he was now left with few nonverbal methods of coercing the United States, Britain, and France. The problem for Stalin was that there was a big difference between closing surface links and shutting down the air corridor. He had already learned about the potential Western reaction in April. Furthermore, the Soviet Union could put up surface obstacles that it would take an act of war by the West to break, but shutting down the air corridor meant that the USSR itself would be initiating an act of war.[25] And despite conventional superiority in Central Europe, the Soviet Union was at a disadvantage because the Americans had a nuclear monopoly. The United States highlighted its nuclear advantage by adding two squadrons of atomic-capable B-29s to those stationed in Germany in late June and then by sending sixty more B-29s to Great Britain in July.[26]

As he had done during the first half of 1948, Stalin continued to apply gradual pressure to coerce the West on Berlin, but because of his unwillingness or inability to stop the airlift, he had to rely on verbal warnings. Consistent with his domestic bargaining style, he used his subordinates to take the low road while he played the grand conciliator. There are two examples in July and August 1948 that illustrate Stalin's typical style of bargaining. First is the gradual increase in July in the sharpness of the rhetoric that established Soviet policy on Berlin. At the start, Stalin's subordinates staked out the position that Berlin was *economically* part of the Soviet zone. But gradually they began threatening that Berlin was literally part of the Soviet zone. The Western Powers never accepted these formulations, but Stalin apparently was willing to raise his rhetorical pressure as long as he was not confronted with direct Western action.

The second example is the series of negotiations among Stalin, Vyacheslav Molotov, and the Western ambassadors in August during which the Soviet leader bargained as he had with Trotsky and Bukharin in the 1920s. Stalin repeatedly communicated a friendliness and desire to negotiate, letting Molotov take the hard line. The records of these negotiations show the Soviet leader pretending to offer concessions that his foreign minister then took away. Unfortunately for Stalin, while this good cop/bad cop strategy had worked well at home in the 1920s, in Berlin it only hardened the Western commitment. In the end, Stalin failed to achieve any of his objectives in Berlin.

The position that Berlin was economically part of the Soviet zone was taken by Marshal Sokolovsky on June 20 in opposition to the Western currency reform. Sokolovsky argued that two currencies would undermine not only the economy of Berlin, "which is located in the Soviet zone of occupation and is *economically a part of it*," but also that of the Soviet zone as a whole. He could not allow two currencies because of the "obligations" imposed by previous "international agreements."[27]

Two days later Sokolovsky again wrote Clay explaining the need for Soviet currency reform on economic grounds. This decision, he argued, was necessary to prevent "economic chaos and the disorganization of monetary circulation." He then warned Clay not to interfere with the Soviet plan: "I hope that you do not create obstacles to the carrying out of this currency reform made necessary by your separate actions in the American sector of Berlin and do not create unnecessary difficulties in the matter of guaranteeing normal currency circulation and economic life both in the Soviet zone and in the region of Greater Berlin."[28]

The Soviet rhetoric became gradually more coercive; whereas the initial claims had been that Berlin was merely *economically* part of the Soviet zone, in early July the Soviet government stated that "after the U.S., Britain and France by their separate actions in the Western zones of Germany broke the system of quadripartite management of Germany and started to create in Frankfurt-am-Main the capital for a government of Western Germany, they therefore undermined the lawful basis that guaranteed their right to take part in the management of Berlin." The statement continued, "Berlin is located in the center of the Soviet zone and is a *part of that zone*."[29] This new position was the one the Western powers faced when they instructed their ambassadors to seek negotiations with Stalin in late July.

In a meeting on August 2, after U.S. ambassador Walter Bedell Smith reiterated the American position on Berlin, Stalin repeated the Soviet declarations of July: It was only natural to have Allied occupation troops in Berlin, the German capital, if Germany was treated as a unit. But Berlin was geographically in the center of the Soviet zone. The London conference called for a West German government with a capital in Frankfurt. Since there were now two capitals, the Western powers lost their juridical right to Berlin. Stalin said that he was not speaking of ousting the West from Berlin but was merely referring to legal rights.[30] As he sweetly put it, "After all, we are still Allies."[31] Good words truly were masks for bad deeds, as Stalin had suggested thirty-five years before.

At these negotiating sessions Stalin proposed that the Western powers temporarily suspend the London decisions, "until such time as the four powers meet" and abolish the special Western currency, the mark B, that had been introduced into Berlin in June; in return, the USSR would lift restrictions on traffic and communications. Smith wrote home that Stalin emphasized that the Soviets simply could not accept a West German government created out of the Western zones: Stalin "did not mind unification of the three zones, and even considered it progress. The Soviet zone also formed a unity but they had not thought of creating a government there, although we seemed to be pushing him towards it. That was the issue."[32]

After two hours of discussions, however, Stalin resorted to a typical deception, saying, "Would you like to settle this matter tonight?" He then proposed the replacement of the Western mark B with the Soviet currency coincident with the removal of all transport restrictions. Furthermore, he seemed to soften on the need to consider the fate of all of Germany: "While the Soviet government will no longer ask as a condition the deferment of the implementation of the London decisions for setting up a Western government in Germany, this should be recorded as the insistent wish of the Soviet government."[33]

Smith cabled home in the presence of the other two ambassadors: "Atmosphere generally much more friendly than I expected and Stalin, on four specific occasions, stated categorically Soviet Government had no intention of pushing Allied occupation forces out of Berlin although he reaffirmed vigorously Soviet position that by London decisions we had lost juridical right to remain there. On the whole, we are all satisfied with the outcome and with the general trend for the conversations."[34] When he was alone Smith wrote of these opening meetings, "Stalin and Molotov were undoubtedly anxious for settlement. . . . [If] one did not know real Soviet objectives in Germany[, one] would have been completely deceived by their attitude as both literally dripping with sweet reasonableness and desire not to embarrass. . . . [Of] course it will be harder to negotiate with Molotov alone."[35]

It was. Stalin had played his typical role as the grand conciliator.[36] But then the ambassadors met later with Molotov, who was, in Smith's words, "a stubborn, intransigent, and difficult bargainer." The ambassador reflected, "Time after time, it seemed to us that he reneged on statements that Stalin had made."[37] At his first meeting alone with the ambassadors on August 6, the Soviet foreign minister was aghast at a new Western proposal that spoke of Western input over currency control in Berlin. He reminded the ambassadors that with the Western zones split from the East, there was no more quadripartite control in Berlin. Molotov's position was that the Soviet deutschemark would be issued by the German emission bank, which was under the control of the Soviet Military Administration. The U.S. and British envoys both tried immediately to soothe Molotov's concerns, which may have led him to believe that they would not hold firm to insisting on quadripartite control over currency in the two Berlins.[38]

In a meeting on August 12 the Soviet foreign minister proposed the creation of an export/import bank in eastern Germany to regulate trade in

Berlin and suggested that the Soviet-zone currency be introduced "in the same quantity as the amount of B Marks issued by the Western powers in Berlin"; he also suggested that after transport restrictions were lifted and the switch to a single currency had been made, questions concerning currency flow could be discussed.[39] These proposals were, of course, unacceptable to the West.

After meeting once more with Molotov, the ambassadors met on August 23 with Stalin, who, Smith wrote, "met us quite jovially with the remark, 'well, I have a new draft.' "[40] As usual, Stalin made several accommodating gestures that seemingly satisfied Western concerns. He proposed a financial commission made up of representatives of the four military governors in Berlin that would govern currency matters in the city. Smith reported that Stalin "was quite categorical that this commission would be the controlling body and said he did not mind using the word control."[41] Furthermore, while Molotov in earlier meetings had agreed only on lifting the transport restrictions imposed in late June, Stalin at this meeting suggested that they use the phrase "the restrictions lately imposed" and, according to Smith, "confirmed that if there were any imposed before that date they would also be lifted." At the time, Ambassador Smith had difficulty assessing the negotiations; he remarked, "Things went so smoothly that I was a little worried, and remembered Stalin's proverb, 'an amiable bear is more dangerous than a hostile one.' "[42]

The negotiations finally culminated on August 27 in an agreement to send a four-power directive to the four supreme commanders in Berlin, who would have to concur on the practicality of the plan within a week of its issuance. Earlier Molotov had insisted that the details would be worked out in Moscow; this shift indicated that Stalin was not interested in a settlement.[43] The directive stated that the Soviets would lift their restrictions ("those lately imposed"), and simultaneously the Western mark B would be removed, with the German mark of the Soviet zone becoming the single currency in Berlin. The German bank of emission of the Soviet zone would regulate the currency, but a four-power financial commission would be set up to control the financial measures undertaken by the bank.[44]

The agreement seemed to satisfy both sides. But Stalin was negotiating with the Western ambassadors in August exactly as he had bargained with his rivals domestically twenty years before. He came to meetings offering new ways to settle problems, but he had no intention of carrying out his concessions. He played the role of moderate, and he let Molotov take the hard line. Stalin played his classic good cop/bad cop routine to the hilt. When the Moscow directive reached the four military governors, disputes soon arose on all points: which restrictions the Soviets would lift, what power the financial commission would have, and who would regulate trade in Berlin.[45] President Harry Truman wrote in his memoirs that the "week of technical discussions in Berlin proved even more futile than the month of negotiations in Moscow."[46]

The Western powers charged that Sokolovsky was deviating from the Moscow agreement; not surprisingly, the Soviets countered that the Western interpretation violated the four-power directive. Furthermore, the ambassadors and Stalin had agreed on August 23 to meet when the military governors had finished their work; Stalin, however, left for vacation and was unavailable.[47] Perhaps his failure to achieve a reopening of the German question led to his lack of interest in agreement on Berlin.[48]

Following the September breakdown, fruitless discussions took place at the United Nations. The so-called six neutrals of the Security Council (i.e., those not directly involved) put forth a resolution calling for an end to restrictions, to be followed by a meeting to establish a unified currency based on the Eastern mark. The Soviets vetoed this proposal because it backed away from the August directive calling for simultaneous actions. The Soviets wanted to settle the currency issue to their liking before lifting restrictions; the West wanted to see the restrictions removed and then gain four-power control.[49]

After the August negotiations, the next time the West heard from Stalin was in a *Pravda* interview of October 29. In the interview, Stalin tried to focus attention back on the August agreement as he disparaged the Security Council as a framework for discussion. He argued that the August agreement was a good one because it "does not offend anyone's prestige, it takes into account the interests of the sides, and guarantees the possibility of further cooperation."[50] Here was the first explicit Soviet acknowledgment that each side had legitimate interests in the dispute, and this interview may have been a signal to the West that the Soviet leader wanted to continue the four-power negotiations. Again, it was Stalin, not Molotov or Sokolovsky, who spoke when the Soviet leader wanted to hint at possible accommodation. These were the last major Soviet remarks regarding Berlin until Stalin's interview in January 1949, which broke the stalemate.

If Stalin had started the blockade to prevent what he perceived as a potential new threat from the West, he could only have been disappointed that by January 1949 his behavior had intensified that danger (although he probably did not attribute the hardening of the Western commitment to his own actions). Accelerated by his actions in Berlin, plans were moving ahead for the creation of West Germany and the North Atlantic Defense Pact. Meanwhile, in June 1948 the West had imposed a counterblockade on the Soviet zone in Germany and Berlin that was proving effective in ruining the economy of the Eastern zone. Finally, the success of the Western airlift even in winter demonstrated that the Soviets could stop it only by force;

barring the use of force, they could achieve nothing by exerting continued pressure on Berlin.

But how could Stalin get out of this situation without losing face? Basically, he settled for a minimal face-saver: the commitment by the Western powers to hold another Council of Foreign Ministers meeting that could discuss all the issues affecting Germany and Berlin. Stalin would try to get a commitment by the West to delay the creation of West Germany; the United States responded that the new state was not scheduled to be established before a council meeting would be held anyway. Despite the failure to achieve any change in the German situation, Stalin settled on the CFM meeting and acquiesced to the status quo ante of March 1948.

Stalin chose an unusual way to indicate his desire to negotiate. In January 1949 Joseph Kingsbury-Smith, the European manager of the International News Service, filed a series of questions with Stalin, as journalists often did.[51] On January 31 Stalin chose to respond to the questions on the front page of *Pravda*. For the first time Stalin's response indicated that the crisis could be resolved without dealing with the currency issue. His failure to mention the currency dispute seemed to be a signal to the West, but this means of signaling allowed him to disavow his interest in negotiating if he was dissatisfied with the response. As was typical, he was avoiding making a commitment—an omission in an interview was an ambiguous public signal designed to test the waters without putting Soviet prestige on the line.

Sending the signal in this way also meant that the Western powers had to notice that it was in fact a signal. Charles Bohlen, one of the leading Soviet experts in the United States and State Department counselor at the time, first noticed that Stalin had failed to mention the issue that had ostensibly created the Berlin crisis in the first place and brought this omission to the attention of Secretary of State Dean Acheson.[52]

The State Department decided that Philip C. Jessup, the deputy chief of the U.S. mission to the United Nations, should open a channel to Jacob Malik, the Soviet permanent representative to the United Nations. Seeing Malik at the delegates' lounge on February 15, Jessup asked the Soviet official if Stalin's omission of the currency issue had been an accident. "Malik said coldly that he had no information of the subject. Well, I said, if he should get any information perhaps he would let me know since I would be interested."[53]

A month later Jessup, then based in Washington as an ambassador-at-large, received word that Malik wished to meet with him. Jessup flew to New York the following day and learned that Stalin's omission had not been accidental: the currency question could be discussed at the CFM meeting along with the other issues. Jessup wanted to know if the blockade would be lifted prior to the CFM meeting, but Malik responded that since this question had not been asked before, he had no information.[54]

On March 21 Malik and Jessup met again, this time with the British and French representatives. Malik, answering Jessup's latest query, said that if a definite date was set for the Council of Foreign Ministers, then the blockade could be lifted before the meeting.[55] Truman commented later that these Jessup-Malik meetings were "an example of how difficult it was to do business with the Russians on a straightforward basis."[56]

By having his representative conduct the negotiations in the United States, Stalin could avoid tying himself personally to humiliating accommodation with the Western Powers. He apparently was accommodative himself only when he was being deceptive. If the Soviets were actually going to concede, a low-level official would present the proposals. At the same time, those associated with the hard-line policies of the previous fall were removed from their positions in March 1949: Andrei Vyshinsky replaced Molotov as foreign minister, and General Vasily Chuikov replaced Sokolovsky as supreme commander in Germany. These replacements were perhaps another way of distancing Stalin from the prior coercive behavior and a way of promoting a new Soviet peace campaign.

The negotiations dragged on throughout the spring, but basically Stalin accepted a return to the preblockade situation in Berlin. As agreed in the negotiations with Malik that culminated on May 5, the Soviets lifted the blockade on May 12, 1949. Stalin received the small face-saver of a CFM meeting on May 23, but he had failed to prevent currency reform and the creation of the West German state, and he was unable to remove the Western presence from Berlin. Eleven months of a blockade had achieved nothing and had only strengthened the American commitment to Europe.

Conclusions on Berlin

Stalin's bargaining over the Berlin issue in 1948–49 in many important ways reflected the style he had developed at home during his rise to power. One aspect of that style was his use of noncommittal tactics. From March to June 1948 the Soviet Union imposed new restrictions gradually and carefully, labeling each one temporary and thus easily reversible. The verbal communications of the summer also introduced the issue of Soviet control gradually and carefully: from a discussion first of Berlin being an economic part of the Soviet zone to Berlin being a literal part of the Soviet zone. Finally, the signal to resolve the crisis was noncommittal: while made by Stalin personally, it was ambiguous and was conveyed through the newspaper, making it easy to disavow.

The overall strategy was primarily coercive, both in word and in deed. Stalin played his typical role of conciliator in the August negotiations, using Molotov and then Sokolovsky to apply pressure. While such behavior may have had some utility in early August, by the end of that month the Western negotiators were clearly fed up with being told first one thing and then another. If Stalin believed that his opponents could not outlast him, he was wrong.

As a power-based explanation might suggest, it is also clear that the international environment placed limits on how far Stalin could go. The Soviet Union avoided using force to interfere with the airlift, as Stalin tried to avoid actions that might lead to war. After the incident in the air corridor in April, no further attempts were made to interfere with Western flights (although verbal warnings persisted during the summer). The Soviet inability or unwillingness to risk war gave the West enough room to maneuver successfully. The limits imposed by the U.S. nuclear monopoly established important boundaries on Stalin's behavior, but they did not fundamentally alter his basic bargaining style.

This encounter with the West was not the only example of Stalin's foreign policy mirroring his earlier domestic style. His negotiating style during the wartime conferences offers another example—and one that turned out better for him.

The Wartime Conferences

While there were many issues that Stalin discussed with his Western counterparts during World War II—including the timing of the launching of the second front, Soviet positions in the Turkish straits and in the Far East, and Soviet reparations from Germany—one of the key sticking points was Poland; the main issues were first, the postwar borders, and second, the composition of the government. The West was willing to agree to some shift westward of the Polish borders, both to compensate the Soviets and to weaken Germany, and the West also understood that any provisional government would include a significant number of Lublin Poles, who were loyal to the Soviet Union. What the West, and particularly the British, did not want was an extension of Poland to the western Neisse River and a provisional government composed *mainly* of Lublin Poles. In the end, Stalin received both of these things, which gave him everything he wanted on the Polish issue. He succeeded not simply because of the location of the Red Army in 1945 but also because of his ability to chip away at the Western position from November 1943 to July 1945. Whereas during the Berlin crisis his stalling hardened the Western commitment, during the wartime conferences it allowed him to cause splits in the positions of Winston Churchill and Franklin Roosevelt. FDR wanted Allied unity so badly, and he so much wanted Stalin to participate in both the United Nations and the war in the Far East, that he put off hard choices about Poland until it was too late.

In these negotiations and their aftermath, Stalin used his typical strategy. He was personally conciliatory, and he avoided making commitments both on the border issue and on the nature of the government. But he clearly had no intention of giving in to his counterparts. And he used Molotov, in follow-on conversations with his Western counterparts, to play the same role that the foreign minister would play three years later in the discussions concerning Berlin.

At Tehran in 1943 Stalin staked out a position only that the Western border of Poland should extend to the Oder River. In discussions with Stalin alone, Churchill expressed his desire for a strong and independent Poland, but he acknowledged his flexibility on the border issue.[57] When FDR met with Stalin alone several days later, the president said that the sizable number of Polish-Americans would preclude public comment on the borders, but that he privately agreed that they needed to be moved.[58] By the end of this first conference Stalin had received vague comments on the Western border; he had also laid out the Soviet desire for the area near Königsberg as well as the claim that the Curzon Line, drawn by the West after World War I, should serve as the eastern border between Poland and the Soviet Union.[59]

By the time of Yalta more than a year later, Churchill and Roosevelt were trying to get some of this area back. They suggested to Stalin that he graciously give Lvov to Poland, but Stalin reminded them that Lord Curzon had drawn the line, and Lvov would stay in the Soviet Union. When FDR and Churchill raised this issue, Stalin changed the subject to Dumbarton Oaks, an issue on which he was prepared to offer what was presented as a major concession: to accept only two extra votes in the United Nations rather than sixteen. Stalin could thus deflect attention from the discussions on Poland while claiming to foster the Allied unity that Roosevelt had called for regarding Polish territory.[60]

The composition of the Polish provisional government turned out to be a disaster for the West. Churchill raised the issue on February 6, 1945, at a meeting of the Big Three in Yalta, arguing that they should put together a government made up of both Lublin and London Poles. Stalin responded, "I am afraid that was a slip of the tongue, for without participation of the Poles it is impossible to create a Polish government. I am called a dictator and not a democrat, but I have enough democratic feeling to refuse to create a Polish government without the Poles being consulted."[61]

Of course, when FDR then suggested the following day that they bring

Poles from the different camps to Yalta to work out the new government, Stalin claimed that he was trying to phone them, but they were away and unfortunately could not be reached. Molotov then presented the Soviet proposal, which was merely to enlarge the current government with "democrats" in some unspecified manner, thus demonstrating that of course the Soviets were not all that concerned about consulting the Poles themselves.[62]

The debate raged for several days about whether to create a new government, as the West wanted, or merely to enlarge the current government, as the Soviets preferred. The British were particularly keen to have a more representative government, and Churchill argued that the Lublin government was not sufficiently popular. The argument fell on deaf ears; from Stalin's perspective what mattered most was loyalty, and he pointed out that since Poland was now in the rear of the Red Army, he needed a government he could trust. In a foreign ministers' meeting, U.S. secretary of state Edward Stettinius and British foreign minister Anthony Eden tried to insert a sentence about the role of the three powers in observing free elections, but Molotov squelched it. And the following day, while Stettinius said he still believed it was important, he backed off, saying, "The President . . . was so anxious to reach agreement that he was willing to make this concession."[63]

Because of FDR's desire for Allied unity and his lack of interest in details, the hard issues surrounding Poland were simply postponed at Tehran and Yalta. Yalta left open questions concerning the percentage of noncommunists in the Polish government, the manner by which key positions would be filled, and the persons who would become president and prime minister.

These issues were left for discussions in Moscow among representatives of the three powers: Averell Harriman, Archibald Clark Kerr, and Molotov. Here Molotov could play his familiar role in the bargaining. As he did at the Berlin negotiations in 1948, Molotov in 1945 added a whole host of new conditions to Stalin's earlier positions. At the first meeting, Molotov repeated the Soviets' position at Yalta that the provisional government should simply be enlarged rather than "reorganized," as the West hoped. He also added new conditions that included having the Tripartite Commission meet with representatives from the Warsaw government first, giving the Soviet and Warsaw governments the right to veto names proposed by the West for consultations, and prohibiting Allied personnel from observing events in Poland.[64]

As Churchill wrote to Roosevelt in early March, "It suits the Soviets very well to have a long period of delay, so that the process of liquidation of elements unfavorable to them or their puppets may run its full course."[65] The Soviet Union repeatedly refused to allow the West's leading candidate,

Stanislaw Mikolajczyk, to come to Moscow, first on the grounds that he refused to support the Yalta decisions and then on the grounds that he had inspired violence against Red Army officers in Poland.[66]

FDR and Churchill agreed on April 1 to confront Stalin directly on the disappointments of the Polish negotiations since Yalta. The two leaders reiterated the West's interpretation of the new government to be created in Warsaw, but FDR did allow that the Lublin Poles could come to Moscow first for consultations. The Tripartite Commission then met two days later, but as Harriman noted, "No agreement was reached on any point." [67]

Stalin replied to FDR on April 7, "Matters on the Polish question have really reached a dead end." He of course argued that the cause was the failure of the West to live up to the Yalta decisions, and he reiterated the Soviet position that the provisional government was to serve as the "kernel" of the new Polish government. If the West agreed to the Soviet position on Yalta, said Stalin, "I think that . . . a harmonious decision on the Polish question can be reached in a short time." At the same time, he also added a sweetener in his message to Churchill: "If you consider it necessary, I would be ready to influence the Provisional Polish Government" to remove its objection to Mikolajczyk if the latter would give public support to the Yalta decisions and to friendly Polish-Soviet relations.[68] Stalin was thus turning what the West saw as a right under the terms of the Yalta agreement into another magnanimous gesture by the grand conciliator.

After a series of meetings between various Western officials (including President Truman) and Molotov in Washington in late April, Stalin sent a message to the new president in which he suggested that the West was "demand[ing] too much" of him; "You demand that I renounce the interests of security of the Soviet Union, but I cannot turn against my country." He then proposed a new way out of the situation: the West simply needed to adopt the Yugoslav example in Poland.[69] Stalin had first raised this analogy several weeks before, and it was truly egregious, given that the Big Three had never agreed on the Yugoslav government but had an agreement on the government in Poland.

Within a few weeks Stalin clearly felt that events on the ground allowed him to abandon his false suggestions for accommodation. He had by now agreed that Mikolajczyk could come to Moscow, but he wrote Truman on May 10, "It seems to me you do not agree to regard the Provisional Polish Government as [a] basis for the future government of national unity and do not agree that the Provisional Polish Government should occupy in this government a place which rightfully belongs to it. I must say that such a position does not give [an] opportunity to reach a harmonious solution on the Polish question." [70]

The West continued to lose ground in the negotiations. Presidential adviser Harry Hopkins visited Moscow in late May and hammered out an agreement with Stalin on which Poles the West could bring to Moscow from Poland and abroad for consultation. Again, Stalin seemed to be making a grand gesture to his esteemed visitor, but as Churchill wrote to Truman, "I cannot feel . . . that we can regard this as more than a milestone in a long hill we ought never to have been asked to climb," given the Yalta agreements.[71] A month later the United States and Great Britain recognized the new Polish Provisional Government of National Unity, two-thirds of whose members had been drawn from the existing Warsaw government. Stalin's puppet government also maintained the posts of president, prime minister, interior minister, and defense minister.[72]

Just as he had done at home, Stalin achieved everything he wanted in these negotiations over Poland. As in the 1920s, he proposed various ways of achieving "harmonious solutions" with no intention of accommodating the West on anything that mattered. He let Molotov play the tough cop in the Moscow negotiations, allowing the issues to drag on while he consolidated his hold over Poland. The West was divided on how to deal with him until April, when it was probably too late. Churchill wanted to confront Stalin earlier, but FDR was hesitant until April 1 because he was nervous about the upcoming meetings in San Francisco to establish the United Nations.

Stalin thus exploited divisions in the West, and he also had a strong position on the ground in Poland that enabled him to achieve victory with his familiar bargaining style. And perhaps this experience confirmed what he had learned in domestic politics about splitting the opposition. Roosevelt was so intent on preserving the Big Three, and so keen on demonstrating that he and Churchill were not in cahoots against Stalin, that he did not press Stalin on the key issues; these were left to discussions among the subordinates, and we saw where that led in Berlin. Perhaps Stalin's use of the good cop/bad cop routine in the 1948 negotiations even when the strategy was not working stemmed not only from the success of this style at home in the 1920s but also from its continued success in the international negotiations at Tehran, Yalta, and Potsdam.

FOUR

Khrushchev and the Cuban Missile Crisis

When President John F. Kennedy ordered a quarantine around the island of Cuba on October 22, 1962, to block Soviet shipments of medium- and intermediate-range nuclear missiles,[1] he set the stage for what became the two superpowers' most dangerous showdown of the postwar era. But it was Nikita Khrushchev who took the superpowers to the brink of war, blustering and bullying as he had always done at home, even after the United States had discovered his secret plan to send missiles to Cuba. Khrushchev's behavior before and during the crisis reflected his earlier domestic bargaining style—until the threat of war became too great, at which point he abandoned his familiar style of raising the stakes and increasing his commitments.

Whereas Stalin in Berlin had used his subordinates to take the hard line while he himself professed conciliation, Khrushchev during the Cuban missile crisis was openly confrontational and used his subordinates merely to complement his own behavior. As he had often done at home, Khrushchev made a bold commitment in Cuba; he tried to orchestrate a *fait accompli* by secretly installing nuclear missiles on the island. When he failed to achieve his surprise, Khrushchev maintained and escalated his commitment early in the crisis by ordering Soviet workers on the island to speed up preparation of the missiles already there. He abandoned the commitment only when the threat of a U.S. attack on Cuba increased dramatically. This pattern of behavior was different from Stalin's in Berlin but was developed in the same way—it was what Khrushchev used to win power at home. As happened to Stalin in Berlin, the international environment altered Khrushchev's style only when the threat of war limited how far the Soviet leader would go in pressuring the United States.

The Setting

The genesis of the Cuban missile crisis involved at least three key judgments made by the Soviet Union. First, the Soviets and Cubans both feared that the United States would repeat the attempt to topple Fidel Castro that had failed so miserably at the Bay of Pigs in April 1961. There was pressure from several quarters in the United States to carry out such a plan, and a number of military exercises and options were drawn up for this purpose. The Soviets were aware of these exercises. They also saw as ominous the January 1962 decision of the Organization of American States to exclude Cuba as a participant, which had further isolated the island.

More important, in November 1961 U.S. deputy secretary of defense Roswell Gilpatric had announced that American surveillance of the Soviet Union revealed that Khrushchev's bluster about Soviet nuclear capabilities was just that—bluster.[2] The Soviets thus realized that their earlier attempts to bluff the United States about their own intercontinental ballistic missile capabilities were also exposed, and presumably Khrushchev worried that the Americans might try to use their nuclear advantage—estimated at the time to be 17 to 1—to coerce the Soviet Union. Khrushchev wanted to settle the Berlin issue, as he had been making clear ever since the wall went up in August 1961, and he may have feared that he might not be able to settle that issue to his advantage with the exposure of a missile gap favoring the United States.[3] In his memoirs Khrushchev suggests both of these reasons: "In addition to protecting Cuba, our missiles would have equalized what the West likes to call 'the balance of power.'"[4]

A third reason for the Soviet missile deployment may have been the U.S. stationing of intermediate-range missiles in Turkey and Italy. After all, from a Soviet perspective, if the United States could place such weapons to defend its allies, then why could the Soviets not do the same for Cuba? In terms of Soviet prestige, the ability to act as the United States had done would show that the Soviet Union was an equal superpower.[5]

Khrushchev apparently made his decision to send missiles to Cuba in late April or early May 1962. He himself wrote later that he thought of the deployment plan while on a trip to Bulgaria in May, but there are indications that while on vacation with Defense Minister Rodion Malinovsky in the Crimea in April, he discussed with Malinovsky the existence of U.S. missiles in Turkey. Khrushchev decided to reciprocate in Cuba.[6] He told his friend and Presidium colleague Anastas Mikoyan about his plan, arguing that the January decision of the Organization of American States to exclude Cuba was a precursor to an invasion. Khrushchev then informed Malinovsky, Presidium member Frol Kozlov, Foreign Minister Andrei Gromyko, and Strategic Rocket Force chief Sergei Biryuzov. At the same time, Khrushchev decided to make Aleksandr Alekseyev, a friend of Castro's, the new Soviet ambassador to Cuba.[7]

In early May Alekseyev met with the group, and they were joined by Uzbek Party chief Sharaf Rashidov. According to Alekseyev, Khrushchev said at the meeting that he wanted the United States to understand that an attack on Cuba would meet the nuclear might of the Soviet Union.[8] Mikoyan had advised Khrushchev that it would be hard to carry out the first secretary's plan in secret, and he also argued that Castro would never agree to it anyway.[9] Khrushchev suggested sending a delegation to Cuba to find out. He picked Rashidov to lead an agricultural mission to Cuba at the end of the month that would serve as a cover for consultation with Fidel Castro on the proposed Soviet plan. Biryuzov joined Rashidov's agricultural group under an assumed name to present the plan to Castro.[10] Castro accepted the plan immediately. Alekseyev reports that he, Rashidov, and Biryuzov told Fidel and Fidel's brother and defense minister, Raúl, of Khrushchev's plan, and "Fidel thought for a minute and then said that if such a decision would serve world socialism and the struggle of oppressed peoples against American imperialism, then Cuba was willing to take on this risk and its share of responsibility."[11]

On June 10 the Presidium ordered the Ministry of Defense to proceed with the weapons shipments. The plans called for sending twenty-four SS-4 medium-range ballistic missile launchers and sixteen SS-5 intermediate-range launchers with two missiles per launcher. Raúl Castro met with Khrushchev in Moscow in early July, and the two sides worked out the final arrangements for delivering the missiles and maintaining them under the Soviet military command. Forty-two SS-4 missiles actually arrived in Cuba, and recent evidence indicates that approximately twenty of the nuclear warheads may have reached Cuba during the summer.[12]

Khrushchev's solution to the strategic nuclear imbalance and to his fears about Cuba's security was typical of him. He made a personal decision to seek a quick fix and solve several problems in a single bold stroke. Instead of seeking a course of gradually building up the Soviet nuclear stockpile, he decided to send nuclear missiles surreptitiously to Cuba. He apparently planned to announce the Soviet *fait accompli* at the United Nations in November for maximum effect. The first secretary made the decision and presented it to his colleagues and to Castro. Unlike Stalin, who had avoided attaching his name to coercive policies, Khrushchev throughout the crisis tied himself personally both to coercive and to accommodative gestures, a strategy that would cost him dearly when he had to back down.

Khrushchev's basic strategy in Cuba was coercive. The Soviet leader was responding to his problems by threatening the United States with a new nuclear weapons deployment only ninety miles from Florida. In carrying out this strategy Khrushchev was committing himself to an unprecedented course of action. The Soviets had never considered deploying such weapons so far from their own soil. Khrushchev carried his bravado a step further by making public statements about the Soviet determination to defend Cuba. And by deceiving Kennedy he was making an even stronger commitment to his bold deployment plan, since he was directly challenging the president's own commitment to prevent Cuba from acquiring offensive weapons.

The Onset of the Crisis

By late summer of 1962 Kennedy had become extremely concerned about the increased volume of shipments from the Soviet Union to Cuba and was warning the Soviets not to send offensive weapons to the island. On September 4 the president warned the Soviets that if offensive ground-to-ground missiles or other offensive weapons were placed in Cuba, "the gravest issues would arise." [13]

Khrushchev responded to Kennedy's commitment with both confrontation and deception. He himself made a number of comments on Cuba in which he adopted a highly confrontational tone and clearly specified how the Soviet Union would respond to particular American actions, while also continuing to deny the presence of offensive missiles in Cuba. He also conveyed the same message through a major statement issued by the Soviet news agency, TASS. And he used his subordinates to deceive Kennedy about the Soviet shipments to Cuba. Through his statements and his actions, Khrushchev committed himself both publicly and privately to protecting Cuba and to challenging President Kennedy. [14]

For example, only two days after Kennedy's September 4 speech, Khrushchev met with U.S. secretary of the interior Stuart Udall at his dacha in the Caucasus. After assuring Udall that the USSR had supplied the Cubans with defensive weapons, he added, "You have surrounded us with military bases. . . . If your Congressmen want to attack Cuba, they are like Tolstoy's aging man. I have stated that we could support Cuba even from our own territory." Less than two weeks later, in a meeting with Austrian vice-chancellor Bruno Pitterman, Khrushchev declared that if the United States blockaded Cuba, Soviet ships were under orders not to stop. If the ships were fired on, Khrushchev warned, it would be an act of war. [15]

Then on September 11 TASS issued a statement that reaffirmed Khrushchev's stance about the defensive nature of the weapons sent to Cuba as well as his resolve to meet any U.S. challenge. The statement reiterated that the Cubans had requested arms to deal with the imperialist threat, and that the Soviets had sent weapons and also specialists to train the Cubans to use them. The statement continued:

The Soviet government has authorized TASS to state also that the Soviet Union does not need to transfer to any other country, for example Cuba, the means it has for repulsing aggression, for a retaliatory strike. Our atomic means are so powerful as an explosive force, and the Soviet Union has such powerful rocket delivery for these nuclear charges that it does not need to look for a place for their deployment somewhere outside the Soviet Union. We have said before, and we will repeat that if war is unleashed, if the aggressor makes an attack on some other state and this state turns for help, then the Soviet Union has the ability from its own territory to give help to any other peace-loving state, and not only Cuba. And let no one doubt that the Soviet Union will give such help since in 1956 it was ready to render military aid to Egypt. . . .

We do not say this in order to frighten anyone. Intimidation is alien to Soviet foreign policy.[16]

This type of rhetoric was far more extreme than the rhetoric that had led up to the Berlin blockade. And there was more. The statement also warned that an attack on Cuba would unleash a war, and that in "modern conditions" the socialist camp "has no fewer" capabilities than the Western camp. TASS also reminded the world of the Soviet view that the USSR had just as much right as the United States to establish bases: "The whole world knows that the USA has circled the Soviet Union and other socialist countries with its military bases. What have they placed there—tractors? . . . This they consider their right. . . . It is necessary to acknowledge equal rights and equal capabilities for all countries of the world." [17]

TASS concluded with a reminder that the German problem remained open, and the Soviets hoped for the "quickest conclusion of a German peace treaty and based on it the regulation of the [Soviet] position in West Berlin." The statement warned, "The problem should be decided and it will be decided. The sovereignty of the GDR should be protected, and it will be protected." [18]

In addition to the confrontational statements about Soviet abilities to counter any U.S. challenge, Khrushchev also used several key subordinates to deceive President Kennedy about Soviet activity. Foreign Minister Gromyko, Soviet ambassador to the United States Anatoly Dobrynin, and Khrushchev's personal emissary Georgy Bolshakov each assured members of the Kennedy administration that the Soviets had no intention of installing ground-to-ground missiles. While Gromyko knew the truth, Dobrynin and Bolshakov were apparently unaware that they were misinforming the United States.[19] The deceptive signals were designed to increase Khrushchev's chances of deploying the missiles secretly, but they also raised the stakes in his relationship with President Kennedy.

The use of Bolshakov made it clear that Khrushchev was using every means he had to deceive Kennedy. Bolshakov had become a valuable emissary who on several important occasions conveyed messages from Khrushchev through Robert Kennedy to the president. The two had become acquainted in early 1961, when Bolshakov gave Robert Kennedy the impression that he was Khrushchev's personal representative. They then met often, and Bolshakov played a role in defusing conflicts over Berlin and Laos.[20] Both Kennedys trusted him, and Khrushchev's willingness to risk sacrificing this channel of communication emphasizes the first secretary's commitment to achieving a *fait accompli* in Cuba.[21]

In early October Khrushchev sent Bolshakov to deliver a message to Robert Kennedy. The emissary informed the president's brother that Mikoyan and Khrushchev *personally* assured the United States that "no missile capable of reaching the U.S. will be placed in Cuba."[22] At the same time, Khrushchev was sending similar messages to the United States through other Soviet officials. On September 4 Ambassador Dobrynin assured Robert Kennedy that the Soviet government would make no trouble for the administration before the midterm congressional elections.[23] On September 6 the ambassador met with Kennedy adviser Theodore Sorensen and told him that Khrushchev might come to the United Nations in late November, again implying that the Soviet leader had no wish to challenge the president prior to the elections. The following day Dobrynin met the American representative at the United Nations, Adlai Stevenson, and informed him that only defensive weapons were being supplied to Cuba. Dobrynin had been instructed from Moscow to give these messages.[24]

On October 16, the day Kennedy learned of the Soviet missiles in Cuba, Khrushchev was meeting with U.S. ambassador Foy Kohler. The Soviet leader reiterated his pledge not to take action in Berlin before the November elections, and he mentioned again that he might visit the United Nations in late November or early December. He expressed concern over the U.S. Jupiter missiles in Turkey and in Italy, and he continued to insist that all Soviet activity was purely defensive.[25]

The best-known example of Soviet deception in this period occurred on October 18, when the American president met with Foreign Minister Gromyko. Kennedy was furious because Gromyko continued to deny the presence of offensive weapons in Cuba. Gromyko himself stated later that since the president had asked about "offensive weapons" and not rockets, he avoided the whole subject of missiles and said simply that only defensive weapons were being sent; the foreign minister argued that since he had not been asked directly about missiles, technically he had not lied.[26]

The deception increased the level of commitment for both leaders. Kennedy had clearly told Khrushchev that he would not tolerate missiles in Cuba. Khrushchev had claimed that he was only defending his ally, and he threatened retaliation in the event of an American attempt to prevent this assistance. When he learned that Khrushchev had deceived him, Kennedy had to do something. Once Kennedy did something, he was challenging Khrushchev's commitment. Khrushchev's deception had put both leaders in a bind.

The Showdown

On October 22 Kennedy explained to the nation and the world that the Soviet Union had placed offensive missiles in Cuba and that he intended to quarantine the island to prevent further military shipments. The threat of superpower war—as Soviet ships steamed toward the island and as the United States made preparations to strike the missiles already deployed there—was the highest it had been since 1945. The two leaders had to respond quickly, since the construction at the weapons sites increased the likelihood that the missiles could be used, and the United States in turn was making preparations for a possible air strike.

During the course of the next week Khrushchev first responded, as he had often done at home, by increasing his verbal bluster. He denied that the missiles were in Cuba, and he warned that the Soviet Union would not back down. He involved himself very personally, as he had done in the preceding weeks, sending letters every day to Kennedy (and to others, such as United Nations Secretary General U Thant and British philosopher Bertrand Russell). He also met for three hours with an American businessman visiting in Moscow and harangued him about the Soviet abilities to withstand the challenge. The Soviet military stressed its battle-readiness, and work continued on the missiles to make them operational.[27]

At the same time as he was taking a confrontational verbal position and threatening the United States by continuing work on the missiles in Cuba, Khrushchev was careful to avoid actions that might initiate hostilities. The ships carrying military cargo did not challenge the blockade and turned back to their home ports. Furthermore, the Soviet Union took no action in Berlin, as some in the U.S. government had feared it might do. There were limits to Khrushchev's actions that were not evident in his earlier domestic political bargaining, and these limits stemmed from the dangers of nuclear war posed by the crisis.

Soviet Rhetoric

On the morning after Kennedy's October 22 address announcing the quarantine of Cuba, TASS began sending out the first Soviet government response. Ambassador Kohler was given a copy of the statement with a letter from Khrushchev to Kennedy. In the letter Khrushchev first adopted a confrontational tone, denying the existence of offensive missiles and arguing that the U.S. quarantine violated United Nations and freedom-of-navigation laws. His tone then shifted as he tried to persuade the United States to change course, and he issued an ambiguous warning about the possibilities for war: "I hope that the United States government will display wisdom and renounce the actions pursued by you, which may lead to catastrophic consequences for world peace."[28]

As expected, the Soviet government's note also put blame for the crisis on the United States and sent a mild warning: "At this alarming time, the Soviet government considers it its duty *to appeal* with serious caution to the government of the USA, to *forewarn it* that by implementing the measures stated by President Kennedy, it brings on itself a serious responsibility for the fate of the world; it plays a reckless game with fire." The note reminded the United States of Soviet nuclear capabilities, warning that while the USSR would never be the first to use its nuclear weapons, "if the aggressor unleashes war, then the Soviet Union will inflict the most powerful retaliatory strike."[29]

This letter was quite measured compared with the one the first secretary sent the following day. In this highly confrontational letter Khrushchev argued that Kennedy was presenting him with an unacceptable ultimatum. While the Soviet leader had used ultimata in his own domestic and international political bargaining, he apparently resented it when someone else presented him with one: "In presenting us with these conditions, you, Mr. President, have flung a challenge at us." Khrushchev continued:

You, Mr. President are not declaring a quarantine, but rather are setting forth an ultimatum and threatening that if we do not give in to your demands you will use force. . . . No, Mr. President, I cannot agree to this, and I think that in your own heart, you recognize that I am correct. I am convinced that in my place you would act the same way. . . . Therefore, Mr. President, if you coolly weigh the situation which has developed, not giving way to passions, you will understand that the Soviet Union cannot fail to reject the arbitrary demands of the United States. When you confront us with such conditions, try to put yourself in our place and consider how the United States would react to these conditions. I do not doubt that if someone attempted to dictate similar conditions to you—the United States—you would reject such an attempt. And we also say—no.[30]

Khrushchev was taking great pains to define the problem his way. He was framing the issue not only so that the United States would shoulder the blame for the events taking place, but also so that a "rational man" like President Kennedy would see that Khrushchev had no other choice except to stand firm. Kennedy should back down, Khrushchev was saying, because the U.S. president was asking something of the Soviet Union that he himself would never accept were it asked of him. Khrushchev was strengthening his personal commitment to his position in a way that Stalin never did in the Berlin blockade crisis, and thus when he backed down, his reputation suffered a more serious blow than it otherwise might have.

Even though Khrushchev had already ordered the military cargo ships to turn back, he stated that the "Soviet government cannot instruct" the ships bound for Cuba to reverse course. The first secretary also issued a threat (one that he apparently had no intention of fulfilling): "Naturally we will not simply be bystanders with regard to piratical acts by American ships on the high seas. We will then be forced on our part to take the measures we consider necessary and adequate in order to protect our rights. We have everything necessary to do so."[31]

Khrushchev also had a three-hour meeting on October 24 with William E. Knox, a U.S. businessman visiting Moscow at the time.[32] He sent several warnings to Kennedy through Knox and also offered a conciliatory gesture. He told Knox that the blockade was illegal, that stopping and searching would be piracy, and that the Soviet Union had anti-aircraft and ballistic missiles armed with conventional and nuclear warheads in Cuba. For the first time he had admitted that the Soviet Union had placed ballistic missiles in Cuba, but Khrushchev also spent a half-hour distinguishing between offensive and defensive weapons and comparing Cuba with Turkey. He said that if Soviet ships were stopped and searched, Soviet submarines would be instructed to sink the U.S. vessels. Khrushchev did stress that these weapons were in Soviet hands and "would never be fired except in defense of Cuba and then only on the personal instructions from Khrushchev as the Commander-in-Chief of the Armed Forces." This statement was an assurance to the United States, but also a commitment—any missile fired would be Khrushchev's responsibility.[33]

At the same time, Khrushchev expressed a desire to meet Kennedy in the United States, in the Soviet Union, at sea, or anywhere the U.S. president wished—except at the United Nations, which he called a "place for arguing not negotiating."[34] Khrushchev also sent a similar signal in response to an appeal from British philosopher Bertrand Russell. On October 23 Russell had written Khrushchev asking for caution in the face of what Russell described as illegal U.S. actions. Khrushchev wrote back assuring Russell that the Soviets sought a resolution: "I want to assure you that the Soviet government will not take any decisions that would be reckless, will not give provocation itself to the unwarranted actions of the USA, and will do everything to liquidate the situation fraught with irreparable consequences that has arisen in connection with the aggressive actions of the U.S. government." After reiterating the Soviet intention to avoid war, Khrushchev also issued an appeal for a summit with Kennedy: "The question of war and peace is such a vitally important question that we would consider useful a meeting at the highest level, in order to discuss all the questions that have arisen, to do everything to reduce the threat of thermonuclear war." [35]

Khrushchev never proposed to Kennedy that the two leaders get together to negotiate a settlement. He made his request personally and publicly, but to a third party, as he had done in suggesting a summit to Knox. In this way Kennedy would not need to reply to the appeal; it was not specifically addressed to him. But Khrushchev had put himself on record as favoring a summit. Perhaps he was searching for possible ways of ending the crisis, or perhaps he was simply trying to stall for time while the missile sites were being completed. [36]

United Nations Secretary General U Thant gave Khrushchev another opportunity to express his interest in ending the crisis. U Thant had made a proposal that would fit well with Soviet intentions. He had suggested that the Soviet Union stop all shipments to Cuba and that the United States lift the quarantine. He proposed that it would aid the negotiation process if each side halted its actions for "two or three weeks." On October 25 Khrushchev replied to U Thant's letter: "I have received your appeal, and carefully studied the proposals it contains. I welcome your initiative. I understand your anxiety over the situation obtaining in the Caribbean, since the Soviet government also regards this situation as highly dangerous and calling for immediate intervention by the United Nations. I declare that I agree with your proposal which accords with the interests of peace." [37]

Not only might U Thant's proposal serve the interests of peace; it would also certainly serve Soviet interests. The USSR could continue to work on the missiles to make them operational, while the United States would have to sit back and watch. But in accepting U Thant's proposals, Khrushchev was again expressing his fear of escalation (and he now agreed that even the United Nations could play a role in resolving the crisis). Taken with the letter to Bertrand Russell, the response to U Thant should be seen as another indication that Khrushchev was putting out feelers for negotiations. On the other hand, he had not yet said anything about removing Soviet missiles from Cuba.

As Stalin had done in early 1949 during the Berlin crisis, Khrushchev was sending accommodative signals in noncommittal fashion so that these could be denied if a satisfactory U.S. response was not forthcoming. Khrushchev was more careful when offering concessions than when trying to bully his opponents. Stalin was much more personally involved when offering false concessions than when pushing a hard line, while Khrushchev was more personally involved when issuing fake threats than when signaling a possible interest in accommodation. Stalin's plan backfired in Berlin because his false conciliatory gestures hardened the Western commitment; Khrushchev's style would backfire in Cuba because he had to back down from personal threats to stand up to the West.

Khrushchev's care in proposing concessions was visible in his two proposals to end the crisis on October 26.[38] The first was a rambling, highly personal and private letter from Khrushchev to Kennedy that seemed to propose a withdrawal of the missiles in exchange for a U.S. pledge not to invade the island, though it had no specific words to that effect. The second, much more formal in tone, upped the ante, proposing a missile swap involving Turkey and Cuba. Unlike the first missive, the second was sent publicly, thus raising the level of Khrushchev's commitment to that position.

In the first letter Khrushchev swung from a slightly confrontational tone to a highly conciliatory one, but the letter was rambling, and his proposals for getting out of the crisis were vague. After discussing the horrors of war, the need to avoid it, and the inability of the two sides to stop a war if one started, Khrushchev issued a veiled threat: "I assure you that the ships bound for Cuba are carrying no armaments at all. The armaments needed for the defense of Cuba are already there. I do not mean to say that there have been no shipments of armaments at all. No, there were such shipments. But now Cuba has already obtained the necessary weapons for defense."[39] This statement was, of course, true. The military cargo ships had turned back, and Cuba did already have part of the shipment of medium-range missiles. Furthermore, the technicians on the island were still working to ready the weapons already there. Khrushchev was reminding the United States of his deployed force without saying anything about retaliatory strikes.

Khrushchev then reiterated his acceptance of U Thant's proposals to stop the arms shipments while the sides negotiated. He also offered several vague proposals for ending the crisis:

If the President and Government of the United States would give their assurances that the United States would itself not take part in an attack upon Cuba and would restrain others from such action; if you recall your Navy—this would immediately change everything. . . .

I propose: we, for our part, will declare that our ships bound for Cuba are not carrying any armaments. You will declare that the United States will not invade Cuba with its troops and will not support any other forces which might intend to invade Cuba. Then the necessity for the presence of our military specialists in Cuba will be obviated.[40]

These words said nothing specific. The second paragraph merely reiterated the U Thant proposal. Khrushchev referred only to the military specialists on the island, and not to the weapons. To this point he had not made any concessions; he had merely hinted at possibilities.

The first secretary then added a section seemingly pleading with Kennedy to help him find a way out while warning that war might be unleashed despite their efforts:

If you have done this as the first step towards unleashing war—well then—evidently nothing remains for us to do but to accept this challenge of yours. If you have not lost command of yourself and realize clearly what this could lead to, then, Mr. President, you and I should not now pull on the ends of the rope in which you have tied a knot of war, because the harder you and I pull, the tighter this knot will become. And a time may come when this knot is tied so tight that the person who tied it is no longer capable of untying it, and then the knot will have to be cut. What that would mean I need not explain to you, because you yourself understand perfectly what dread forces our two countries possess.[41]

The letter that followed had a much different tone. It was more formal, and it raised the ante. Now Turkey was to be part of the equation. The United States, Khrushchev wrote, believed that it could place missiles in Turkey and yet still ask the Soviets to remove theirs from Cuba. "How then can recognition of our equal military capacities be reconciled with such unequal relations between our great states? This is irreconcilable." He then made his new offer: "I . . . make this proposal: We are willing to remove from Cuba the means which you regard as offensive. We are willing to carry this out and to make this pledge in the United Nations. Your representatives will make a declaration to the effect that the United States, for its part, considering the uneasiness and anxiety of the Soviet state, will remove its analogous means from Turkey."[42]

This proposal was unambiguous. Khrushchev would take his missiles out of Cuba. The United States would take its missiles out of Turkey. The clarity of the message was in striking contrast to the previous letter. And it was public. Furthermore, the Soviet leader imposed a one-month time limit for this deal to take place.[43]

In his proposal Khrushchev reaffirmed Soviet control over weapons in Cuba.[44] He may have meant it as a reassurance, but it also made him accountable for the firing of any missiles. And the United States believed that Khrushchev had ordered such a strike when an American U-2 reconnaissance aircraft was shot down later that day. Khrushchev had written, "The means situated in Cuba, of which you speak and which disturb you, as you have stated, are in the hands of Soviet officers. Therefore, any accidental use of them to the detriment of the United States is excluded."[45]

The members of Kennedy's Executive Committee (ExComm) had plenty to speculate about after receiving the second letter. They were concerned not only with the difference in content and style but also with the public/private distinction. On the first point, former U.S. ambassador to the Soviet Union Llewellyn Thompson argued that either the Presidium had overruled Khrushchev and had forced him to take a stronger line, or Khrushchev had seen comments by journalist Walter Lippmann and Austrian foreign minister Bruno Kreisky on a Turkey/Cuba swap and thought these were signals by the U.S. government.[46] Lippmann's piece had appeared in the *Washington Post* on October 25, and in it the journalist argued, "The only place that is truly comparable with Cuba is Turkey."[47]

As for why the second letter was made public, President Kennedy argued that Khrushchev had done so because the proposed swap was a good one. McGeorge Bundy added that it was "a way of pinning themselves down" to a position.[48] In other words, if the Soviets were making a commitment to end the impasse, these were the terms they were offering. Again, in making a commitment to those terms, Khrushchev was putting his reputation at stake, as he had done so often at home in his favorite sphere—agriculture.[49]

At the same time, the ExComm was puzzled by the line of communication opened during the crisis by Aleksandr Fomin, the KGB station chief in Washington. Fomin approached ABC newsman John Scali on the morning of October 26 and suggested that Khrushchev might be willing to withdraw the missiles under United Nations supervision in exchange for a U.S. pledge not to invade Cuba. Along with the withdrawal, Castro would pledge not to accept offensive weapons in the future. Fomin said that if Adlai Stevenson made this proposal at the United Nations, the Soviet representative there, Valerian Zorin, would be interested.[50]

Because Fomin floated his proposal at the same time that Khrushchev's letter vaguely outlining such a deal arrived in Washington, many on the ExComm inferred that Khrushchev was using Fomin as a supplement to his letter; perhaps Khrushchev made no personal commitment in his letter because he was using Fomin to present the specific proposal. The Soviet leader could disavow it easily if the United States did not respond.

After checking with Secretary of State Dean Rusk, Scali responded, "I have reason to believe that the U.S. Government sees real possibilities on this and supposes that representatives of the two governments could work this matter out with U Thant and with each other. My impression is, however, that time is very urgent." Fomin replied that he would send the message to the "highest authorities" in Moscow and to Zorin.[51]

Years later Fomin said that he had acted on his own. His statements have been backed up by Georgy Kornyenko, the political counselor in the Soviet embassy in Washington at the time. Raymond Garthoff, who has researched these events in great detail, has also argued that if Fomin was in fact a Khrushchev messenger, then presumably the first secretary would have waited to hear the results of the probe. The October 26 letter was sent before Fomin's account was received in Moscow.[52]

Neither Kornyenko's comments nor Garthoff's arguments necessarily support Fomin's contention. If Fomin was directly connected to Moscow, he need not have acted through the embassy. And presumably the KGB station chief in Washington had his own channels to Moscow.[53] Furthermore, if Khrushchev meant to use the Fomin channel in *conjunction* with his own letter that outlined the deal more ambiguously, then Garthoff's point on the timing of the two signals is misleading. Garthoff himself argues that U Thant's October 26 suggestion to Adlai Stevenson and John McCloy that the United States need offer only a noninvasion pledge to settle the crisis may have been planted discreetly by the Soviets themselves.[54]

There are other reasons to believe that Khrushchev did instruct the KGB to send Fomin. One is simply that it is difficult to imagine a KGB officer deciding to act on his own at such a time by offering a deal to the United States. A second is Fomin's mention of Zorin during his meetings. If Fomin was urging the United States to make the proposal at the United Nations, and if he was stating that Zorin would respond favorably, then presumably Fomin had been in touch with the Soviet ambassador to the United Nations. And if he had, the independence of the action is placed in greater doubt.

Khrushchev may have wanted to propose his deal through multiple channels so that he would not have to commit himself to the specifics of his offer, which was the pattern with his earlier letters to U Thant and Bertrand Russell. One observer has written, "Khrushchev was returning to his preferred method of defusing confrontation with the United States— sending a secret agent to make a suggestion for which the Chairman did not wish to take public responsibility."[55] Again, Khrushchev was cautious when offering concessions in a way that he was not when making threats.

Soviet Actions

What about the Soviet actions that accompanied Khrushchev's rhetoric during the crisis in Cuba? When Kennedy announced the imposition of the quarantine on October 22, twenty-four Soviet ships were steaming toward the island. At the same time, work was continuing on the missiles already deployed, and if they become operational they would pose a serious threat to American security. At the start of the crisis there were several actions Khrushchev could have considered taking to demonstrate his commitment to Cuba in addition to his blustery rhetoric. First, he could try to break the blockade, or at least to test it. Second, he could bring his nuclear missiles to operational readiness or increase the alert status of other forces. Third, he could use his surface-to-air missiles (SAMs) around Cuba to shoot down U.S. reconnaissance planes. Fourth, he could take action in another area; for example, he might reimpose a blockade around Berlin. But Khrushchev was much more circumspect in his actions than he was in his rhetoric, and the reason was the threat of nuclear war, a threat he had not had to consider in his domestic political battles.

Soviet action in Berlin was something several ExComm members apparently feared, but there was no indication that Khrushchev ever considered threatening Berlin in order to ease the pressure on Cuba. Nor did he try to break the blockade. And while Soviet forces did shoot down an American U-2 over Cuba on October 27, Khrushchev apparently did not order this action. He did, however, have the missile crews continue their work.

Khrushchev must have made an immediate decision to order the ships carrying military cargo to reverse course, since they began doing so by midday on October 23, a day before the quarantine was to take effect.[56] Five tankers and three dry cargo ships were still heading toward Cuba, but the latter appeared to be carrying nonmilitary material.[57] All sixteen Soviet ships carrying military cargo, five of which had missiles on board, including one with nuclear warheads, reversed course prior to the imposition of the quarantine.[58]

Khrushchev could, however, still threaten the United States with the missiles on the island. And he did not order Soviet technicians to stop their work; quite the opposite, he had them speed up their preparations, which was his most serious action in the crisis and which was consistent with his typical bargaining style of raising the stakes by increasing his coercive actions. If the missiles were made operational and some warheads had reached the island, then the quarantine would not eliminate the threat the Soviets would pose from Cuba.

As early as October 19 U.S. intelligence estimated that the SS-5s would be operational sometime in December and that two SS-4 sites had been completed. And in the two days prior to Kennedy's address, the Central Intelligence Agency reported that a possible nuclear warhead building at the San Cristóbal site had been completely assembled. By October 25 the CIA was reporting that all twenty-four SAM sites were operational, and Soviet construction and equipment material for one of the nuclear storage buildings had arrived on September 29.[59] The former meant that Khrushchev could indeed hamper U.S. reconnaissance efforts, and the latter was an ominous sign of Soviet capabilities already on the island.

In the next several days low-level U.S. reconnaissance showed that three of the four medium-range ballistic missiles at the San Cristóbal site and two at the site at Sagua "appear[ed] to be fully operational." By the last day of the crisis the CIA was reporting that all twenty-four medium-range ballistic missile launchers appeared to "have reached full operational readiness."[60]

If the United States was going to strike the island and wipe out the missile force, it would want to carry out the attack before any of the missiles could be used. By continuing work on the missiles, Khrushchev was showing that he was sticking to his commitment to provide Cuba with nuclear forces. It was not the kind of direct challenge that trying to break the quarantine would have been. On the other hand, he did not need to challenge the quarantine directly if he could deploy part of his force. By accepting U Thant's proposal and perhaps stalling negotiations, he might still achieve his *fait accompli* before the United States acted. He apparently believed through October 27 that completing the work on the missiles might still be possible.

In addition to the activity in Cuba, the Soviets talked a great deal about raising the alert status of their forces, although these actions were not terribly threatening. On October 5 the Soviet Ministry of Defense newspaper, *Krasnaia Zvezda*, called on all branches of the military, especially the Strategic Rocket Forces, to be at high combat-readiness. The article referred to the low level of preparations that had allowed German forces to achieve a surprise attack in the summer of 1941. Highest combat-readiness was defined as the "state in which troops are able at any moment to repel successfully a surprise nuclear attack of an aggressor and, at the first signal, to undertake resolute combat operations aimed at the complete destruction of the enemy." The article noted that rocket and air defense troops must be able "to begin to execute combat missions in a matter of minutes or even seconds after signals and commands are received." These exhortations still said nothing specific about what increased alert levels meant in practice.[61]

At the start of the crisis Kennedy ordered U.S. strategic forces to increase their alert level to Defense Condition 3. By the early morning of October 24 the Strategic Air Command had raised its alert level to DefCon 2. All battle staffs were placed on twenty-four-hour alert duty, B-47 bombers were dispersed, B-52s were put on airborne alert, all leaves were canceled, and ninety Atlas and forty-six Titan intercontinental ballistic missiles were put in a heightened state of readiness.[62]

Despite statements in the Soviet press from various defense officials, the Soviets did much less with their forces. The CIA reported that it had not detected "any unusual activity or alerting of Soviet forces during the first few hours after the President's speech."[63] The Soviet armed forces canceled all military leaves, and the scheduled release of overage personnel in rocket, anti-aircraft, and submarine units was delayed. Warsaw Pact armed forces went on alert. Foreign diplomats and other foreigners were recalled or had their trips canceled.[64] Only the Soviet navy took significant action in the crisis. *Krasnaia Zvezda* reported on October 26 that submarines had been dispersed from their home ports in the Soviet Union out to sea, and Vladivostok radio announced on October 25 that the Soviet Pacific Fleet was in a state of readiness.[65]

There has long been speculation about why the Soviet Union did not use military alerts to send signals of commitment in crises as the United States did on several occasions during the Cold War. Possibly the Soviet unwillingness to take such steps reflected a concern with force control—sending out planes armed with nuclear missiles or mating warheads with launchers might lead to unauthorized use. Or perhaps the Soviet Union was unable to put forces on alert for long periods of time and hence would not do so until war was imminent.[66]

It is therefore possible that Khrushchev was limited in the actions he could take to signal that he was ready to go to war if Kennedy did not back down. Perhaps the Soviet Union could do no more than talk a great deal about "highest combat-readiness." These actions did not compare with U.S. bomber dispersal and the nuclear arming of air force interceptors. One analyst has argued that since the Soviets did not even take "ad hoc measures (such as putting some of their bombers on strip alert) to reduce the vulnerability of their strategic forces," perhaps the USSR was most concerned with U.S. preemption and wanted to give no cause for it by making war preparations.[67]

Khrushchev did threaten war in one tangible respect, however. Every day he came closer to having combat-ready nuclear forces in Cuba. Furthermore, the air defense forces in Cuba reached the highest state of readiness, and they shot down a U-2 plane over the island on "Black Saturday," October 27.

The shooting down of the U-2 was apparently not authorized by Khrushchev (thus Soviet fears about the possible dangers of increased-readiness moves and their unwillingness to take concrete steps with strategic forces may have been well founded). Unfortunately, the incident occurred just when the United States received Khrushchev's "second letter" proposing the missile swap. President Kennedy viewed the U-2 incident as a major escalation and considered taking out the responsible SAM site in retaliation.[68]

Apparently two Soviet commanders on the spot had ordered the firing of the SAM at the American U-2. The crews were on a war footing, and the military leaders had little time to decide whether to let the plane pass or to bring it down. Of course, if the orders were not to shoot under any circumstance, then they need not have contemplated this choice. Ambassador Alekseyev recently argued that the orders were "to fire on any aircraft that flies overhead in wartime." Such wording allowed sufficient ambiguity to lead to a mistake.[69]

The Crisis Is Over

The crisis ended abruptly on October 28. Believing that a letter would take too long to get to Kennedy, Khrushchev had his acceptance of Kennedy's terms read out on Moscow radio.[70] In doing so, Khrushchev not only failed to consult Castro; he also seems to have overruled his own military advisers. He himself later said this:

When I asked the military advisors if they could assure me that holding fast would not result in the death of five hundred million human beings, they looked at me as though I was out of my mind, or, what was worse, a traitor. The biggest tragedy, as they saw it, was not that our country might be devastated and everything lost, but that the Chinese or Albanians would accuse us of appeasement or weakness. So I said to myself: "to hell with these maniacs. If I can get the United States to assure me that it will not attempt to overthrow the Cuban government, I will remove the missiles." That is what happened. And so now I am being reviled by the Chinese and the Albanians. They say I was afraid to stand up to a paper tiger. It is all such nonsense. What good would it have done me in the last hour of my life to know that though our great nation and the United States were in complete ruins, the national honor of the Soviet Union was intact?[71]

Khrushchev told Castro several months after the crisis that he and his colleagues were in such a hurry, fearing an imminent U.S. invasion of Cuba, that the text was read out before the final section had even been edited. He had no time to inform Havana, said Khrushchev, because "peace hung by a thread."[72]

In his message ending the crisis Khrushchev wrote, "I regard with great understanding your apprehension and the apprehension of the people of the United States of America over the fact that the weapons which you describe as offensive are indeed terrible weapons." He then implied that he had already ordered the work at the missile sites stopped, and now he was ordering that the missiles be taken apart and returned to the Soviet Union: "In order to eliminate as rapidly as possible a conflict which endangers the cause of peace, to give confidence to all peoples of the Soviet Union, the Soviet Government, in addition to previously issued instructions for the cessation of further work at the weapons construction sites, has issued a new order to dismantle the weapons, which you describe as offensive, and to crate and return them to the Soviet Union."[73]

Khrushchev then tried to put the best face possible on the settlement package. After all, he had made a personal decision to place the missiles, and made a personal decision to remove them. His actions were to cost him dearly politically, both at home and in the socialist community at large. But he wrote that since the United States had promised that there would be no invasion of Cuba in the future, "the motives which prompted us to give aid . . . to Cuba no longer prevail."[74] He thus tried to make it appear that he had achieved his goals in the end.

There has been much speculation about why Khrushchev ended the crisis so abruptly. One theory was that he lost control of the SAM batteries to the Cubans. U.S. intelligence later believed that it had evidence of a fire-fight between Cubans and Soviets on October 26, and perhaps the Cubans had taken over the SAMs that brought down the U-2 the following day.[75] More recent evidence suggests that the "firefight" was simply an accidental explosion at an ammunition dump.[76] Fomin's report of U.S. anger over the public second letter may also have contributed to Khrushchev's sense of urgency.[77] In fact, Fomin told Scali on October 28, "I have been instructed to thank you and to tell you that the information you supplied was very valuable to the Chairman in helping him make up his mind quickly. And that includes your 'explosion' Saturday."[78]

The swift conclusion of the crisis also apparently stemmed from meet-ings between Robert Kennedy and Anatoly Dobrynin on October 26–27 at which the attorney general offered the Soviet ambassador both carrots and sticks. The two men have described those meetings quite differently. RFK recounted in his book on the crisis that Dobrynin came to his office at the Justice Department on the night of October 27. Kennedy told him that work on the missile sites had accelerated, and he emphasized the serious-ness of the U-2 incident. Kennedy wrote of the exchange, "We had to have a commitment by tomorrow that those bases would be removed. I was not giving them an ultimatum but a statement of fact. He should understand that if they did not remove those bases, we would remove them." Kennedy also added that there could be no missile swap but said that he believed the missiles in Turkey would be removed shortly.[79]

Dobrynin has recently given a slightly different account. The former ambassador says that he met with Robert Kennedy several times from October 23 to 27 at both the Soviet embassy and the Department of Justice. During a meeting on October 26 at the Soviet embassy, Dobrynin claims, he mentioned Turkey in the context of equal rights. Kennedy took the ini-tiative in raising the idea of a missile swap. Kennedy then went out of the room to talk to the president, and when he came back he explicitly stated that the United States would remove the missiles from Turkey after the crisis. The Soviets then sent the "second letter" proposing this same deal.[80]

Dobrynin agrees that at the meeting the following day, Robert Ken-nedy said that if the Soviets failed to take the missiles out, the United States would do it. Therefore, it appears that the United States was publicly accepting the vague Soviet proposals on a noninvasion pledge, privately accepting the demands for a missile swap, and giving an ultimatum.[81] At the start of the crisis Khrushchev had rejected what he deemed a Kennedy ultimatum; this time he did not.[82]

Conclusions on Cuba

During the biggest international crisis of his rule, Khrushchev confronted, blustered, bullied, and bluffed as he had done at home in the 1950s. He made the decision to send missiles to Cuba and then bragged about Soviet abilities to defend the island. He did not shy away from bold, personal commitments as he planned his operation and tried to carry it out—even after his plan was discovered in mid-October 1962.

During the period leading up to the crisis, Khrushchev, in meetings with officials from various Western countries and in Soviet government statements, issued a variety of warnings and threats on Cuba and Berlin. He warned that U.S. actions in Cuba would lead to war, and he threatened that the Berlin issue needed a solution. At the same time, he used this period to try to establish the legitimacy of the Soviet position. He talked about the need for equal rights, referring to the U.S. bases that surrounded the USSR. And he and his cohorts continually reminded the world that the imperialists posed a grave threat to Cuba. These themes would reappear during the crisis, as Khrushchev tried to justify the actions he had taken and so persuade the United States to back down.

At the start of the crisis Khrushchev placed the blame on the United States and argued that the Soviet Union could not back down. He was highly confrontational at first, saying that the USSR would do whatever was necessary for the defense of both the Soviet Union and Cuba. But he also expressed hope that the events would not lead to war, and he signaled publicly through third parties that he would be willing to meet President Kennedy to discuss an end to the confrontation.

Unlike Stalin in Berlin, Khrushchev was personally confrontational; his letters at the start of the crisis, especially the one in which he said that the Soviets simply could not back down, were tough. Also unlike Stalin in 1948, Khrushchev did not take an incremental approach. He tried for a *fait accompli,* choosing the bold step of placing the weapons surreptitiously, and he hoped to unveil his actions publicly for maximum effect later.[83] When he finally conceded, he pulled out as quickly as he could and did so personally and publicly.

Khrushchev used multiple channels of communication to convey both his threats and his concessions. Prior to Kennedy's discovery of the missiles, Khrushchev not only deceived the president personally but also used Gromyko, Dobrynin, and Bolshakov to convey the same message. During the crisis he not only wrote to Kennedy but also responded to U Thant and Bertrand Russell as well as meeting with William Knox. It is also probable that he used Fomin as a supplement to his vague letter to Kennedy on October 26.

In one important respect, however, Khrushchev's behavior in Cuba was not reminiscent of his domestic bargaining style. As events appeared to be edging toward war, Khrushchev pulled back. Perhaps he had achieved what he wanted. Kennedy promised publicly not to invade Cuba, and he agreed privately to remove the missiles from Turkey. But Khrushchev had lost a great deal of prestige for himself and the socialist community, and his relations with Cuba suffered as well. Khrushchev could not even claim publicly that the planned withdrawal of Jupiter missiles was linked to his demands.

At home, when he was doing badly, Khrushchev had redefined the problem, raised the stakes, and pushed ahead. He acted this way as well at the start of the Cuban crisis, but not at the end. He conceded swiftly on October 28, and he suffered for it later. But it was clear that Khrushchev was impressed with the dangers posed by nuclear weapons, and this awareness caused a shift in his basic bargaining style as the superpowers approached the threshold of war.

One scholar of Soviet foreign policy, Hannes Adomeit, has concluded that Khrushchev's behavior regarding Cuba was an exception for him, and that in the Berlin crisis of 1961 he acted similarly to Stalin in 1948, showing a pattern of "calculated risk-taking" on the part of Soviet leaders in general.[84] But as is clear from the comparison of Khrushchev's behavior at home and in the Cuban crisis, it is wrong to view the latter as an "exception" to be dismissed. Furthermore, if we look at the broader conflict surrounding Berlin, which began with Khrushchev's ultimatum of November 1958, and we think about more than simply "risk-taking propensities," we see that the conflict that led to the Berlin Wall is much more comparable to the Cuban crisis than it is to Stalin's blockade of Berlin in 1948. Khrushchev's behavior toward Berlin is consistent with the pattern that has been described in this book.

Khrushchev in Berlin, 1958–1961

Starting in 1958 Khrushchev made strong personal commitments to altering the situation in Berlin, first with his ultimatum to President Dwight Eisenhower in 1958 and later with his ultimatum and browbeating of Kennedy at the Vienna summit of 1961. And he successfully achieved a *fait accompli* as he later tried in Cuba, this time erecting the Berlin Wall without a Western response. This behavior was highly reminiscent of his style at home and in Cuba.

For example, Khrushchev presented his ultimatum to the Western powers on November 27, 1958, in typical fashion. The note itself was from the Soviet government to the other governments, but along with it Khrushchev held a ninety-minute press conference—a personal appearance at which he publicly committed himself to the demands set forth in the note. One Western scholar has suggested that this press conference added flexibility to the note,[85] but it also raised the stakes by strengthening the Soviet leader's commitment. As Eisenhower suggested at the time, "There seemed to be no avoiding a showdown because Khrushchev had apparently laid his prestige on the line."[86]

In the note, the Soviet government proposed that West Berlin become a demilitarized free city; it added that "the Soviet government proposes not to introduce changes in the existing order of military transport of the U.S., Great Britain, and France from West Berlin to the FRG for one-half year. . . . If the stated time is not used for the achievement of an appropriate agreement, then the Soviet Union will bring about an agreement with the GDR."[87] This type of ultimatum and commitment was far different from Stalin's approach in 1948. Stalin never proposed a time limit to the West in the spring of 1948 as he prepared his blockade.

In his press conference on November 27 Khrushchev stressed that the Soviet Union would not act during those six months, and he also suggested that his government was not issuing "an ultimatum."[88] But as Alexander George and Richard Smoke have pointed out, "The note . . . contained all three elements of the classical ultimatum: a demand upon the recipient powers, a time limit for the fulfillment of the demand, and a threat of sanctions in the event of nonfulfillment."[89]

The six months came and went, but this did not prevent the Soviet leader from trying again. In talks with former New York governor Averell Harriman just prior to the foreign ministers' conference in Geneva in the summer of 1959, Khrushchev said that the Soviet Union would act unilaterally if the West failed to agree on a settlement; in remarks similar to those he would make in 1962 concerning Cuba, the first secretary added, "If you send in tanks, they will burn and make no mistake about it. If you want war, you can have it, but remember it will be your war. Our rockets will fly automatically."[90] The following spring, after his walkout from the Paris summit scheduled with Eisenhower, Khrushchev again called for a conference in six to eight months' time, and said the Soviet Union would wait no longer to solve these issues.[91]

Then in June 1961 Khrushchev went to Vienna and confronted the new American president, delivering a new Berlin ultimatum. Many people have suggested that Khrushchev acted this way because of Kennedy's youth, but in fact this confrontational mode was standard operating procedure for Khrushchev. He thrived on confrontation, and he seemed unconcerned about the consequences of issuing yet another ultimatum whose terms he might not fulfill.[92] At Vienna Khrushchev again threatened to sign a peace treaty with the GDR unilaterally; he also handed over an aide-mémoire saying that if the issue was not resolved within six months, East and West Germany should sign separate peace treaties.[93] On June 15, in a televised address, Khrushchev reported on the summit and stated, "If the Federal Republic of Germany does not agree to sign a peace treaty, then we will sign one with only the German Democratic Republic, which has already stated its desire to conclude a peace treaty and has agreed to the creation of a free city of West Berlin on its territory." He repeated himself in another televised address on August 7.[94] By this time he was beginning to sound like the boy who cried wolf.[95]

At home and abroad, Khrushchev seemed to revel in issuing ultimata, whether they concerned his 1956 Secret Speech denouncing Stalin, the Cuban crisis, or Berlin. He seemed oblivious to the political costs normally associated with hollow ultimata of this kind. Having failed to achieve anything by the summer of 1961, and facing a huge outpouring of people from East Berlin, Khrushchev moved ahead with the construction of the wall. As he reportedly told his generals, "We'll just put up serpentine barbed wire, and the West will stand there like dumb sheep. And while they're standing there, we'll finish a wall." [96] This was the kind of *fait accompli* he was presumably hoping to achieve the following year in Cuba. Khrushchev succeeded in Berlin and failed in Cuba, but in both cases he followed the same pattern of public confrontation, bluster, and bluff that had carried him to the top of the Kremlin hierarchy in his rise to political power.

FIVE

Brezhnev and the 1973 Middle East War

O n October 6, 1973, at the height of U.S.-Soviet detente, Egyptian and Syrian forces unleashed a surprise attack on Israel. The arms and training that allowed Egypt and Syria to start the war had come from the Soviet Union, but General Secretary Leonid Brezhnev was wary of standing firmly behind his Mideast clients, given his stake in promoting a new era of cooperation between the superpowers. Brezhnev tried both to please everyone and to anger no one as the war progressed—a course both coercive and accommodative, and seemingly contradictory.

This range of behavior has led to a variety of explanations for the Soviet activity in October 1973. Those analysts who argue that the Soviets were cautious cite as reasons a regional military balance that favored the United States, a predominance of U.S. interests, or a desire to preserve detente.[1] Those who argue that the Soviets were confrontational believe that the source of the behavior was a desire to promote regional competitive interests at the expense of, or despite, global detente.[2] Generally, the interpretations of the Soviet behavior have varied because scholars have focused on different phases of the conflict. Those who see the behavior as cautious have focused on the Soviets' early attempts to gain a cease-fire, on their vague verbal warnings, or on their threat to intervene late in the crisis (a threat these analysts view as empty). Those who see the behavior as confrontational have focused on the Soviets' decision to begin airlifting supplies early in the war and on their preparations to intervene later on (preparations these analysts view as examples of a willingness to escalate).

But when we examine the full range of Soviet behavior in the crisis, we find that what it most reflects is Brezhnev's own bargaining style. Brezhnev was in a difficult position in 1973, and he responded as he had typically done at home: he tried to please everyone, which in this case meant trying to preserve both his relationship with the United States and the Soviets' influence with Arab states in the Middle East.

Brezhnev's first response after the war began was to stall, and even after the Soviets decided to resupply the Egyptian war effort, they seemed more concerned about preventing Syrian losses than about pushing Egyptian gains. During the war Brezhnev called U.S. secretary of state Henry Kissinger to Moscow to negotiate a cease-fire agreement; in his memoirs Kissinger describes his surprise at Brezhnev's willingness to accommodate U.S. demands so swiftly. Brezhnev never used confrontational rhetoric during the October war, as Khrushchev had done before and during the Cuban missile crisis.

Brezhnev also avoided making bold statements that would commit him to a position. His warnings and threats were vague, and even when the Soviets did show that they were committed to preventing the destruction of the Egyptian Third Army, Brezhnev's letter to President Richard Nixon said that if the Israelis continued to violate the cease-fire, the Soviet Union would find it necessary to *consider* intervening unilaterally. The general secretary did not commit himself to a position whereby he would actually have to intervene if the cease-fire efforts failed, although he was apparently considering that option, at least with a token force. This caution was much different from Khrushchev's hollow bluster about ordering his ships to proceed in the event of a U.S. blockade of Cuba.

On the other hand, the Soviets in 1973 did take actions that committed them to the war effort. During the conflict the USSR undertook a massive airlift and sealift to resupply Egypt and Syria, permitted or supplied proxies, stationed advisers, raised troop alert levels, and sent an advance staff of an airborne division to Syria. As in 1962 in Cuba, the Soviets did not upgrade the alert status of strategic forces as the United States would once again do, but the increased readiness of conventional forces made the potential threat to intervene more credible.

These examples of coercion and commitment are at odds with the typical Brezhnev style. In 1948 and 1962 the threat of war had altered Stalin's and Khrushchev's bargaining behavior. In 1973 Brezhnev's style also shifted in the face of an overwhelming threat, in this case the danger of unacceptable losses to Syria and Egypt, which would have weakened the Soviets' international position. Once again a Soviet leader's bargaining schema would guide him in the international arena until a major threat from the external environment caused a shift.

The Setting

Unlike the Berlin blockade and the Cuban missile crisis, the 1973 superpower conflict grew out of a war initiated by smaller countries, which meant that the superpowers had less control over the situation than they had had in those earlier events. Also unlike the events in Berlin and Cuba, this crisis was preceded by a period in which the superpowers were seeking a reduction of tension in the global relationship. Brezhnev was a champion of the Soviet-American detente that had produced agreements to limit offensive and defensive nuclear systems and to provide for a lessening of the risk of confrontation in third areas.[3] The war in the Middle East would directly challenge these superpower initiatives and thereby put the Soviet leader in the difficult position of having to balance his interests in supporting his allies against promoting detente with the United States.

Despite his interests in detente, Brezhnev did seek the expansion of Soviet influence in the region, which meant supplying Egypt and Syria with substantial conventional weaponry. The Soviets and Egyptians had signed a Treaty of Friendship and Cooperation in 1971, but the Egyptians had expelled Soviet advisers in July 1972 because Egyptian leader Anwar Sadat believed that the Soviet commitment to helping him regain former Arab territory was a weak one. Given the policy of detente with the United States, Brezhnev had encouraged the Arabs to pursue their goals through diplomacy, not force. Sadat then turned to the United States for assistance in regaining lost land, but the Americans gave him no reason to believe they would help him either. The Egyptian leader then turned back to the Soviet Union, and when he did so, the Soviets responded more enthusiastically, stepping up their arms supply after February 1973.[4]

The Soviets had supplied the Egyptians and Syrians with the wherewithal to fight a war, but they did not seem to favor one. Brezhnev and Foreign Minister Andrei Gromyko had warned the United States several times during the summer of 1973 that war in the Middle East was a distinct possibility.[5] After May 1973 Soviet commentary on the region ceased referring to the Arabs' right to liberate their land and concentrated on their need to negotiate a return of their territory.[6] At the June summit in Washington Brezhnev harped on the danger of war in the Middle East and urged the United States to put pressure on Israel for a settlement.[7] In August in Alma-Ata the Soviet leader spoke of the need to resolve the Arab-Israeli dispute peacefully.[8] As late as September 28 Gromyko told Nixon at the White House, "We could all wake up one day and find there is a real conflagration in that area."[9] But while Brezhnev did not want a Middle East war, Sadat did.

War Begins

It is unclear when the Soviets actually knew of the Arab decision to launch a surprise attack on October 6. Presumably, given the number of Soviet advisers in Egypt, Brezhnev had a general knowledge of a war decision months in advance. But the Egyptians have said that they told the Soviet Union of the plan only two or three days before the war began (presumably they did not want to hear a plea for postponement or cancellation of the attack). Egyptian adviser Mohammed Heikal has written that on October 1 Sadat told the Soviet ambassador to Egypt, Sergei Vinogradov, that Egypt might be moving soon. Vinogradov reportedly replied that even without hearing from Brezhnev, he could say that the decision was Egypt's to make, and that "as friends we will do everything we can to help you." [10] To offer his government's support, Vinogradov must have communicated with Moscow earlier.

The Arab decision to go to war, communicated to the Soviet Union on October 3, put Brezhnev in a difficult position. The Soviet leader would have a hard time preventing the Arab attack, given his country's commitment to supporting Israel's foes in the past, and yet he presumably did not want these actions to harm detente. His position was made more difficult by the fact that he and Nixon had signed an agreement earlier in the year that committed each of the superpowers to inform the other of events that might escalate to global war. [11]

Brezhnev responded to the news of the impending attack in his typical fashion. He tried to accommodate both the Egyptians and the United States, and he avoided commitments. When they told the Soviet Union of the impending attack, the Egyptians asked the Soviets what their attitude was. Brezhnev replied the following day that the decision was Sadat's to make, and that the Soviets would give the support of a friend. This statement committed him to nothing and seemed to indicate that the Soviets were planning to do very little. [12]

Brezhnev also asked permission to evacuate civilian advisers and their families from Egypt. The Soviets had apparently played no role in the *decision* to go to war—while giving the Arabs the supplies to conduct one— and Brezhnev perhaps hoped to communicate to the United States the lack of Soviet involvement. [13] More important, if the United States had even considered the possibility of an Egyptian attack on Israel, the evacuation could have been a signal of imminent war. Sadat in fact was concerned that the Soviet move might have blown his surprise. He was also angry that the planes used to take the Soviet dependents out of Egypt did not come loaded with supplies for the Egyptian war effort. [14] Brezhnev's request for evacuation may have been an attempt on his part to signal to the United States what was about to happen without publicly abandoning the Arab plan to retrieve territory lost in 1967.[15]

The Soviet Union's lack of commitment and its desire to accommodate both U.S. and Arab interests continued in the early phase of the war. Prior to the war the Soviets and Syrians had apparently discussed calling a cease-fire within hours after the initiation of hostilities. Thus, if Syria was doing well, it could preserve its gains; if it was not, then a cease-fire would prevent serious losses.[16] Given the previous Arab experiences, the Soviets probably expected serious losses.

Sadat was not aware of these Soviet-Syrian discussions, and when the Soviets approached him with what they called a Syrian plan only six hours after the war began, he believed that the Soviet Union was acting duplicitously. His feelings were "confirmed" when Syrian president Hafez al-Assad denied his role to Sadat.[17] According to Heikal, Assad had told the Soviets that "no harm would be done if a resolution calling for a cease-fire was put forward." The Soviets believed that a cease-fire in place was the optimal strategy and repeated their request to the Egyptians the following day.[18]

Soviet ambassador Anatoly Dobrynin brought to Kissinger on the afternoon of October 6 the Kremlin's first communication to the United States after the start of hostilities. Not only did the letter reflect a Soviet desire to stall for time; in it the USSR also sought to distance itself from the events: "The Soviet leadership got the information about the beginning of military actions in the Middle East at the same time as you got it. We take all possible measures to clarify [the] real state of affairs in that region, since the information from there is of a contradictory nature. We fully share your concern about the conflagration of the situation in the Middle East. We repeatedly pointed in the past to the dangerous situation in that area."[19]

The Soviets were stalling either because they could not make a decision or because they could not get Egypt's agreement on a cease-fire, or some combination of the two. They continued to stall in the next several communications.[20] The United States was proposing a United Nations cease-fire with a return to the status quo ante. Brezhnev finally replied to this proposal on the afternoon of October 7. To Kissinger's disappointment, the letter to Nixon referred not to ending the war but to the familiar Soviet proposal for a superpower-imposed peace in the Middle East that would assure Israeli withdrawal from occupied territories. The Soviet leader called on Israel to withdraw immediately from those territories. Kissinger concluded, "Clearly, the Soviets wanted to let the war run its course a little longer or else they did not have as much influence with their Arab friends as we had thought."[21]

The first official Soviet statement on the war, unlike Khrushchev's early statements during the Cuban missile crisis, reflected neither a strong commitment nor an attempt to confront the United States. The Soviets explicitly blamed Israel for the conflict and did not mention the United States directly. There was not even an appeal for Arab solidarity and assistance. The Soviets did not warn of action on their part, nor did they refer to vital Soviet interests; furthermore, Soviet warships were withdrawn from the area.[22] The Soviets did warn, however, that if Israel failed to heed the voice of reason, "this may cost the people of Israel dearly. The responsibility for the consequences of such an unreasonable course will be fully borne by the leaders of the State of Israel."[23]

By saying that the Israelis bore full responsibility for the war, the Soviets were implying that the United States bore none. There was no demand that the United States restrain its ally. There was no reference to the global forces of imperialism. The statement suggests that Brezhnev had no desire to harm the detente relationship, and he was walking a tight line, trying to give Egypt and Syria verbal support without confronting the United States.

The Soviet general secretary sent a message to the United States on the morning of October 8 that again hinted at his difficulties: "We have contacted the leaders of the Arab states on the question of cease-fire. We hope to get a reply shortly. We feel that we should act in cooperation with you, being guided by the broad interests of maintaining peace and developing the Soviet-American relations. We hope that President Nixon will act likewise."[24] Befitting someone who had come to power by not rocking the boat, Brezhnev was taking a highly accommodative tone, but he was in a quandary as long as the Arabs did not agree on the need to stop the war.

Having failed to gain Egyptian support for a cease-fire, the Soviet leader now faced new choices. The Syrians had begun to suffer heavy losses and were being pushed back to Damascus. The Egyptians, meanwhile, had unexpectedly stormed across Israeli defenses along the Suez Canal—the Bar-Lev line—and had finally secured a stronghold on the East Bank of the canal. Brezhnev could not allow the Syrians to lose badly if he wanted to preserve Soviet influence in the Arab world. And the Egyptian successes presented the USSR with an opportunity to change the Arab position on the ground in the Middle East before any negotiations on the future of the Sinai.

Soviet rhetoric continued to be fairly noncommittal during the war, but Soviet activities escalated and increased the level of commitment to the Arab position, in a way that seems uncharacteristic for Brezhnev. In fact, Brezhnev's rhetoric and actions in the war reflect his typical bargaining style, which he used consistently except when major threats to the two Arab states caused him to alter his strategies and tactics.

Soviet Rhetoric

Brezhnev's first public comments on the war came on October 8: "Naturally, all our sympathy is on the side of the victims of aggression. As regards the Soviet Union, it was and remains a firm supporter of a just, secure peace in the Near East and of guaranteed security for all countries and peoples in the region that is so close to our borders."[25] While Brezhnev mentioned Soviet interests arising from the proximity of the region to the USSR, he spoke only of sympathy for the Arab states and guaranteed security for all states, including Israel, making this statement a mild one indeed. During the course of that day and the next, however, Brezhnev, Prime Minister Alexei Kosygin, Ideology Secretary Mikhail Suslov, and Defense Minister Andrei Grechko all endorsed the Arab war effort.[26]

Also on October 8 Brezhnev wrote a letter to Algerian president Houari Boumedienne in which he called on the Arab states to assist Egypt and Syria in the conflict:

Syria and Egypt must not be alone in their struggle against a treacherous enemy. There is an urgent need for the widest aid and support of the progressive regimes in these countries. . . . The Central Committee of the CPSU and the Soviet Government are firmly convinced that the Algerian leaders, who are widely experienced in the anti-imperialist struggle, understand full well all the peculiarities of the present situation and that, guided by the ideals of fraternal solidarity, [they] will use every means and take every step required to give their support to Syria and Egypt in the tough struggle imposed by the Israeli aggressors. . . . As for the Soviet Union, it gives to the friendly Arab states multilateral aid and support in their just struggle against the imperialist Israeli aggression.[27]

In this letter Brezhnev called on the Arab states to provide aid to their brethren. He again placed the blame on Israel and not on the United States. By speaking of "the peculiarities of the present situation," the letter implied that the Soviets were constrained by the global relationship. And it said that the USSR was giving multilateral aid. While trying to appear as the chief supporter of the Arab actions, Brezhnev was not committing himself to a major effort; furthermore, as these words of "support" were being written, the Soviets were still trying to get Egypt to agree to a cease-fire; according to Sadat, Brezhnev even tried to enlist the help of Marshal Josip Broz Tito of Yugoslavia in these efforts.[28]

Early on the morning of October 10 Dobrynin read Kissinger a message from Moscow. The Soviet ambassador described the discussions with Syria and Egypt as "protracted" and "not easy." Dobrynin implied that the USSR would abstain if a cease-fire in place was proposed but would veto a call for a return to the prewar boundaries. The Soviet statement also expressed the desire to seek a negotiated settlement based on an Israeli withdrawal from the occupied territories. Kissinger has noted that if the Soviet Union had "conducted a decisive policy" and pushed hard for a cease-fire in place at that time, it would have been difficult for the United States to reject the proposal, Arab gains would have been ratified, and the Soviets would have achieved a "clear-cut victory." He added, "What the Soviets hoped to achieve is hard to fathom. Their ambivalence gave us a chance to play for time and recoup." [29] This ambivalence was typical of Brezhnev.

Then on October 12 the Israelis sank a Soviet merchant ship. Coming only several days after a bombing of the Soviet cultural center in Damascus, the action prompted a Soviet warning to Israel:

If Israel's ruling circles presume that their actions against peaceful cities and civilian targets in Syria and Egypt will remain unpunished, they are profoundly deluded. Aggression cannot remain unpunished, and the aggressor must bear harsh responsibility for his actions. The Soviet Union cannot regard indifferently the criminal actions of the Israeli military, as a result of which there are victims also among Soviet citizens in Syria and Egypt. The continuation of criminal acts by Israel will lead to grave consequences for Israel itself.[30]

The threats against Israel were sharp, but again the Soviet Union failed to mention the United States. Dobrynin, however, also privately warned Kissinger that Israeli population centers would not remain untouched indefinitely, and the Soviet Union would defend its ships and other means of transportation.[31]

On October 13 the U.S. resupply effort finally began in earnest. Kissinger writes that in response to the new American decisiveness, Brezhnev sent an "oral message" stating that the Soviet Union had been prepared for two days to join a cease-fire effort. The Soviet leader argued that because the United States had delayed its support for a cease-fire, the Arab states had decided to abandon their cease-fire efforts. Kissinger told Dobrynin that the Soviet Union should not be misled into thinking that it could pressure the United States through military efforts. Dobrynin assured Kissinger that he would send Brezhnev the American response.[32]

Israel turned the tide of battle on October 15–16, and the Soviets increased their efforts to gain Egyptian support for a cessation of hostilities. On October 16 Kosygin flew to Cairo carrying with him a cease-fire plan.[33] On the following day Brezhnev sent a private message to Washington through Dobrynin stating that while the Soviets might be willing to fight the war by proxy, they would stop short of a confrontation with the United States.[34]

On the night of October 18 Dobrynin called Kissinger with an "urgent message" from Brezhnev. The Soviet Union was ready to submit a proposal to the United Nations that called for a cease-fire in place, that appealed for a phased Israeli withdrawal in accordance with UN resolution 242, and that sought "appropriate consultations" for peace.[35]

Events on the ground were rapidly shifting in Israel's favor. The following morning Dobrynin arrived with another urgent message from the general secretary. Brezhnev wrote to Nixon that the war posed "harm" to U.S.-Soviet relations. He added, "Since time is essential and now not only every day but every hour counts, my colleagues and I suggest that the U.S. Secretary of State and your closest associate Dr. Kissinger come in an urgent manner to Moscow to conduct appropriate negotiations with him as with your authorized personal representative. It would be good if he could come tomorrow, October 20. I will appreciate your speedy reply."[36] Kissinger flew to Moscow with full authority from Nixon to conduct negotiations— which made Kissinger anxious about his bargaining position, because he would not be able to stall for time by citing the need to check every position with the president. He need not have worried. Kissinger found a typically accommodative Brezhnev.

Kissinger remarked, "No evening with the Soviet leadership could be complete without some bluster." But his conversation that first evening in Moscow was far different from one he might have had with Khrushchev. Brezhnev spoke of the threat of war inherent in the events, but Kissinger says he did so "more in sorrow than in anger." Kissinger was stunned by the Soviet leader's behavior. He wrote later that when he met with Brezhnev on October 21, the Soviets were "so eager to settle that there was really no negotiation in the strict sense." He continued, "Usually the Soviets stick to their formal positions for extended periods and then sell their abandonment of an outrageous proposition as a concession. On this occasion, Brezhnev conceded my points before I had even raised them." A cease-fire agreement was reached within only four hours.[37]

The cease-fire that went into effect on October 22 was promptly broken by the Israelis on October 23. Brezhnev quickly sent a note addressed to Kissinger—not to Nixon, as was customary—which indicated that he was desperate.[38] Brezhnev described the Israeli advance as "unacceptable" and a "flagrant deceit." After all, Kissinger had stopped in Israel on his way home from Moscow, and Brezhnev could have expected him to ensure Israeli support. Several hours later Brezhnev again expressed his anger with "Israeli treachery" and assured the United States that the Arabs would abide by the cease-fire. He also called for a joint superpower action to impose a settlement.[39] According to Nixon, Brezhnev at this time also used the U.S.-Soviet hotline to protest the Israeli violations, and "he curtly implied that [the United States] might even have colluded in Israel's action."[40]

In addition to the communications with the United States, the Soviets publicly warned Israel not to continue its actions against Egypt, but in terms no stronger than they had used eleven days before.[41] The powers then agreed to a new cease-fire, but it was violated on October 24. Apparently the Israelis wanted revenge for earlier losses and were in no mood to release the Egyptian Third Army.

The situation was becoming quite dangerous for the superpowers. Sadat sent a letter asking that both superpowers send troops to impose the agreement they had reached. Israeli troops continued to encircle Egypt's Third Army and threatened to destroy it. Meanwhile, the United States had assumed "full responsibility" the day before for ending hostilities on the part of Israel.[42] As the cease-fire had again been broken, Moscow may have wondered what the United States was doing to fulfill its obligations.[43]

Earlier in the crisis Brezhnev had been careful to place full blame on Israel for the actions taking place. As the threat to Egypt grew, he was shifting blame to the United States. Such a shift made the tone of his October 24 letter "menacing," as Kissinger described it. Brezhnev wrote about the broken cease-fire:

We, naturally, have questions as to what is behind all this. I wish to say it frankly, Mr. President, that we are confident that you have possibilities to influence Israel with the aim of putting an end to such a provocative behavior of Tel Aviv.

We would like to hope that we both will be true to our word and to the understanding we have reached.

I will appreciate information on your steps towards Israel's strict and immediate compliance with the decision of the Security Council of this October 22 and 23.[44]

On the afternoon of October 24 Foreign Minister Gromyko sent a message through Dobrynin. A communication from the foreign minister was less threatening than one from the general secretary. The purpose of the message was to allow Gromyko to report new Israeli military activity and thereby put responsibility for future problems on the United States.[45] Putting responsibility on the United States rather than on Israel would give the Soviets greater pretext for action should that become necessary.

Later in the day the Soviets privately expressed to the United States an interest in having the United Nations provide troops, including Soviet troops, to enforce the cease-fire that continued to come unstuck. Then at 9:35 P.M. Nixon received the most serious letter yet from Brezhnev, one that Kissinger describes as "in effect an ultimatum." Brezhnev repeated Sadat's demand for the joint dispatch of troops to ensure implementation of the cease-fire. Brezhnev then wrote, "I will say it straight that if you find it impossible to act jointly with us in this matter, we should be faced with the necessity urgently to consider the question of taking appropriate steps unilaterally."[46]

Nixon later described this statement as the most serious threat to a U.S.

president since the Cuban missile crisis.[47] In response, the United States put its strategic forces on a higher stage of alert, Defense Condition 3, and also warned Brezhnev in writing that the United States could "in no event accept unilateral escalation . . . [for] such action would produce incalculable consequences."[48] Nixon and Kissinger worried that the letter and alert would not communicate U.S. intentions quickly enough, so they also decided to alert the Eighty-second Airborne Division, to move two more carriers to the Eastern Mediterranean, and to return the Guam-based B-52 bombers to the United States.[49]

Brezhnev's letter was a serious threat. But he could have made a stronger verbal commitment to intervention. He did not write, "If you fail to act, we will take all necessary measures to defend our ally." He said that it would be necessary to "consider" acting unilaterally, which gave him more room to maneuver.

On the afternoon of October 25 Sadat finally agreed to receive an international force—one that would exclude U.S. and Soviet troops—to observe the new cease-fire. Less than two hours later the United States received another letter from Brezhnev. The general secretary told Nixon he was sending seventy Soviet "representatives" to the scene and added, "Since you are ready now, as we understand, to send to Egypt a group of American observers with the same task, we agree to act jointly in this question."[50] Brezhnev was defining the problem in a way that would allow him to save face. The night before, he had proposed joint action. By offering to send nonmilitary observers jointly with the United States, he could claim to have carried out the action he had suggested in his October 24 letter.

The issue of observers soon became moot. The United Nations dispatched its forces, and the United States urged that the Soviet and American observer contingent be a minimal one. Kissinger and Dobrynin haggled over the issue and finally agreed to send thirty-six observers each. Egypt then decided that it no longer wanted superpower representatives on the scene.[51]

Events took a turn for the worse when Israel increased its pressure again. On October 26 Brezhnev sent another warning, although it was not as serious as the one he had issued on October 24: "If the next few hours do not bring news that necessary measures have been taken to resolve the question raised by President Sadat, then we will have the most serious doubts regarding the intentions of the American side." Brezhnev also complained about the alert. But the message was crafted in the usual Brezhnev style. Kissinger writes, "It was a strange message. It spoke of threats to universal peace but not about what the Soviet Union would do about them. It asked for an American response within a few hours but threatened no consequences other than serious doubts about our intentions."[52] In fact, it was not at all strange; it was typical Brezhnev—talk tough but avoid specific threats or challenges.

Finally, Israel relaxed its grip. The war was essentially over. The Soviet government issued one more statement several days later about the U.S. alert: "This step of the United States that in no way promotes international detente was taken obviously in an attempt to intimidate the Soviet Union. But those who are behind this step should be told that they have chosen the wrong address." [53]

Soviet Actions

While Brezhnev's rhetoric during the war was on the whole quite accommodative and noncommittal, reflecting the style of bargaining that had worked well for him at home, some of his actions—for example, sending arms and advisers—signaled a commitment atypical of him. International events forced Brezhnev to take stronger action than was typical, but he was still careful not to provoke the United States to act, and his actions were never serious enough to change the outcome of the war.

The Soviets had begun sending arms and advisers even before the war began, which is why Egypt and Syria were able to contemplate attacking Israel. By October 1973 Egypt and Syria had available to them several hundred MiG fighters, several thousand antitank missiles, and more than two thousand tanks. Egypt had also received thirty SCUD missiles—a strategic weapon in the Middle East, since it could strike from Egypt anywhere in the Israeli homeland and was capable of delivering nuclear warheads. [54]

The Soviets committed themselves more strongly to supporting the Arab states soon after the war began by lifting supplies into the region in a substantial manner on October 10. Galia Golan has written that the "airlift (and sealift) was one of the most controversial Soviet actions during the war, a direct intervention which, the Soviet leadership must have calculated, would invite similar American action, prolong the war, endanger detente, and raise the risk of superpower confrontation." [55] The Soviet effort did demonstrate a commitment to supporting the Arab states, but it was not intensive enough to ensure an Arab victory. As Kissinger has written of the Soviet resupply, "Probably the Soviet leadership tried to keep several options open and managed to combine all disadvantages. It did enough to ensure the continuation of the war but failed to affect the outcome." [56]

There are several possible explanations for the resupply effort. First, it may have been a response to Israel's bombing of the Soviet cultural center in Damascus, which had caused Soviet casualties. Second, it may have been a reaction to early Arab victories—something that would allow the

Soviets either to claim credit or to push for a more sizable victory. Third, it may have been a response to the Syrian retreat.[57] Apparently the Soviets informed Sadat on October 8 at the earliest that there would be an airlift. On October 7, when Sadat raised the problem of tank losses with Ambassador Vinogradov, Moscow had suggested that because of the length of time a Soviet response would require, Sadat should turn to Iraq.[58] Perhaps the Soviets had simply not yet decided what to do. The following evening Vinogradov informed the Egyptians that the airlift would begin. Typically, Sadat viewed the belated decision as an example of Soviet bandwagoning on Egypt's earlier success.[59] On the morning of October 10, the United States learned of the airlift.[60]

Was the resupply effort undertaken in order to push the Arabs to victory or to forestall their collapse? Perhaps Brezhnev hoped to save Syria from destruction as well as to bribe Egypt by helping Sadat gain a stronger position before negotiations began. Meanwhile, Brezhnev sought to soften the effects of the Soviet activity by engaging in a series of contacts with Nixon on October 7 urging that the fighting in the Middle East not be allowed to damage detente.[61]

The Soviets were apparently concerned both with the Egyptian military plan and with the Syrian losses.[62] The Egyptians had decided on an "operational pause" after crossing the Bar-Lev line, Israel's line of defense along the Suez. The pause lasted four days and may have cost Egypt dearly. Sadat later admitted that his main goal in the war was to demonstrate that he could cross the Suez Canal and thus smash the myth of Israeli invincibility.[63] He wrote later, "I used to tell Nasser that if we could recapture even four inches of Sinai territory (by which I meant a foothold, pure and simple), and establish ourselves there so firmly that no power on earth could dislodge us, then the whole situation would change—east, west, all over."[64]

If all Sadat wanted to do was demonstrate his ability to cross the canal, then it is more difficult to understand why Egypt did not agree to a cease-fire in place once it had achieved this objective. Sadat understood well that an Egyptian position in the Sinai would change the whole character of Arab-Israeli negotiations on the occupied territories. If Brezhnev was trying to win Egyptian support for a cease-fire, confirming this position, why was he not successful?

When Sadat told the Soviets that he had limited objectives, they might legitimately have asked what he meant in practice. And Brezhnev did ask Vinogradov, "What is the limit of their limited objectives?"[65] Vinogradov, speaking later, was highly critical of Egyptian strategy, arguing that Sadat had no idea what he wanted to achieve after crossing the canal; everything had been geared to that one, highly improbable military objective.[66]

Vinogradov told the Egyptians on October 10 that he had spoken with

Brezhnev and Defense Minister Grechko, who told him that they believed Israel would try to knock Syria out of the war and then turn on Egypt. The Soviet military believed that Egypt should push ahead to the Sinai passes in order to take pressure off the Syrian front. The Syrians were apparently the Soviets' major concern.[67] Even later, when Kosygin was in Cairo and Sadat yelled at him for not sending the tanks he had been promised, the Soviet prime minister said, "We've concentrated on Syria because she took a thrashing and lost twelve hundred tanks in one day." [68] Brezhnev and the military may also have believed that if Israel was concentrating on Syria, then Egypt had a window of opportunity to gain some territory and enhance its hand for the postwar bargaining. The Soviet efforts to get Egypt to support a cease-fire suggest that the USSR's main regional concern was not only saving its allies but also preparing for the political process that would follow the war.

Whatever Brezhnev's motivation, the airlift was significant, and it was a coercive action that increased the Soviet commitment, even though it was taken in conjunction with what was described above as fairly gentle and vague rhetoric. Once the USSR had shown its support for Egypt and Syria by stepping up aid, it put itself in a position where it would have been difficult simply to pull the plug.

The airlift began on October 10, and by October 12 its magnitude had reached sixty to ninety flights per day.[69] By October 15, 125 An-12s had traveled to Syria (each capable of carrying ten tons of supplies); 42 An-12s and 16 An-22s had flown to Egypt (the An-22 carried up to fifty tons); and 17 An-12s had lifted supplies to Iraq.[70] The total Soviet airlift during the crisis amounted to fifteen thousand tons of supplies on 934 trips by Antonov 12s and 22s; the sealift added another eighty-five thousand tons on thirty ships.[71]

On October 13, after the bombing of Damascus and the Soviet merchant ship, the Soviet Union sent an advance staff of an airborne division to Damascus and moved a Soviet destroyer off Cyprus to protect merchant vessels. In addition, on October 10–11 the Soviets alerted all seven operational divisions of the airborne troops, a total of fifty thousand men.[72] These moves appear to have been a reflection of concern about the fate of Damascus.[73]

The next major actions the Soviets took were in conjunction with the Brezhnev warning of October 24. These added greatly to the seriousness of the verbal warning and indicated a Soviet commitment to saving the Egyptian Third Army. One of the airborne divisions may have gone on an even higher stage of alert at this time.[74] The airlift had stopped, which may have signaled the possible readying of those planes for troop transport. Five or six new ships entered the Mediterranean, which brought the number to eighty-five (compared with sixty at the start of the crisis). An airborne command post was established in the southern Soviet Union.[75]

On the ladder of commitment, these actions were also clearly a step above sending arms and advisers. If the Soviets were planning to use their own troops, then the prior step was to ready them for activity. Alerting airborne divisions, augmenting naval forces, establishing an airborne command post, and preparing planes to move troops to the region were strong signals that Brezhnev wanted the crisis settled before the Third Army was destroyed. In some ways the physical commitment was softened by the vagueness of Brezhnev's letter. But at the same time, the letter took on a more ominous tone because of the military preparations. At no time, however, did the Soviet Union increase the readiness of strategic forces as the United States had done.[76]

Conclusions on the 1973 War

Like Stalin and Khrushchev, Brezhnev bargained in the international arena as he had done at home. He tried to accommodate both the Arabs and the United States, and in doing so he irritated both his allies and his rival superpower. Furthermore, Brezhnev seemed careful to preserve his options, which caused both the United States and Egypt to suspect his motives.

Soviet behavior just prior to the war was a perfect example of Brezhnev's attempts to accommodate and avoid commitments. When informed of Egypt and Syria's decision to launch an attack, he verbally assured them the support of a friend. At the same time, apparently to distance himself from the decision and perhaps to signal to the United States that something was afoot, Brezhnev ordered the evacuation of Soviet dependents from the region.

Brezhnev's behavior after the start of the war continued to reflect indecisiveness and/or an unwillingness to commit either to support of the Arabs or to agreement with the United States. The Soviets asked Egypt to support a cease-fire after only six hours. They continued to make this request for several days. Kissinger has described well the inconsistencies in Soviet behavior early in the war that apparently derived from a wish to accommodate both the Americans and the Arabs and ended up leaving the Soviets worse off than they might have been had they chosen to accommodate one side and confront the other. Kissinger concluded, "What seems to have occurred is that the Soviets sought to combine the advantage of every course of action: détente with us, enough support for their Arab friends to establish their indispensability if things went well, but not so much as to tempt a confrontation with the United States."[77]

At the same time, after two days Brezhnev agreed to support the Arabs with a resupply effort. The airlift was a coercive action that did raise the level of Soviet commitment to the Arab cause. But it was not an all-out effort. If its intent was to save Syria, then Soviet actions sufficed. If it was designed to help Egypt in its drive in the Sinai, then it was not satisfactory. The Soviets tried to shift blame onto the Egyptians for a poor strategy after they crossed the Bar-Lev line, but the Soviet Union seemed unwilling to escalate by sending more supplies.[78]

The Soviet desire to end the war and to accommodate the United States was readily apparent during Kissinger's trip to Moscow. Brezhnev did not stonewall, nor did he threaten, bully, or confront Kissinger in any way. Khrushchev might have done so. Stalin would likely have played good cop to Gromyko's bad cop. Brezhnev conducted the negotiations personally in a conciliatory way that certainly surprised Kissinger. Even earlier during the war Kissinger had noticed that the Soviets were avoiding confrontational gestures: "They never launched a diplomatic offensive to embarrass or isolate us at the United Nations."[79]

The Soviet Union did issue coercive statements during the war, but these were framed in a careful way. The early warnings were directed at Israel, and there was no attempt until the very end to challenge the United States for actions taking place in the region. The most coercive letter came, of course, on October 24. As serious as this communication was, Brezhnev framed his remarks so that he could preserve his options; he made no clear verbal commitment, as Khrushchev had often done.

But the preparations the Soviets made to intervene were serious. Putting divisions on alert, setting up a southern command post, and readying planes to ferry troops were actions not taken in the earlier crises. They demonstrated that the Soviets had a strong commitment to protecting Egypt.

One explanation for the commitment might be that for the first time the Soviet Union had the capabilities to take these actions. Stalin and Khrushchev were in a weaker position vis-à-vis the United States. Under Brezhnev the Soviet Union had achieved strategic nuclear parity with the United States, and the USSR's conventional capabilities had also grown significantly. One line of reasoning might suggest, then, that the Soviet Union *could* put military pressure on the United States, and so it did. But simply having the capabilities does not explain why the Soviet Union acted as it did. These capabilities may have given Brezhnev options his predecessors lacked, but it cannot explain why he chose them.

Perhaps hard-liners on the Politburo pressured Brezhnev to act. Analyses of the Soviet press in this period have suggested strong differences of opinion within the leadership on how desirable it was to maintain detente as opposed to supporting an anti-imperialist cause.[80] This type of argument would suggest that a coalition built by the likes of Marshal Grechko and ideological hard-liner Suslov pushed Brezhnev to take a tougher stand vis-à-vis the United States.[81]

An argument focusing on the internal workings of the Politburo is certainly plausible. Brezhnev had become the dominant voice in foreign policy by 1973, but as Khrushchev's downfall had shown, a leader could never afford to alienate too many of his colleagues. The varying positions taken by different newspapers indicated that there were debates within the top leadership. But if there was conservative pressure on Brezhnev to take a harder line against the United States and Israel, then how can we explain the evacuation of dependents, the early efforts at arranging a cease-fire, and the accommodation of Kissinger in Moscow?

The range of behavior shows that the primary thrust of Brezhnev's behavior was consistent with his domestic style of relying on accommodation and the preservation of options. But Brezhnev could not tolerate major losses—the destruction of either Egypt or Syria. The two major coercive actions he took that also demonstrated commitment to the Arab cause were initiated in response to severe threats to the Arab, and thus Soviet, position. The airlift began when Israel turned the tide in the north and began to move against Syria. The alerts of the airborne divisions and the establishment of the southern command post also served as warnings that the Soviets could not suffer a major loss to Syria. The preparations to intervene were prompted by a serious threat to Egypt. Only when the negotiated cease-fire had broken down and the Israelis continued to strangle the Egyptian Third Army did Brezhnev take actions that showed a willingness to confront the United States.

During the Cuban missile crisis the threat of nuclear war finally caused a shift in Khrushchev's basic bargaining style. The international environment imposed a constraint that had not existed at home. Similarly, during the 1973 war the international environment—in particular, unacceptable threats to important Soviet allies—caused Brezhnev to alter the bargaining style he had learned at home. The accommodative, indecisive, cautious leader used coercion and demonstrated commitment when his vital interests were threatened. But as was typical of Brezhnev, both the airlift and the threat to intervene were moderated by continued ambiguities in his position. While he did enough to concern the United States, he did not do enough to help satisfy the demands of his Arab allies. The long-term Soviet power in the Middle East suffered as a result.

While the Middle East war offers an excellent illustration of Brezhnev's international style, it was not the first time he followed this pattern of behavior in foreign affairs. The series of negotiations that culminated in the Soviet invasion of Czechoslovakia in 1968 show the same style—make a commitment only as a last resort and even then, do everything you can to placate everyone involved.

Brezhnev and Czechoslovakia

When the full Politburo pulled into the Slovak town of Čierna-nad-Tisou for negotiations with the government of Czechoslovakia on July 29, 1968, Brezhnev was more constrained politically than he would be five years later in the October Middle East War. Still, the descriptions of his behavior during these negotiations show a style quite similar to the one he had been using in domestic politics. Much as he would later do in the Middle East, Brezhnev tried to accommodate all sides and to avoid intervention until events in Czechoslovakia forced his hand and pushed him into the camp of the interventionists.

The military option had apparently been approved in May by the Politburo for use if events warranted it.[82] But Brezhnev behaved as if he hoped intervention would not be necessary. He opened the negotiations on July 29 with a statement on the need for personnel changes as well as a request that the Czechoslovaks postpone their upcoming Fourteenth Party Congress. He also expressed concern about the free press in Czechoslovakia.[83]

On August 1 Brezhnev met alone with Czechoslovak leader Alexander Dubček. The two leaders agreed on a multilateral meeting in Bratislava to follow the Čierna discussions. They agreed that this next meeting would not address the internal situation in Prague, while Dubček would reaffirm Czechoslovakia's solidarity with the Eastern bloc. The general result of the Čierna meetings was an informal agreement that the Czechoslovaks would stabilize their internal situation, incorporating some of the main Soviet suggestions, and in return the Soviets would withdraw Warsaw Pact troops from the country.[84] From his reading of the internal report of the sessions as well as from discussions with Dubček, one of the members of the Czechoslovak government concluded later, "As far as I know, the impression Dubček gained from this private meeting was that Brezhnev was in conflict with the 'hawks' in his own Politburo . . . and was genuinely looking for a way out of the predicament that would vindicate his moderation and enable him to stand up to pressure from Ulbricht and Gomułka, who were united with the Soviet 'hawks' in pushing the situation toward open conflict and a military intervention in Czechoslovakia."[85]

On August 3 the Czechoslovak and Soviet leaders were joined in Bratislava by representatives of Hungary, Bulgaria, Poland, and the German Democratic Republic to ratify the Čierna "agreement" and to restate the unity of the Communist bloc. The Soviet draft declaration did, of course, contain elements that related to Czechoslovak internal matters, and it also said, "It is the common international duty of all socialist countries to support, defend, and consolidate these achievements, which have been made through the heroic efforts and dedicated labor of each country's people." This was the pretext that would underlie the "Brezhnev Doctrine" justifying intervention. The draft declaration went on to add, "This is the unanimous opinion of all participants in the meeting." When Zdeněk Mlynář then suggested adding, "While respecting the sovereignty and national independence of each country," to be joined with a dash to the earlier part, Brezhnev commented nervously, "The dash in this instance would go against the spirit of the Russian language!"[86] As usual, Brezhnev was trying to preserve his flexibility.

Brezhnev apparently still opposed intervention at this point, and he later, on August 13 and 16, sent personal letters to Dubček urging him to fulfill the provisions of the meetings held earlier that month. The Czechoslovaks, however, were not taking the measures they had promised the Soviet Union, including banning groups such as the Social Democratic Party and establishing control over the media. The Soviet leadership then decided to send the tanks.

Brezhnev's behavior in Czechoslovakia was quite similar to his behavior at home during the previous four years and to his actions before and during the 1973 war. Karen Dawisha wrote later that a recurring theme in Brezhnev's conduct throughout the Czech crisis in the spring and summer of 1968 was "a leadership style strongly inclined toward conciliation and collective leadership. This appears to have been the product not just of the balance of forces within the Politburo but also of his own personal orientation. . . . He both helped to form a political consensus and reflected that consensus; he was an architect of both the hard-line Warsaw Letter and the Čierna compromise." She also wrote, "If Brezhnev opposed invasion, as he apparently did for so long, it was not out of sympathy with the Prague Spring; it was attributable to the cautiousness of his own personal style" as well as to the belief that the trouble in Czechoslovakia was limited and could be dealt with.[87]

Similarly, Jiří Valenta, in his study of this crisis, often describes Brezhnev as "wavering" between the more clearly pro- and anti-interventionists in the Politburo. Others may have taken a stand on what they thought should be the correct course, but not Brezhnev. Valenta in fact attributes the ambiguity in the agreements reached with Dubček in early August partly to Brezhnev's desire to remain flexible.[88] Dawisha, Mlynář, and Valenta all describe the Soviet leader as a vacillator who hoped that the Czechoslovaks would solve the issues for him, but who was then forced into siding with the hard-liners in order to preserve his political position.[89]

As was typical for him, Brezhnev tried to accommodate all sides and to remain noncommittal as long as possible. And as would happen in 1973, the threat of an overwhelming loss finally compelled him to make a commitment and to act coercively. In 1968 it was only when faced with the threat of the loss of Czechoslovakia from the Soviet camp that Brezhnev altered his typical bargaining style.

SIX

Gorbachev and German Unification

The fall of the Berlin Wall in 1989 and the unification of Germany less than one year later signaled the end of the Cold War between the United States and the Soviet Union. Soviet concerns about Germany and Berlin had, as we have seen, led in earlier periods to the Berlin blockade and to the building of the wall. With Mikhail Gorbachev's program of *perestroika* at home and "new thinking" abroad, the last Soviet general secretary was unwilling to use force to maintain the division of Germany.

Neither the pace nor the form of German unification was a foregone conclusion in November 1989, however, and bargaining among the United States, the Federal Republic of Germany, and the Soviet Union was intense during the next eight months. In these negotiations Gorbachev and his foreign minister, Eduard Shevardnadze, first tried to stall the process of unification itself, and then, after this failed, they attempted to delay or even preclude full German membership in the North Atlantic Alliance.

This set of negotiations was different from those of 1948, 1962, and 1973, because the bargaining was done entirely through verbal diplomacy; there were no troop movements, alerts, or any other kind of military activity. The potential for military activity existed, since the Soviet Union had almost four hundred thousand troops stationed in the GDR that Gorbachev could have used to disrupt the process and turn it into the type of international crisis we have seen in the earlier cases. But Gorbachev's domestic program required a benign international environment, and he chose not to use those troops to affect the bargaining over Germany.

In this bargaining, Gorbachev was careful as he had been at home, to avoid making a firm commitment to any one position. He floated proposal after proposal in the months after the wall fell as he had often done in domestic economic affairs. The United States was concerned at various times that Gorbachev might neutralize Western advantages, in this case by staking out a minimum position that would satisfy German desires for unification but would preclude the U.S. goal of full membership for Germany in the North Atlantic Treaty Organization.[1] As in domestic politics, however, Gorbachev outlined general principles but did not take a stand on a specific position.[2] He did make public, personal statements, saying first that German unification and later that German NATO membership was unacceptable. But the statements were ambiguous. He never said what the Soviet Union would do to stop the process.

At home Gorbachev was successful because he could complement this behavior with the stick of popular pressure as well as with threats to resign if he did not win backing for the broad proposals he introduced. In the negotiations over German unification he stated several times that the Western positions were simply unacceptable. But in domestic politics, since his adversaries had no program of their own and needed Gorbachev, he could coerce them into accepting his leadership. In this international bargaining the West had a coherent proposal and could plunge ahead.

An important difference, then, between the international bargaining style exhibited by Gorbachev in 1989–90 and his earlier behavior at home was his inability to adopt a coercive strategy, given his concern not to jeopardize his relationship with the West. At home, when adversaries stood in his way Gorbachev used public pressure to force them aside, or at least to get them to assent to the positions he staked out; he could always play his trump card of threatening to resign. In this international case Gorbachev's hands were partly tied by his inability to use or threaten to use force to get his way. In purely diplomatic bargaining a leader can apply pressure only by staking out a firm position. Gorbachev occasionally warned the United States and Germany about the anti-German passions that might be unleashed in the Soviet Union if the outcome was counter to Soviet interests, but this pressure was sufficient only for gaining a few face-savers in exchange for Soviet capitulation.

At home Gorbachev's avoidance of commitments helped him implement his coercive strategy. Since in the international bargaining over Germany's fate he could not confront the West, given his need for American and German support, his avoidance of commitments made his position worse— had he taken a strong stance early in the bargaining he might have prevented full German membership in NATO, as many of his conservative opponents at home were hoping he would do.

The Setting

During the course of the Cold War the German Democratic Republic had become the Soviet Union's most important ally in the Warsaw Pact because of its size, location, and economic performance. Emotionally it was still the Soviets' most important prize from the Great Patriotic War against Nazi Germany. The problems surrounding Berlin, which had led to Stalin's blockade in 1948 and to Khrushchev's wall in 1961, seemed to have stabilized in the early 1970s, when, in pursuit of detente with the USSR, the Americans and West Germans ratified the postwar borders that consigned Eastern Europe to the Soviet sphere of influence—even if the West German constitution still expressed the hope of eventual unification. And as long as the Soviet Union hung on to the Brezhnev Doctrine, which had guaranteed Soviet intervention to save "fraternal" governments, there seemed to be no hope that borders or alliances would shift. The presence of Soviet troops in the GDR guaranteed a continuation of the status quo.

But in December 1988 Gorbachev delivered a stunning speech at the United Nations that unleashed dramatic changes. Repeating a statement he had made the previous summer at the Nineteenth All-Union CPSU Party Conference, Gorbachev said that every country had "freedom of choice." This time he backed up the statement with a bold announcement: the Soviet Union would unilaterally reduce its armed forces, including those stationed in Eastern Europe, and would also withdraw some of its most threatening military hardware. Two months later, in Kiev, Gorbachev said that Soviet–East European relations would be conducted on the basis of "unconditional independence, full equality, and strict non-intervention in internal affairs."[3] The Brezhnev Doctrine was dead.

The Soviets' new approach stemmed in large part from Gorbachev's domestic needs. Controlling the external empire by force was no longer advantageous to the Soviet Union. From an economic standpoint, Eastern Europe had become a drain on the Soviet economy, while winning aid from Western Europe and the United States had become a key foreign policy goal.[4] And from the standpoint of security, Soviet possession of nuclear weapons made a buffer zone in Eastern Europe unnecessary, although some people in the military certainly disagreed. Furthermore, the political and economic benefits that Gorbachev could gain by allowing the East Europeans their freedom were immense. Finally, Gorbachev could not afford to leave successful conservative apparatchiks in power in other socialist states if he was arguing that the Soviet Union and its Communist Party needed to restructure in order to function more effectively.

Despite the changes, Gorbachev in 1989 neither expected nor wanted to see Germany unify. He wanted to transform the nature of the Warsaw Pact, as well as that of NATO, but he did not want to see his country's main World War II adversary reunified as a full member of NATO. In discussions of the issue Gorbachev continually emphasized the historical fact of two states. As he had said in 1987 in conversations with Richard von Weiszäcker, the West German president, "There are two German states with different social-political systems. They have their own values. They both learned lessons from history, and each can contribute to Europe and the world. And what will be in 100 years, history will decide. Any other approach is unacceptable. If anyone were to take a different path, the consequences would be very serious. In this, we should be absolutely clear."[5] He would repeat this formulation many times,[6] but his insistence on maintaining separation was not enough to stem the flow of events. Furthermore, while he continued to say that alternatives were unacceptable and that "we should be absolutely clear," he never said what he would do if "anyone were to take a different path." It was a hollow ultimatum, as his resignation threat at home had been, but it was ineffective with adversaries who were not prepared to concede.

By late summer 1989 the situation in the GDR had become quite tenuous. East Germans were swarming into Hungary, hoping to cross the recently opened border between Hungary and Austria. The Hungarians had signed an agreement with the GDR in 1969 that prevented East Germans from leaving for a third country without a proper visa. In September the Hungarian foreign minister, Gyula Horn, asked a deputy to sound out how the Soviets would react if Hungary scrapped the agreement, and the deputy reported that the USSR would clearly not stand in the way. On September 10 Hungary suspended its twenty-year-old agreement with the GDR, and within three days fifteen thousand East German refugees had fled west.[7]

By the time Gorbachev arrived in East Berlin on October 6 to celebrate the fortieth anniversary of the GDR, forty-five thousand East Germans had fled. In 1961, faced with massive emigration from East to West, the Soviet Union had built a wall. Now Gorbachev was leaving the East Germans on their own. While stressing that his relations with East German leader Erich Honecker were good and that the GDR situation was not dangerous, Gorbachev said that the West should understand that the affairs of the East Germans were to be "decided not in Moscow but in Berlin."[8]

On October 9 local Communist Party leaders in Leipzig refused to attack seventy thousand demonstrators as Honecker had ordered.[9] On October 18 the East German leader stepped down and was replaced by Egon Krenz. Within a few weeks half a million people were demonstrating in East Berlin, and a similar number had taken to the streets across the GDR.

Krenz asked Gorbachev for advice. The latter replied that the East Germans should open the border to stabilize the situation.[10]

Bargaining over German Unification

The negotiations that followed the fall of the Berlin Wall fell into roughly three phases. The first phase lasted from the fall of the wall in November until a meeting on January 30, 1990, between Gorbachev and East German prime minister Hans Modrow. In this phase the Soviets focused on forestalling or delaying unification itself. Gorbachev continued to stress that the two Germanys were a fact of history, and he warned against tampering with the alliances. He sought to keep four-power control at the front of the agenda, and he reached out to possible anti-unification partners such as France. But by the end of January events on the ground made it clear that unification was inevitable.

In the second phase of negotiations, from January 30 until the Washington summit at the end of May, the focus shifted to German membership in NATO. The Soviets threw out a variety of proposals to prevent a complete capitulation to the U.S. position, including a neutral and demilitarized united Germany; German participation in both alliances for some specified period; a dissolution of the blocs, along with the creation of a new European security structure to accommodate a unified Germany; and partial German participation in NATO's military structures. Gorbachev was trying to come up with some proposal that would satisfy his Western partners short of full German participation in the Atlantic Alliance.

Finally, from the Washington summit in late May 1990 until his meeting with West German chancellor Helmut Kohl in the Caucasus in mid-July, Gorbachev basically accepted German participation in NATO as long as there was a ceiling placed on the size of the German armed forces; but the Soviet leader did not finally accept the reality of a unified Germany in NATO until after receiving certain face-savers, and until after the Twenty-eighth CPSU Party Congress in July, which further strengthened his hand at home.

As at home, in each phase Gorbachev failed to stick with one proposal in his bargaining with the West. His only form of commitment was his hollow ultimatum, in this case declaring that the Western position was unacceptable. Since he never credibly threatened Germany and the United States, he was unable to prevent the implementation of their plan.

In the first phase of negotiations Gorbachev clung to the notion that the creation of two Germanys was a fact of history, and he issued vague warnings to the West not to take advantage of Soviet domestic changes to impose a solution to the issue without taking Soviet interests into account. After sending a message to U.S. president George Bush on November 12 stating his hope for a "calm and peaceful" situation, Gorbachev made his first public remarks a few days later in meetings with French foreign minister Roland Dumas. Gorbachev warned the West, "It is not useful to shout about winning the Cold War or about the failure of this or that social system." [11] His foreign minister, Eduard Shevardnadze, added, "Great anxiety is caused by attempts being undertaken by certain circles in West Germany to place the issue of the reunification of Germany on today's political agenda." [12]

On November 28 Chancellor Kohl staked out a ten-point plan for German unification that called for a gradual process of building closer ties between the two Germanys within the European Community and the Conference on Security and Cooperation in Europe, a process that would lead in five or ten years' time to unification. [13] Kohl's Western allies heavily criticized him for failing to consult them ahead of time; the German chancellor, however, was laying out not a detailed program but merely a general vision of the future: "No one knows today what shape a reunited Germany will ultimately take," he said. "But I am certain that unification will come if the people in Germany want it." [14]

The initial Soviet responses were mixed and came from the Foreign Ministry. Shevardnadze took a strong stand against Kohl's remarks; his press spokesman, Gennady Gerasimov, said that the Soviet foreign minister feared West German "revanchism" and added, "There is not one country in Europe today that would thirst for German reunification because of the questions it raises for stability. It is not on the agenda." [15] But another Foreign Ministry official, Yuri Gremitskikh, said that reunification could occur only as part of a larger process that ended the division of Europe, including dissolution of the two alliances. Here, at least, there seemed to be acceptance of the idea of unification under certain conditions. The Soviet position at this point appealed to the universal desire for stability but did not appear to reject unification outright.

At a summit with Bush in Malta in early December, Gorbachev repeated his phrase that "history has willed" two Germanys, as he would also stress in a subsequent meeting in Moscow with Warsaw Pact chiefs. [16] And a week later Shevardnadze stepped up the attack on the ten-point plan, saying it was "fraught with dangerous consequences" and bordered "on outright diktat." Referring to the "vital interests of the Soviet Union," Shevardnadze said, "[The] Soviet people remember well the history, the tragic lessons of the Second World War. Our public opinion is highly sensitive to everything that is related to its results and this should not be forgotten by anyone."

Upset with what he called "unilateral, egoistic" attempts to take advantage of the Soviet domestic situation, the Soviet foreign minister warned that the "artificial speeding up of events can bring about unpredictable consequences."[17]

Largely through his foreign minister, Gorbachev was expressing his concern about the process taking shape, and while the public nature of these comments put his government on record as opposing German unification, he was sending only mild warnings that were not backed up in any way. There was certainly no similarity between these Soviet pleas not to change the status quo and Brezhnev's 1973 letter to Nixon warning of possible Soviet intervention in the Middle East. Brezhnev too had been careful not to make a firm commitment, but his tone and his military actions had made it clear that the Soviet Union was serious about preserving the Egyptian Third Army. In 1989 Gorbachev did not take a serious stand to preserve the GDR.

But he could have done so. At this stage Gorbachev had at least two other choices as he bargained with the West, both involving a higher level of commitment. The more risky and costly option would have been to say that the Soviet Union would never allow unification and would use force to prevent it. This option would of course have initiated a major crisis and posed diplomatic costs that Gorbachev could not afford, given his other domestic and foreign policies. But this highly coercive policy was not the only option available to the Soviet leader. President Bush had proposed his so-called four conditions on German unification on December 4, including continued German membership in NATO. Gorbachev could have stated *in December* that he accepted the right of the Germans to unify, but not on the terms the West was offering. Had he warned that a major international crisis loomed if German unification involved full NATO membership, but said such a crisis could be averted if the Germans chose a more reasonable course, then Gorbachev might have divided German and American opinion enough to secure a more favorable outcome for the USSR.[18] Even this latter choice posed diplomatic costs, but many Germans, such as West German foreign minister Hans Dietrich Genscher, were sensitive to Soviet interests, as would become evident during the second phase of negotiations.

At home Gorbachev's rivals had not made the kind of coherent, alternative proposals that the United States and West Germany would issue during these negotiations, and he thus had fewer challenges when he formulated his program of *perestroika*. Now, Gorbachev's inability to stick to a clear position was costly. He kept expressing his concern at the way events were moving, but the warnings he issued were mild ones. For example, a few days after the Malta meetings, in a joint appearance in Kiev with French president François Mitterand—who also opposed unification at this point—Gorbachev merely said, "We proceed from the assumption that each people has the right to choose, to solve its own problems of independence in its own interests, but also taking into account the interests of other countries."[19]

Several days later Gorbachev made a seemingly stronger statement before of his Central Committee, but a close examination of the speech shows the hollowness of his warnings:

> With all means we will try to guarantee progress and stability—stability in Eastern Europe, stability of the whole continent, and the inviolability of postwar borders of all existing states in Europe. . . . We with all decisiveness emphasize that we will stand up for the GDR—it is our strategic ally and a member of the Warsaw Treaty. It is necessary to proceed from the complex postwar realities—the existence of two sovereign German states, members of the UN; departure from this threatens the destabilization of Europe.[20]

Did Gorbachev really mean that the Soviet Union would use "all means" and would "with all decisiveness" stand up for its strategic ally? Gorbachev was making a public and personal statement about Soviet vital interests— the GDR as strategic ally—and he was warning about the destabilization of Europe, but he did not provide concrete proposals for what he would do to stop or alter the process taking place. He certainly did not mean that the Soviet Union would use all means, since he clearly had no intention of keeping his strategic ally by using Soviet troops, and in a sense this statement was evocative of Khrushchev's bluffs in 1962 (although Gorbachev never used such Khrushchevian phrases as "our rockets will fly automatically"). The statement *sounded* mildly coercive, with no hint of compromise with the West, but without any actions to back up this position, Gorbachev's warnings were ineffective. And the West was more certain in 1989 that Gorbachev would not use force in Germany than it had been about Khrushchev's potential actions in Cuba in 1962.

But events on the ground were simply moving too quickly for diplomatic delays. In the first half of January 1990 more than twenty-five thousand East Germans left for the West.[21] At the end of the month Gorbachev met with East German prime minister Hans Modrow in Moscow. Gorbachev accepted that "time itself is having an impact on the process,"[22] and it was in these meetings that the Soviet leader shifted his focus from delaying unification to affecting its outcome. As Egon Bahr, a prominent member of the Social Democratic Party, noted, Gorbachev's comments during his meetings with Modrow signaled that "it is no longer a question of if, but when, how and what form a unified German state might take."[23]

In this first phase, then, Gorbachev missed several opportunities to take a stand because of his familiar tactic of avoiding commitments. He warned about unacceptable Western positions, but since he could not couple these warnings with a coercive strategy given his other policy goals, he was much less effective than he had been in domestic politics. And his inability to put forward a clear position that would constrain Germany's NATO membership continued into the second phase of the bargaining.

In this next phase of negotiations the Soviet Union put on the table a number of proposals, including a call for a neutral, united Germany, for German participation in both alliances, for new European security structures, and for partial German participation in NATO.[24] Gorbachev acted like a man grasping at straws, never holding to any position long enough for there to be any semblance of a coherent Soviet approach.

Gorbachev probably lost his best chance to preclude full German membership in NATO in the first few weeks of February.[25] For a brief time there were glaring inconsistencies in the Western position, and Genscher in particular was inclined to take Soviet security concerns quite seriously. Had Gorbachev made a firm commitment to a proposal that prohibited NATO from extending into East German territory, he might have succeeded, given the potential divisions in the West. But Gorbachev was still focusing not on limiting German membership in NATO but on preventing German membership entirely, which was not a realistic outcome by this time.

Perhaps Gorbachev was constrained by continued domestic opposition to German unification itself. He was certainly facing public criticism at home over the course of events in Germany. In a speech to a Central Committee plenum in early February, Yegor Ligachev warned, "We should not overlook . . . the growing danger. I have in mind the forced reunification of Germany, in fact, the swallowing up of the German Democratic Republic. It would be an unforgivable myopia and mistake not to see that on the world horizon looms Germany with a huge economic and military potential. We need the realistic forces of the world community, all the democratic forces of the world, in order to prevent a reexamination of post-war borders and . . . not to allow a pre-war Munich."[26]

How much this domestic criticism hampered Gorbachev is unclear. But it was precisely at this time that the position of the Western governments was as fluid as it was ever to be. By the end of January Genscher had come up with a formula that included what he thought was necessary to gain Soviet approval: a united Germany would be a member of NATO, but the alliance's military structure would not extend to the territory of the GDR. On February 3, in Washington, prior to their separate trips to Moscow, Genscher and U.S. Secretary of State James Baker agreed on this plan.[27]

The precise meaning of this formula had not yet been worked out, as was clear from the statements of the participants in the United States and

West Germany. The *Washington Post* wrote that Baker was coming to Moscow with plans for a united Germany to be a "limited" member of NATO. President Bush gave a speech in San Francisco on February 7 in which he said that a united Germany should "remain tied into NATO in some way" but "maybe not in NATO in exactly the same form it is." And NATO secretary general Manfred Woerner said that a united Germany should be in NATO, but he declined to comment when asked whether the GDR would be demilitarized or whether German troops outside NATO could be deployed in eastern Germany.[28]

The lack of clarity in the United States and West Germany concerning the precise meaning of the Genscher plan would continue for several more weeks, and it provided Gorbachev with an opportunity that he did not take.[29] Baker, for example, told Gorbachev in Moscow that the United States did not favor "neutrality for a unified Germany" but instead favored "a continued membership in, or association with, NATO." While Baker told the press that his comment about "association" was meaningless, he did say that there would be no extension of NATO forces into GDR territory.[30] He would repeat this position as late as February 18, during a television appearance on ABC's *This Week with David Brinkley*. When reminded by George Will that "the *Bundeswehr* is a NATO force," Baker replied, "Now, you're getting—you want to take me beyond where we've already . . . beyond where we've gone and we will be—well, we're going to be discussing." And NATO secretary general Manfred Woerner said on the same show that he could guarantee the Soviets that NATO would "not extend the military integration over the borders of the now Federal Republic of Germany."[31] The conflict within the West German government on this issue emerged publicly at the same time; Defense Minister Gerhard Stoltenberg argued for NATO's extension to the GDR, and Genscher denounced him for fear of Soviet intransigence.[32] The issue was not cleared up until February 25, when Bush and Kohl at Camp David said, "We share a common belief that a unified Germany should remain a full member of the North Atlantic Treaty Organization, including participation in its military structure."[33]

The Soviet Union might have taken advantage of the confusion by embracing the Genscher proposal, which could perhaps have led to the full demilitarization of GDR territory after the eventual Soviet troop withdrawal, or at least something less than full German membership in NATO. But Gorbachev was proposing other solutions. After Baker said at their February 9 meeting in Moscow that NATO's jurisdiction would not change, Gorbachev did state, "Certainly any extension of the territory of NATO would be unacceptable."[34] He and Shevardnadze did not focus on this solution, however. On February 10 Shevardnadze spoke not about limited NATO membership but rather about gradual unification coincident with both Germanys leaving their respective alliances, and he reminded the West that the idea of a neutral, unified Germany was a longstanding Soviet position dating back to the 1950s.[35] The Soviet position in February 1990, however, was not altogether clear. One U.S. official said of the Soviets in these Moscow meetings, "They did not commit themselves to a position; they were noncommittal."[36]

Just after these meetings in Moscow, the Soviet Union in Ottawa accepted negotiations on German unification within a two-plus-four framework, as Baker had proposed to Gorbachev in Moscow the week before.[37] In announcing Soviet acceptance Shevardnadze gave no indication that the Soviet Union had a coherent vision of an outcome. First he said that a neutral Germany was "the most sensible," but he added that this solution was "not the only way." Then, after saying, "I think the ideal solution would be a neutral Germany," Shevardnadze returned to the old line that "our preference is for the existing reality of two sovereign independent Germanys, the German Federal Republic belonging to NATO and the German Democratic Republic belonging to the Warsaw Pact."[38] As one Soviet official noted, neutrality no longer seemed to be the bottom line, but "we have lost our ability to exploit German domestic politics. We no longer have time for a long-term foreign policy strategy."[39]

Having abandoned the neutrality option, Gorbachev went back to a proposal the Soviets had put forward in November and December: German unification within a new European security structure that could replace the blocs. In an interview in *Pravda* on February 21, Gorbachev said that while the Germans had a right to unification, this process could not upset the "military-strategic balance" of the two alliances. This, he said, "should be completely clear." He then argued that the process was "organically linked" and "should be synchronized" with the creation of the new European security arrangement.[40] At the same time, his foreign minister was reminding everyone that Moscow did not want Germany in NATO and would not "remain indifferent" should this occur.[41] In early March Gorbachev said on West German television, "We will not agree to [German membership in NATO]. This is absolutely ruled out."[42]

Gorbachev had been "absolutely clear" before. But what did it mean for the Soviets not to "remain indifferent," or for them to "rule out" German membership in NATO? As he had done throughout the negotiations, Gorbachev was publicly committing himself to the general idea of nonmembership without being specific about what he would do, much as at home he had publicly and personally committed himself to the general idea of *perestroika* without stating specific positions. This behavior was qualitatively different from Khrushchev's introduction of the Virgin Lands program and his bluff about stopping U.S. actions with submarine and rocket forces.

Although Gorbachev, in a speech to the Congress of People's Deputies, again said that German membership in NATO was unacceptable, Shevardnadze, at a meeting of Warsaw Pact foreign ministers in Prague, said, "We for instance think that is impossible, but this question is one which requires further discussion and clarification."[43] If it was impossible, then presumably there was no need for discussion. Shevardnadze also said that the main issue now was the level of armaments in a united Germany.[44] At this point the Soviet position had greatly weakened, with the results of the East German elections showing overwhelming support for Kohl and unification.[45]

Gorbachev continued holding to his typical style of never sticking to any position long enough to follow through on it.[46] For example, in early April he sent his foreign minister to Washington to meet with Baker. Shevardnadze formally dropped the idea of a neutral Germany but continued to insist that NATO membership was unacceptable. Shevardnadze spoke about the pan-European security structure and the possibility of German membership in both NATO and the Warsaw Pact,[47] but these proposals were vague and unrealistic. A few days later Gorbachev repeated the idea, proposing that a united Germany would remain in both NATO and the Warsaw Pact for five to seven years, and then a new European security system could come into being in place of the blocs. The Bush administration responded privately to the Soviet Union that since everyone except the Soviet Union wanted Germany in NATO, then that was what would happen. Gorbachev, however, was not ready to accept this outcome.[48]

The two-plus-four talks opened in Bonn on May 5.[49] At these meetings Shevardnadze repeated the Soviet position on NATO membership for Germany, and he also tried to use the threat of a right-wing reaction inside the Soviet Union as leverage on the process. Given the Soviet Union's unwillingness to use force, as well as its inability to tie Germany's future to other things the West might want, the only means of pressure available to the Soviets at this point was the threat of a coup in the event that they were humiliated in this process. Shevardnadze told his negotiating partners, "The population of our country, which sustained such frightening losses in the last war, cannot accept the idea of including Germany in NATO. . . . If an attempt is made to push us into a corner on matters touching our security, it will lead to a situation—I will say it candidly—in which our political flexibility would be severely curtailed, because emotions would boil up inside the country."[50] Baker in fact took pains to say, "We must find a solution where there won't be any winners and losers, but where everybody wins."[51]

Given Soviet weakness, Shevardnadze's comments about the potential popular outcry over German membership in NATO were designed to help persuade the West that it was not a good idea to proceed along those lines. Gorbachev could not use his military forces to threaten the West, but he could make a nonmilitary threat—a possible public backlash in the Soviet Union that might lead to a change in his country's foreign policy. This threat echoed his use of public pressure against domestic foes such as Grigory Romanov back in 1985.

In the final phase of negotiations the threat of a right-wing coup in the Soviet Union was Gorbachev's only bargaining chip, and he came to Washington in late May with no clear alternative to the U.S. proposal. At that time Bush and Baker offered the Soviet Union a package of face-saving measures in return for its acceptance of German membership in NATO; this package was in fact to serve as the basis for the eventual agreement. These "nine assurances" included allowing Soviet forces to remain on East German soil during a transition period; assuring the Soviet Union that no NATO forces would be stationed in East Germany during that transition period; committing Germany to its borders as well as to non-nuclear/chemical/biological weapons status; changing NATO's orientation to allow for new links with former Warsaw Pact members; and providing substantial German economic aid to the Soviet Union.[52]

Gorbachev was still calling for German membership in both alliances, but Bush pointedly reminded him that under the 1975 Helsinki accords that laid out a set of principles for NATO and Warsaw Pact members, nations were allowed to choose their own alliances. Gorbachev agreed. Bush's statement at a joint press conference highlighted the contradiction; after noting that he and Kohl as well as others sought a united Germany as a full member of NATO, Bush noted, "President Gorbachev, frankly, does not hold that view. But we are in full agreement that the matter of alliance membership is, in accordance with the Helsinki Final Act, a matter for the Germans to decide."[53] If Gorbachev agreed that Germany could choose its own alliance, then he was agreeing to NATO membership. Several days later Shevardnadze assured Baker in Copenhagen that, given an agreement on German troop limits, a unified Germany in NATO was acceptable.[54]

At the spring NATO ministerial meeting in Scotland, Baker reiterated the nine assurances given the Soviets. The assurance that caused the greatest stir was the fifth: "NATO forces will not be extended to the former territory of the GDR for a transition period." When pressed on what that meant, Baker said the transition period remained unspecified. But he also reminded his audience that in Washington, Gorbachev "seemed to accept" that Germany had the right to choose its own alliance.[55]

At the second round of the two-plus-four meetings in Berlin on June 22, the Soviet Union backtracked briefly when Shevardnadze proposed the retention of some four-power rights in Germany even after unification, as well as a reduction of foreign troops on German soil. The West rejected any notion that Germany would have a special, limited status in Europe as a less-than-sovereign nation. Shevardnadze added that much depended on the decision of the upcoming NATO meeting to reorient NATO and make it less threatening to the East.[56] The Soviet foreign minister reiterated this point several days later in a critique of rising "McCarthyism" in the Soviet Union:

Yes, the prospect of a united Germany has stirred up memories and has put many on guard not only in our country. But we will endeavor to approach this question with other countries. How much longer could the division of Germany be maintained? Years, decades, an eternity? How much longer could our soldiers guard the Elbe—years, decades, an eternity?

   I am far from intending to say that the possibility of broadening NATO should not concern us. We are not at all indifferent to the future military-political status of Germany. But this question will be, probably, examined differently depending on those changes which will take place in Europe.[57]

In other words, with troop limits and a changing orientation for NATO, the Soviet Union could accept the inevitable.

   In early July two crucial meetings took place that enabled Gorbachev finally to accede to the Western position: the Twenty-eighth CPSU Party Congress met in Moscow, and the NATO summit convened in London. At the latter the NATO heads of state and government, meeting in London, issued their Declaration on a Transformed North Atlantic Alliance. The NATO powers reached out to their former adversaries, proposing a joint commitment to nonaggression and inviting Gorbachev and the other Warsaw Pact leaders to address NATO and to establish links with the Alliance. NATO promised that a commitment to German troop levels would be given when the agreement on conventional forces in Europe (CFE) was signed. NATO promised to change its strategy of forward defense to a "reduced forward presence" and offered to eliminate NATO nuclear artillery shells from Europe if the Soviet Union did likewise. Furthermore, NATO adjusted its "no first use" doctrine, saying that nuclear weapons would now be weapons of "last resort." Not only were NATO leaders adjusting to the changing realities, but they were giving Gorbachev the ability to say that Soviet security would not be threatened—and in fact would be enhanced—by German unification.

   Meanwhile, in Moscow, Gorbachev asked the delegates to the Party Congress, "Have we been correct in not interfering in matters that got under way in East Europe? What, ought the tanks again have been sent? Are we again to teach others how to live?"[58] At the congress Gorbachev finally got rid of his conservative nemesis, Yegor Ligachev, as the latter was humiliated in his attempt to win the post of deputy general secretary.[59] Gorbachev thus had less to fear from any criticism he might get for capitulating on German unification.

Having disposed of Ligachev, and having received the NATO declaration—and, perhaps most important, the promise of German economic aid—Gorbachev wasted no time in assenting to the Western position on German unification in a meeting with Chancellor Kohl in the Caucasus. Saying that the two leaders had "acted in the spirit of the well-known German expression: 'Realpolitik,'" Gorbachev announced Soviet acceptance of German unification in NATO.[60] The Soviets accepted the Kohl-Bush stance that after Soviet troops left the territory of the GDR, German forces in NATO's integrated command could be stationed there, albeit without nuclear weapons. It was on this point that Foreign Minister Genscher had criticized Defense Minister Stoltenberg in February.[61] But by the summer of 1990 Bush and Kohl had achieved their maximum objectives.

Conclusions on German Unification

In an important respect, Gorbachev behaved during the negotiations over German unification as he had in domestic politics when bargaining with his rivals. He avoided making commitments to specific positions while trying to take clear, public, and personal stands first on the impossibility of German unification and then on the unacceptability of German membership in NATO. He continually put new proposals on the table to try and get the deal he wanted.

What had made this strategy work at home was Gorbachev's use of popular pressure and his ability to spring surprises on his opponents. Furthermore, when he was faced with overwhelmingly hostile opposition he would threaten to resign, which then exposed the weakness of his adversaries since they needed him to lead the party. In the international negotiations leading up to German unification, however, Gorbachev was unable and unwilling to use this important element of his political strategy. These constraints stemmed in large part from his overall foreign policy goals. Gorbachev needed Western assistance to carry out his domestic agenda. He could not afford the diplomatic, political, and economic costs that using or threatening the use of force would entail. Stalin could buzz the air corridors of Berlin; Khrushchev could threaten to use his submarines in the Caribbean; and Brezhnev could ready his troops for deployment in the Middle East. But Gorbachev, despite having nearly four hundred thousand troops in the GDR, could do nothing like this because he, unlike his predecessors, needed to maintain Western goodwill to assure the success of his domestic political programs.

Thus, in the case of German unification Gorbachev was not coercing his allies, because he lacked the tools for doing so. His only bargaining chip was the threat of a right-wing coup against him that would turn back the clock on U.S.-Soviet relations, but the West sought to minimize this danger by providing the face-savers, in particular the NATO declaration and the promise of billions of German marks.

Gorbachev's favorite tactic—the resignation threat—was also not of great use in these international negotiations. By stating how unacceptable unification and NATO membership were, he could imply to the United States and Germany, "If you don't agree to a neutral Germany, I'm going home." But while at home Gorbachev's adversaries had no coherent alternative vision to *perestroika,* in the German unification talks he faced a determined opponent with a relatively clear vision of the future of Western Europe—a vision that included a united Germany in NATO.

There was a window of opportunity for Gorbachev when the Western position was not so clear, but he missed it. In February the Western leaders seemed uncertain about the exact arrangement they had in mind for German participation in NATO. Gorbachev could have made things more difficult for the Americans and West Germans by accepting a unified Germany with a limited membership in NATO, along the lines outlined by Foreign Minister Genscher at the end of January 1990. He simply would not commit himself to a firm position at that time, however, and this tactic would prove costly.

Despite the West's overwhelming victory in the negotiations over Germany's future, the United States and Germany did see the need to offer Gorbachev a face-saver for his capitulation. NATO reoriented itself by adjusting military doctrine and reaching out to the East, and Gorbachev did get the German aid he wanted and needed for his domestic economic programs. Kohl promised the Soviet leader that he would pay for the stationing of Soviet troops in Germany during the transition period, and he also offered an aid package to house the troops once they went home. Even with a weak hand, Gorbachev was offered important incentives to back down.

Several years earlier, at a time when he had been successful at home in outmaneuvering his early rivals, Gorbachev also used some of his typical bargaining tactics in arms control negotiations at Reykjavík with U.S. president Ronald Reagan. Here again Gorbachev was also more constrained than he was at home, and while his surprise tactics almost succeeded, his international version of the "resignation threat" did not work as it had at home.

Reykjavík

After a year and a half of throwing his rivals at home off balance, Gorbachev went to Reykjavík and tried to do the same to President Reagan. Although the Soviets had led the Americans to believe that the summit would deal merely with Euromissiles and nuclear testing, Gorbachev came to the Icelandic capital armed with a surprise.[62] When the two leaders sat down on October 11, Gorbachev put forward a set of dramatic proposals: he offered to cut strategic weapons by 50 percent across the board, including the Soviet "heavy" missiles that were of such concern to the United States, and he dropped the longstanding Soviet insistence on taking British and French nuclear forces into consideration in any discussion of intermediate-range nuclear forces in Europe. But along with these concessions he proposed a ten-year commitment to the Anti-Ballistic Missile (ABM) treaty and confinement of Strategic Defense Initiative (SDI) research to the laboratory.[63]

The proposals were startling, but Gorbachev made it clear to Reagan that they were a package. The Soviet leader was clearly setting the terms. He was offering Reagan dramatic results if only the president would give up his cherished strategic defense program, but Gorbachev made clear that the president had to give in order to receive. In the Sunday morning talks Reagan tried to put SDI aside for later discussions, but Gorbachev responded, "No, let's go home. We've accomplished nothing." [64] This threat was similar to the resignation threats he had used and would use again at home: If you won't give me what I want, I'm walking out the door. At home this tactic worked because Gorbachev's opponents had no other choice but to follow him. Here he tried it, but Reagan was not going to give.

The United States did offer a counterproposal in the follow-on session between George Shultz and Eduard Shevardnadze, but the Soviet foreign minister repeated his boss's position, telling Shultz that if Reagan agreed to Gorbachev's terms on SDI, the rest would fall into place. If he did not, "there'll be no agreement on anything." Shultz responded with an unofficial proposal that would combine a five-year commitment to the ABM treaty with 50 percent reductions; in the second five years the sides would seek to eliminate all offensive ballistic missiles but would continue restrictions on defenses. After the ten years, however, either side could deploy defenses. Reagan approved the package, since it gave Gorbachev the ten-year commitment to ABM while still allowing for SDI after the ten years were over.[65]

Gorbachev countered with a proposal that included eliminating all strategic nuclear weapons in the ten-year period, after which the two countries would make "mutually acceptable decisions" on space defense systems. Again Reagan tried to put off the discussions of defense, suggesting that they deal with that issue in Washington. Gorbachev reiterated his commitment to the package. The two leaders then moved to an agreement to eliminate all nuclear weapons, but Gorbachev still insisted on confining SDI to the laboratory. "It's not a trivial thing," he argued, "it is everything." When Reagan said he had given his final position and would not agree to the restrictions Gorbachev wanted on SDI, the Soviet leader responded, "Then we can say good-bye and forget everything we have discussed."[66]

Gorbachev's use of surprise and his "take it or leave it" tactic seemed to be a good strategy either way from the Soviet perspective, and in fact one scholar has suggested that the Soviet leader knew Reagan would not give in on SDI.[67] If Reagan had agreed to the deal, Gorbachev would have succeeded in killing a program that his military feared, but even if Reagan refused, Gorbachev could put the onus of the failure to eliminate nuclear weapons on Reagan's shoulders. The down side, however, was that by laying his concessions on the table, he made it clear to the United States what was possible for future negotiations.[68]

Thinking that he could score big points with the Europeans—who in fact were horrified at the prospect of losing the American nuclear protection—Gorbachev kept up the pressure at his press conference in Reykjavík on October 12. Noting his significant concessions on heavy missiles and on British and French weapons, the Soviet leader said he was leaving his proposals on the table for the United States to think about, and citing the need for "bold, unusual decisions," he called on "realistic" people around the world to act to reverse the arms race.[69]

These attempts to reach the masses to put pressure on Reagan were highly reminiscent of Gorbachev's use of public pressure in 1985–86 as he went about defeating his domestic rivals. He repeated his proposals in a televised address on October 23, describing the deal as a "balance of interests and concessions" and repeating that "if there's no package, there won't be any concessions."[70] He had tried to surprise and to pressure his adversary into action, but unlike Gorbachev's domestic rivals, Reagan would not budge.

SEVEN

Reexamining the Model

The evidence from the international events we have examined shows that leaders do rely heavily on their experiences as domestic politicians when they bargain in international affairs. Each of the four Soviet leaders behaved differently from the other three, and yet each was quite consistent in his behavior from domestic to international politics. Stalin's style was to avoid bold commitments while using a highly coercive strategy masked by accommodative gestures. Khrushchev, on the other hand, delighted in open confrontation and the use of commitments to keep his adversaries off balance. Brezhnev was the most cautious of the four, preferring to accommodate his adversaries and to preserve his options. And while Gorbachev followed Khrushchev's strategy of pressuring his opponents, he avoided the kind of personal commitments that had become a liability for Khrushchev.

Unfortunately for these decision makers, strategies and tactics that worked well for them in domestic politics were not as suitable—and thus not as successful—in the four major cases of international negotiation we have examined. In each case these leaders could probably have done better for themselves, and for their country, if they had not relied on their prior experiences to guide them.

Other Possible Outcomes

Bargaining style was clearly not the only factor that determined the outcomes. Given the balance of power and interests in favor of the United States, we might have expected that Stalin would not succeed in ousting the Western powers from Berlin, that Khrushchev would not get away with putting missiles in Cuba, and that Gorbachev would not succeed in stopping German unification and membership in NATO. Given the more even balance of power and interests in the Middle East in 1973, we could have predicted that neither superpower would allow an ally to be destroyed in a war. The strategies and tactics that the leaders chose in those cases did, however, have a major influence on the specific terms on which each conflict was settled, and those terms had important ramifications for each leader. There are good reasons to believe that different outcomes could have occurred in each of the major cases considered here.[1]

In 1948 Stalin's goals apparently were to prevent the formation of a West German state, to forestall the development of a hostile West European bloc, and to consolidate the Eastern zone of Germany by squeezing the Western powers out of Berlin. Stalin had discussed an agreement with the West in August that might have helped him achieve some of his goals if only he had accepted it.

If Stalin had negotiated in good faith and had helped to implement the agreement, he could have improved his position considerably, even if he did not force the Western powers out of Berlin. The August agreement called for the use of Soviet-zone currency in the Western zones of Berlin and for the creation of a four-power financial commission to oversee its circulation. Stalin would have thereby achieved influence in the affairs of West Berlin. Furthermore, by following the August directive, Stalin would have given the Western powers hope for a long-term four-power solution to the German problem. The French were not keen on the creation of a West German state, and the "united front" of the three Western powers might have cracked in the face of genuine Soviet participation in a four-power plan. The creation of a West German state and even of NATO might have been placed in doubt if Stalin had adopted a different strategy.

Instead, his behavior in August hardened the Western commitment. His good cop/bad cop strategy drove the three Western powers closer together. By January, when he was ready to concede, Stalin had nothing to show for his efforts. He would get no Soviet-zone currency in West Berlin; he had no hand in the affairs of the Western zones. Both the West German state and NATO were created in 1949.

Khrushchev too bargained badly in Cuba. Khrushchev's goals in 1962 were to redress the nuclear imbalance exposed by the United States in 1961 and to defend a new ally, thereby shoring up his position both at home and in the international socialist community. His biggest mistake was to continue to deny the presence of the missiles in Cuba for several days after Kennedy announced his discovery, thereby giving the U.S. position more legitimacy.

What if Khrushchev had chosen a different strategy?[2] Instead of confrontation and deception, instead of raising the stakes on Kennedy, Khrushchev might have admitted immediately after Kennedy's October 22 television address that the missiles were in Cuba. He might have acknowledged U.S. security concerns as well as emphasizing his own. He could have proposed that he would stop his ships *and* declare a moratorium on missile construction, if the two sides could sit down immediately and discuss Khrushchev's concerns over Cuba and over the U.S. missiles in Turkey.

If Khrushchev had done so, he would likely have still failed to keep his missiles in Cuba. But it would have been difficult for Kennedy not to negotiate, because the call for negotiations would probably have taken consideration of a military option off the Executive Committee table. The United States could not have used force against Cuba in the face of a Soviet call for negotiations.

Without the military option, the American quarantine would have been much less successful. Kennedy's quarantine worked because the threat of the military option lay behind it. What Khrushchev feared was the next step: a U.S. strike on the island. Support for this strike in the United States would have been weakened if Khrushchev had not lied and had called for immediate negotiations. Khrushchev hardened U.S. resolve as Stalin had done during the Berlin blockade crisis.

By negotiating immediately, Khrushchev probably could have received the American no-invasion pledge at this stage and possibly the removal of the missiles from Turkey. If he had achieved these goals through negotiations begun at the start of the crisis, he would not have suffered the loss of prestige that came with conceding after a week of blustering, denying, and confronting. Khrushchev would have been able to demonstrate that he could force a nuclear-superior power to sit down and negotiate, and perhaps he would then have felt less pressure to close the missile gap.[3] By using his typical bargaining style, Khrushchev made his own position worse. He gave Kennedy more reason to stand firm, and he allowed Kennedy to take the high ground because the Soviet leader had lied in front of the entire world.

In 1973, as Kissinger has noted, Brezhnev also could have achieved more of his goals, at least in the Middle East, by following a different strategy. If he had pressured Sadat more strongly to accept a cease-fire on October 8 or 9 after the Egyptians had established themselves on the East Bank of the Suez Canal, Brezhnev would have made it hard for the United States to find a reason to oppose a cessation of hostilities. If he had achieved a cease-fire in place after the limited Egyptian success, he would have shown that the Soviets could help the Arabs regain territory, and he might then have been able to play a role in the peace process from which he was shut out after the war. Brezhnev did succeed in preventing Syria and Egypt from suffering unacceptable losses during the war, but by trying to please all sides and waffling on the cease-fire issue early on, he gained less than he might have for the future position of the Soviet Union in the region.

Of course, Brezhnev might have been unable to force Sadat to agree to a cease-fire at that stage, so perhaps he could not have chosen this alternative strategy. He could have pressured Sadat by refusing to resupply the Egyptian war effort if the Egyptians did not comply with the Soviet request, but that might have so embittered the Egyptians that Brezhnev would not have been the beneficiary of an early cease-fire. Stalin and Khrushchev clearly had choices in the 1948 and 1962 crises. Brezhnev may have been more limited in his options in 1973. A different strategy might have led to a more favorable outcome, but perhaps that strategy was simply not feasible in the context of Soviet-Egyptian relations.

In February 1990 Gorbachev had a potential window of opportunity when the United States and West Germany seemed unsure of the precise role they foresaw for Germany in NATO, and when Foreign Minister Genscher in particular was sensitive to Soviet security concerns. If Gorbachev was both worried about hard-line reaction at home and hopeful of gaining Western aid, a solution along the lines proposed by Genscher and Baker in early February might have satisfied both concerns, whereas the July solution that was ultimately adopted satisfied only the West. Perhaps Gorbachev still felt more constrained in February by domestic constituencies than he did after the Twenty-eighth Party Congress, but in accepting the Genscher proposal, he had a chance to satisfy some of the domestic concerns about a rising Germany. Presumably he could have still obtained the aid he needed as well as the shift in NATO doctrine; Baker had spoken of NATO's evolution in December, and since it was a German rather than a Soviet proposal in early February that spoke of restrictions on the territory of what was then the GDR, Gorbachev would not be sacrificing potential German economic aid.

A key element of U.S. success in the four cases was that Soviet strategy gave more legitimacy to the American position, which gave the United States more domestic and international support. There were many in the West who understood Stalin's concerns about the impact of currency reform on the Eastern-zone economy. That his position had some legitimacy is evident from the course of the August negotiations in Moscow. But he lost any leverage he might have had because of the way he engaged the West in those negotiations and in the ones that followed in Berlin.

Similarly, Khrushchev had legitimate security concerns for his new ally, Cuba, and he had a reasonable grievance about the U.S. belief that it alone could surround its adversary with nuclear missiles. But by adhering to his strategy of deliberate deception even after his plan had been discovered, Khrushchev gave Kennedy a more legitimate stance from which to confront the Soviet Union.

In the early days of the October Middle East War Brezhnev could legitimately have called for a cease-fire in place that would have given Egypt a better bargaining position for future negotiations on the occupied territories. Nixon and Kissinger would have been under domestic and international pressure to go along with such a cease-fire. But the continued Soviet resupply effort, the inability or unwillingness of Brezhnev to get Arab support for a cease-fire, and the further weakening of the Israeli position strengthened the U.S. position in legitimately helping Israel regain the advantage.

Finally, Gorbachev could point to legitimate domestic and security concerns that would arise from a unified Germany with full membership in NATO, and Genscher in particular was concerned that the West should not humiliate the Soviet Union. An acceptance by Gorbachev early on of the Genscher proposal for German unification with restricted NATO membership would have put the United States in a difficult position. But Gorbachev lost the legitimacy he had by clinging to his ambiguous position that Germany should not be in NATO, and not offering realistic alternatives.

The Soviet leaders did try to gain legitimacy for their positions in these cases. In the spring of 1948, after the Western powers decided to plan for a West German state, the USSR continually issued statements that placed responsibility on the West for whatever happened in Berlin. In 1962 Khrushchev cited Cuban security needs in the face of the American threat thwarted once at the Bay of Pigs, and he spoke often of the "equal rights" of each superpower to deploy weapons near the territory of the other. In 1989–90 Gorbachev tried at first to put forward his "fact of history" idea to maintain the status quo, and he kept Soviet suffering at the hands of the Germans during World War II in the public consciousness.

Brezhnev, as the most accommodative bargainer, was careful in staking claims to legitimacy. Soviet statements in October 1973 placed the onus of blame on Israel, not on the United States and the global forces of imperialism. A more coercive strategist, like Stalin or Khrushchev, would have avoided acknowledging the legitimate interests of the other side by placing blame for the tension entirely on the adversary. Brezhnev was careful not to do that in 1973, and as Kissinger noted, the Soviet leader's behavior made things easier for the United States in the United Nations.

In all four cases the strategy adopted by the Soviet leader enhanced the legitimacy of the U.S. position and led to a more favorable outcome for the American side. It is interesting to speculate about whether the Soviet leaders recognized that the strategies and tactics they chose affected subsequent U.S. behavior. Did Stalin, for example, realize that he pushed the United States to adopt a more hard-line position toward him by failing to conduct the August and September negotiations seriously? It is unlikely that he did. Given his prior experiences, he most likely expected to force his opponents to concede to his position, as he had done with his domestic rivals. When they did not concede, he probably imputed it not to his strategy but to the nature of imperialism.[4]

The failure of strategies applied from earlier experiences has been cited by Robert Jervis as a major problem: "When a policy has brought notable success, actors are likely to apply it to a range of later situations. Seeing these cases as resembling the past one, the actor will believe that they are amenable to the policy that worked previously. But when insufficient attention is paid to the reasons why the policy worked in the past, the new situation will not be scrutinized to see if it has the attributes that made the earlier success possible."[5] The 1948 and 1962 cases are good demonstrations of the danger of relying on prior experiences to inform current policymaking without fully understanding the lessons of the past. One of the issues raised by this phenomenon that is worthy of future research is why a set of strategies may be so appropriate for one situation but not another.

Domestic bargaining styles can sometimes work in international politics: witness Stalin's success in the discussions over Poland in 1945. Whether or not a bargaining style developed in domestic politics succeeds in an international encounter perhaps depends on some structural similarities or differences between events. In 1945 Stalin was able to divide Churchill and Roosevelt as he had done with Trotsky and Bukharin at home; he was unsuccessful in dividing the Western adversaries in 1948. Perhaps Stalin's success in the 1920s and in 1945 was due to the multilateral structure of the bargaining, which made it easier for him to divide his adversaries. The 1948 negotiations were more clearly bilateral and perhaps for that reason less conducive to the good cop/bad cop strategy. Furthermore, success in 1945 may have induced further rigidity in Stalin's approach to bargaining, since the outcome in Poland may have confirmed those lessons he drew from the domestic political battles of the 1920s.

Other Factors in Foreign Policy Making

Simply because a leader is predisposed to act in a certain way because of prior experiences does not mean that he or she will do so under all circumstances. Khrushchev and Brezhnev both changed their typical bargaining style in the face of an overwhelming threat, and Gorbachev's style was altered by the constraints imposed both by the position of the Soviet

Union and by his own foreign policy goals. At this point, it is helpful to reintroduce the other factors relevant to foreign policy behavior discussed in chapter 1, to understand not only which behavior they fail to explain, but also how they can complement the approach presented here.

Relative Power and Interests

Did the decision makers respond rationally to their external environment? All of the leaders demonstrated in these cases a rigidity that suggests that predispositions can hinder the ability to perceive the external environment.[6] In the Berlin blockade crisis, for example, Stalin never adjusted to the change in his relative position except to give up entirely in early 1949. His position in Berlin relative to the Western powers prior to June 1948 was unclear. Would the Western powers stand firm to maintain their presence in their zones of the city? He could not know, since the West had not made a clear commitment to Berlin prior to the blockade. Stalin tested the strength of the Western commitment by imposing the restrictions gradually, and there was no direct challenge to the Soviet land blockade.

But Stalin's relative position did decline over the course of the summer. The Western powers demonstrated a tremendous commitment to their zones of Berlin by airlifting supplies. If Stalin was unsure of his adversaries' commitment to their position in June, by August he was faced with a strong Western interest in not acceding to his surface blockade.

One might still argue that Stalin had good reason to believe that he could wear his opponents down, given uncertainties over the viability of the airlift. But even if questions were raised about the ability of the West to continue the airlift, Stalin's relative position had still declined during the course of the summer. Western interests were stronger in August than they had been in June (because of Stalin's policies), and in conducting the airlift the United States and its allies had demonstrated not only their new commitment but also their impressive capabilities. The United States had a nuclear monopoly in 1948 and along with Britain and France was defending the status quo, giving it a strong interest in holding firm. Stalin, however, did not adjust.

The Soviet leader continued to follow his old ways. He did not negotiate seriously. By offering concessions that Molotov and Sokolovsky would then renege on, he demonstrated that he had little interest in reaching an agreement. He approached the negotiations as if he believed that he could wear down his opponents by frustrating them. The airlift should have signaled to him that his opponents would not wear down easily. Apparently it did not. And the frustrations his adversaries felt led not to concessions but to a hardening of their commitment and to a strengthening of their resolve.

The change in Stalin's position also highlights a weakness of the George and Smoke explanation based on an image of the adversary's commitment.[7] George and Smoke reasonably suggest that Stalin's uncertainty of the U.S. commitment to Berlin was the reason he chose a limited probe in the form of the blockade. But they then suggest that having learned that the United States and its allies were committed to defending the status quo, Stalin continued to pressure Berlin in the belief that he could erode a commitment that still seemed "soft."

But why would anyone characterize the U.S. commitment as "soft" at that point? The United States and its allies were putting a tremendous amount of resources into saving their position in Berlin. While the commitment could have more justifiably been viewed as soft in June, by August it was both clearer and firmer (even recognizing the uncertainties about Western capabilities, which is another issue). Of course, we do not know how Stalin perceived the Western commitment. George and Smoke's argument about Stalin's perceptions is plausible, but so is the argument that he recognized the firmness of the Western commitment. As has been suggested here, it was not necessarily the Western actions that shaped his views about his ability to erode their commitment; rather, it was his own beliefs in the viability of his typical strategy that led to his misunderstanding of that commitment.

Like Stalin, Khrushchev also failed to adjust rapidly enough to a decline in his relative position during the 1962 affair. When Kennedy announced that the United States had discovered the missiles and was establishing a quarantine around Cuba, Khrushchev suffered a serious blow. The actions Kennedy proposed demonstrated the strength of U.S. power and interests. In 1962 the United States had conventional superiority in the Caribbean and a nuclear advantage of 17 to 1. It also had a firm public commitment both to the Monroe Doctrine in general and to preventing Cuba from acquiring nuclear weapons in particular. Did Khrushchev alter his behavior to reflect the Soviet position?

He did not. Even though the United States knew of the missiles, Khrushchev denied that they were there. And he told Kennedy that the quarantine was an ultimatum the Soviets could not accept. If he was simply responding to his external environment, he would not have acted this way. Kennedy had made a commitment to prevent the influx of offensive ground-to-ground missiles in Cuba. He reaffirmed the commitment with his televised address and with the quarantine. Khrushchev had made a commitment to the position that no offensive weapons were in Cuba and that he could defend the island. He also reaffirmed the commitment by telling Kennedy that he could not accept the ultimatum even though his relative position of weakness vis-à-vis the United States had been exposed on October 22.

Again, this case highlights a problem with the George and Smoke argument about Khrushchev's understanding of the Western commitment. They argue that Khrushchev likely believed that there was no U.S. commitment to Cuba, since Kennedy did not make one explicit until September 1962. They then argue that Khrushchev could have justified this belief because the United States had made a similar deployment in Turkey. This latter point is not the same as a belief that the United States had no commitment; it is simply a justification for deployment.[8]

Furthermore, one could just as plausibly argue that Khrushchev knew that the U.S. commitment was firm but hoped to get the missiles in place so as to change the status quo before Kennedy could do anything to stop him. The United States did have a longstanding policy concerning involvement in the hemisphere (the Monroe Doctrine), and the Kennedy administration had shown a willingness to use force in Cuba in April 1961. In fact, a reason for the secretiveness may have been precisely that Khrushchev knew that the U.S. commitment *was* firm, and that a public, gradual deployment would have been met with firm resistance. Again, we do not know what his perception of the U.S. commitment was, but we can argue that a reliance on bold commitments and public announcements of *faits accomplis* was a consistent element of Khrushchev's bargaining strategy.

George and Smoke also point out that even after the U.S. commitment was made clear, Khrushchev continued to try to achieve the *fait accompli* by speeding up work on the missiles. They are unable to explain this outcome using their model, since if now Kennedy's commitment was "unequivocal but soft," Khrushchev should, according to their argument, have switched to a controlled-pressure strategy. If we want to understand why he continued to seek the *fait accompli,* we can better explain his behavior by looking back at his earlier domestic political behavior.

Khrushchev's behavior was extremely costly to him personally, and he was criticized after the crisis first for having deployed the missiles and then for having backed down after he had made a commitment to keeping the missiles there. His reputation suffered, and this example reinforces the notion that leaders should be careful about making commitments that are difficult to carry through.

Khrushchev compounded the problems for his reputation by making stronger commitments to threats than to concessions. His personal letter to Kennedy of October 24 was highly confrontational, explicitly rejecting what he termed Kennedy's ultimatum. On the same day he sent a more accommodative letter to a third party, Bertrand Russell, suggesting his interest in a summit with Kennedy. Similarly, Khrushchev's first letter of October 26 vaguely outlined a deal on the missiles; he made the public commitment to the second letter stating that he wanted the quid pro quo in Turkey. The commitments associated with coercion were a more typical element of the Khrushchev bargaining style; these cost him dearly when he failed to stand firm.

One might argue that Khrushchev could not change his strategy even as his position weakened because he knew that his reputation both at home and abroad would suffer if he abandoned his position too quickly. But to continue to deny that the Soviets had deployed missiles on the island made him look foolish before the world and only strengthened President Kennedy's position.

Khrushchev adjusted only when the threat of war became overwhelmingly clear. At the brink, the Soviet leader recognized that the danger was too great. Instead of bluffing or raising the ante, he conceded swiftly. An argument focusing on the balance of power and the constraints imposed by nuclear weapons could predict his concession to Kennedy. It could not predict his behavior leading up to October 28. This concession does, however, suggest that an overwhelming external threat can alter a leader's typical bargaining style.

In 1989, since Gorbachev was not going to use the Soviet troops stationed in East Germany, and since the Soviet leader depended on American and West German goodwill for his program of *perestroika,* the structure of the situation heavily favored the United States. As noted above, the structure of the situation meant that the West was likely to win on German unification. But we could not have known beforehand that the Soviet Union would lose as badly as it did. The West was uncertain about the nature of German membership in NATO in February 1990, but Gorbachev did not take advantage of the opportunity. He was used to his opponents backing down when he said, "This is unacceptable." By the time the Soviet leader was ready to adjust to the reality before him, all he could do was concede.

In these three cases an argument based on the balance of power and interests can explain why the stronger power prevailed and how threats can alter typical bargaining styles, but it cannot explain why Gorbachev, Khrushchev, and Stalin adopted such different strategies from one another, nor can it explain why each leader failed to adjust his strategy before finally conceding.

A power-and-interests argument also cannot explain why in 1973 Brezhnev adopted a predominantly accommodative style. The balance of both power and interests was much more even in 1973 than it was in the other cases. Both superpowers had significant interests in the Middle East. And the Soviet Union had achieved military parity with the United States, at least in terms of nuclear capabilities. Any number of strategies would have been consistent with the symmetrical balances that existed. What was particularly inconsistent was Brezhnev's behavior during the Moscow bargaining. Kissinger expected tough negotiations. He should have expected them, given the existing balances and the problems Nixon faced at home. Yet Brezhnev did not push the United States at all during that bargaining, which is inexplicable if one is following a structural argument about the source of foreign policy.

What can be explained by the relative position of the Soviet Union is why Brezhnev adopted a more coercive strategy in the face of Syrian and then Egyptian losses. Given the serious threat to the Soviet allies, Brezhnev's relative interests became much stronger. When the balance of interests was overwhelmingly in his favor and when faced with a serious loss, Brezhnev adjusted his strategy.

The 1973 war and the Cuban missile crisis suggest that *major* changes in the external environment can impress upon a leader that his strategies are inappropriate and can lead to significant changes in bargaining style. The events of 1989–90 suggest that the structure can actually deprive a leader of some of the tools he needs to be successful. Snyder and Diesing have written that "a change of strategy . . . occurs much less frequently than changes in tactics. It occurs only when new information, by a cumulative build-up of a sudden massive input, indicates clearly that a key expectation upon which the whole strategy is based is wrong."[9] The nuclear threat in 1962 and the danger posed to Syria and then to Egypt in 1973 served the role of "sudden massive inputs."

Domestic Politics and the Operational Code

No one would dispute the notion that a successful leader has to satisfy his constituency. But perhaps that poses constraints more on a leader's goals than on the strategies he uses to pursue them. Jack Snyder has used a coalition-politics approach to contrast Gorbachev's general foreign policy to his predecessors' approach of "offensive detente." He argues that Khrushchev and Brezhnev shared a common need to satisfy both the military and ideological elites who favored expansion and the economic managers, technocrats, and intelligentsia who favored detente. But while they may have had a common source for the goals they pursued in international politics, their style of behavior was quite different, as we saw when we compared the Cuban crisis with the war in the Middle East, as well as the Berlin Wall crisis with the intervention in Czechoslovakia. Coalition-politics arguments can help us understand the kind of foreign policy goals Khrushchev, Brezhnev, and Gorbachev had, but not necessarily how they would pursue them.

As for the operational code, the idea that leaders follow maxims like "push to the limit but know when to stop" misses many of the nuances of behavior. How, for instance, does a leader know where the limit is? There are also different ways of pushing to the limit and of stopping, which might themselves change the location of the limit. Should one push all at once, or should one take incremental steps? Stalin and Khrushchev both appeared to push to the limit in Berlin and Cuba, respectively. But they did so in different ways. Stalin moved gradually, avoiding premature commitments and using subordinates to announce those policies that tested the limits he was pushing against. Khrushchev made a bold commitment and personally engaged in confrontational behavior as he tested the steel of Kennedy's resolve. Neither, however, knew soon enough when to stop, and they suffered in the negotiations with the United States because of it.

The notion of an "optimizing strategy" is also problematic. If a leader fails to achieve any of his apparent goals, maximum and minimum, does this mean that he failed to optimize, or that he was simply a bad optimizer? Was Stalin optimizing by scuttling the agreement reached in August 1948? After all, he achieved none of his objectives in the end. Did Khrushchev optimize by continuing to deny the presence of missiles in Cuba and not negotiating until precious time had slipped away? In the end he received the pledge on Cuba, but at tremendous political cost both domestically and internationally. Did Gorbachev optimize by insisting until June that German membership in NATO was unacceptable? If Stalin, Khrushchev, and Gorbachev failed to optimize, how can their behavior be explained by an operational code that stresses the importance of an optimizing strategy?

The notion of an optimizing strategy fails to account for the possibility that leaders may not adjust to unfavorable changes in their position quickly enough to achieve their lesser goals. The concept of an "optimizer" suggests that one should recognize when maximum goals are unlikely to be achieved and then pursue minimum goals instead. Alexander George argued that "if the optimizing strategy is not correctly perceived as such by the opponent, it may well unduly arouse his sense of danger and mobilize his potential for resistance and counteraction in a way that pursuit of more modest objectives might avoid doing."[10] What he failed to note is that the strategy he describes might leave the decision maker in a position in which he is then *unable* to achieve those more modest objectives, as happened in three of the four major events we have studied.

Final Thoughts

While we have examined here only the behavior of four Soviet leaders, the pattern of applying to international bargaining the strategies and tactics learned in domestic politics should hold true for any world leaders who are shaped primarily by domestic politics and are relatively insulated from international affairs in their political careers. The basic premise—that leaders develop certain kinds of political skills at home that they apply in foreign policy—is not Soviet-specific. Biographers of other world leaders have described similar correlations between domestic learning and later international behavior. Lyndon Johnson, for example, learned in Texas and in Congress how to be a master of compromise and how to persuade his adversaries in one-on-one talks. Hugh Sidey wrote of Johnson's later frustration in Vietnam, "Ho Chi Minh's silence in Hanoi was unfathomable to Johnson, who had often said that he had never known a man with whom he could not find some area of understanding if the two could sit down and talk face to face." A. J. P. Taylor wrote of Hitler, "The story of how he came to power in Germany seems to me relevant to his later behavior in international affairs." And one biographer of Neville Chamberlain noted, "Much has been made—and rightly so—of his 'businessman's approach,' his belief that the best way to settle problems in international diplomacy was to utilize the tested techniques of settling difficulties between business enterprises or between management and labor, that is by sitting down amicably together and negotiating in a spirit of good will until a compromise solution was reached." [11]

Major foreign policy makers of the twentieth century, such as Hitler, Stalin, Truman, Khrushchev, Johnson, and Gorbachev, were politicians first. They learned about bargaining in formative domestic experiences, and they applied those lessons when they sought strategies and tactics for dealing with foreign adversaries. If we are going to develop better theories of foreign policy behavior, we need to understand how domestic political experiences shape decision makers' approaches to international problems. We have seen here that the connection is an important one, and the events we have studied suggest that any complete analysis of foreign policy making must integrate this model with approaches based on an understanding of the constraints imposed by international and domestic structures. The Cold War conflicts we have studied show that the strategies and tactics that decision makers choose in international affairs can have important effects on outcomes. And lessons learned in successful domestic battles may be inappropriate for foreign policy making—a fact the four major Soviet leaders of the Cold War failed to understand in critical conflicts with the United States.

Notes

ONE / The Domestic Roots of Foreign Policy Making

1. Fiske and Taylor, *Social Cognition*, 2d ed., p. 13.

2. Fiske and Taylor, *Social Cognition*, p. 139. For more on "schema" or "script" theory, see Abelson, "Script Processing"; Axelrod, "Schema Theory"; Ruth Hamill and Milton Lodge, "Cognitive Consequences of Political Sophistication," in *Political Cognition*, ed. Lau and Sears, pp. 69–93; Nisbett and Ross, *Human Inference*.

3. Nisbett and Ross, *Human Inference*, p. 36.

4. Axelrod, "Schema Theory," p. 1265. For an illustration of the lack of consensus, compare the two editions of Fiske and Taylor, *Social Cognition*.

5. Nisbett and Ross, *Human Inference*, p. 45.

6. Jervis, *Perception and Misperception*.

7. Khong, *Analogies at War*.

8. Jervis, *Perception and Misperception*, p. 283. Jervis, however, relegated his discussion of domestic experiences to an appendix, and his rationale for not exploring the domestic angle was as follows: first, that his lengthy analysis of the role of history applies to domestic politics as well as international politics; second, that few psychological theories are of much use in studying the link between domestic politics and foreign policy; and third, that testing the argument would involve comparing different leaders' perceptions of the same situation. None of these provides a satisfactory reason for not exploring further the role of domestic politics. The psychological theories that apply to the role of international events should be as useful in studying past domestic experiences.

9. Larson, *Origins of Containment*, p. 194.

10. Jervis, *Perception and Misperception*, p. 145.

11. Read, "Once Is Enough"; Nisbett and Ross, *Human Inference;* Vertzberger, "Foreign Policy Decisionmakers," p. 240.

12. On confirming events, see Rothbart, Evans, and Fulero, "Recall for Confirming Events."

13. Fiske and Taylor, *Social Cognition,* 2d ed., pp. 98–99, 136ff.

14. The authors thus conclude that "subcategories develop in response to isolated cases that disconfirm the schema." Ibid., pp. 98–99, 136ff., 141, 150, 152.

15. For a similar argument applied to a different set of international issues, see Jones, *Soviet Leadership Politics.* Jones also argued that "national leaders tend to apply to the international scene those views, approaches, and practices that they developed and applied in the national domestic scene during their rise to the top" (p. v). His focus was on how the experiences of Soviet leaders shaped their approach to fighting a war with the United States. I would like to thank Jack Snyder for pointing out this monograph to me.

16. The importance of the "first independent political success" is underscored in Barber, *Presidential Character.*

17. George and George, *Woodrow Wilson and Colonel House,* pp. 45–46, 114. See also Glad, *Charles Evans Hughes;* Barber, *Presidential Character.*

18. On the general problem of data, see Tetlock, Crosby, and Crosby, "Political Psychobiography." As the authors note, even if the researcher has letters, recollections, and the like, the subject has not been psychoanalyzed in childhood, and there is no precise way of knowing the person's emotional needs at that time. See especially pp. 194–95.

19. Etheredge, "Personality Effects." A second test by Graham Shepard confirmed the first hypothesis and disconfirmed the second. See Shepard, "Personality Effects."

20. Shepard's second test assesses dominance as it relates both to subordinates and equals and is thus an improvement on Etheredge's study in this respect. See Shepard, "Personality Effects," p. 95.

21. Etheredge, "Personality Effects," p. 437. My emphasis.

22. Dawson, "Formation and Structure of Political Belief Systems," p. 101.

23. See George, "Case Studies and Theory Development."

24. See, for example, Jervis, *Perception and Misperception;* Larson, *Origins of Containment.*

25. For a good summary, see Snyder and Diesing, *Conflict among Nations,* chap. 2.

26. See Schelling, *Strategy of Conflict.*

27. Thucydides, *Peloponnesian War,* p. 119.

28. Ibid., p. 221. Diodotus was responding to Cleon, who was arguing in favor of coercion: "It is a general rule of human nature that people despise those who treat them well and look up to those who make no concessions" (p. 215).

29. See Snyder and Diesing, *Conflict among Nations,* pp. 513–14.

30. See Schelling, *Strategy of Conflict,* especially chap. 2. The nature of the choice between making commitments and preserving options is also discussed in Snyder and Diesing, *Conflict among Nations,* pp. 211–54.

31. In the well-known chicken analogy, if I throw my steering wheel out the window, committing myself to driving straight ahead, the danger is that the other driver will do the same, causing us to crash.

32. Glenn H. Snyder, "Crisis Bargaining," in *International Crises*, ed. Hermann, p. 245.

33. Snyder and Diesing, *Conflict among Nations*, chap. 3.

34. Snyder, "Crisis Bargaining." For more on clarity vs. ambiguity, see Snyder and Diesing, *Conflict among Nations*, pp. 245–46. For a useful discussion of indirect communications, see Pruitt, "Indirect Communication."

35. See Jervis, "Bargaining and Bargaining Tactics"; also Snyder, "Crisis Bargaining," p. 222.

36. See the concluding chapter of Snyder and Diesing, *Conflict among Nations*. For a discussion of the concept of "usable capabilities," see George, Hall, and Simons, *Limits of Coercive Diplomacy*.

37. Jervis considers the problems a decision maker faces in making these decisions in his discussion of spiral and deterrence models. He asks, "When will force work, and when will it create a spiral of hostility? When will concessions lead to reciprocations, and when will they lead the other side to expect further retreats?" Jervis argues that the key factor is the adversary's intentions, which are often unknown to the decision maker. If the adversary is an aggressor, concessions will not work; if the adversary is a status quo power, concessions can break an escalating spiral of hostility. See *Perception and Misperception*, pp. 96–102.

38. Power as a concept has come under increasing scrutiny in recent years in the international relations literature, as some analysts have argued that military power has declined as a factor governing a variety of international matters. Snyder and Diesing have suggested that crisis "bargaining power" derives from a combination of capabilities and interests. See *Conflict among Nations*, chap. 3. For a criticism of their approach, see Aggarwal and Allan, "Evolution in Bargaining Theories." This paper provides a useful typology of different schools of bargaining. The authors also argue that the term *bargaining power* needs more specificity; a side might have power to determine the outcome of one set of issues in one location but not in another.

39. Thucydides, *Peloponnesian War*, p. 402. Zeev Maoz suggests that not only may states with greater capabilities lose, but they may lose *because* they have greater capabilities. Maoz, "Power, Capabilities, and Paradoxical Conflict Outcomes."

40. For the conceptual distinction between the carrot and the face-saver, see Snyder and Diesing, *Conflict among Nations*, p. 491.

41. Waltz, *Man, the State, and War;* Singer, "Level-of-Analysis Problem"; Jervis, *Perception and Misperception*, chap. 1.

42. See Jervis, *Perception and Misperception*, chap. 1.

43. Waltz, *Theory of International Politics*, p. 121.

44. Thucydides, *Peloponnesian War*, pp. 400–409.

45. Snyder and Diesing, *Conflict among Nations*, especially chap. 1.

46. Putnam, "Diplomacy and Domestic Politics," p. 436.

47. Major works that explored this linkage include Aspaturian, "Internal Politics and Foreign Policy"; Dallin, "Soviet Foreign Policy and Domestic Politics"; Dallin, "Domestic Sources of Soviet Foreign Policy"; Valenta, "Bureaucratic Politics Paradigm"; Valenta, *Soviet Intervention in Czechoslovakia;* Valenta and Potter, eds., *Soviet Decisionmaking;* Spechler, *Domestic Influences on Soviet Foreign*

Policy; Snyder, "Gorbachev Revolution"; Ross, "Coalition Maintenance"; Ross, "Risk Aversion"; Richter, "Action and Reaction in Khrushchev's Foreign Policy"; Anderson, "Competitive Politics and Soviet Foreign Policy."

48. Ross, "Risk Aversion," p. 240; Ross, "Coalition Maintenance," pp. 266–68.

49. Ross, "Risk Aversion," p. 237. In Ross's work the latter proposition derives not just from the character of the decision-making system (which induces caution) but from what he calls the fear of failure with which the leadership was politically socialized when introduced to politics in the Stalin era. Normally this fear of failure induced caution, but when not acting posed high costs, then the leadership would act. This emphasis on political socialization begins to converge with my own argument.

50. Snyder, "Gorbachev Revolution"; Snyder, *Myths of Empire,* chap. 6.

51. See Leites, *Operational Code of the Politburo;* Leites, *Study of Bolshevism;* George, "Operational Code."

52. And where does this optimizing strategy come from? Despite George's general focus on adversary images, in "Operational Code" he suggested that the optimizing strategy derived from lessons Lenin learned at home. These include the idea that only political struggle reveals what is possible and that one should seek maximum objectives but be willing to settle on lesser goals if the struggle proves difficult.

53. George and Smoke, *Deterrence in American Foreign Policy.*

54. A number of scholars who do not necessarily subscribe to the operational-code approach have considered the role of adversary images. Snyder and Diesing argue that leaders enter international crises with prior expectations of how to bargain with the adversary. Leaders then use those strategies and tactics to manipulate perceptions of relative interests and relative capabilities. In contrast to a completely structurally based argument, Snyder and Diesing argue that while leaders may try different tactics, their basic strategy is much less likely to change even if the structure changes. They attribute this phenomenon to cognitive dissonance—that is, leaders find it difficult to process incoming information that jars their preconceptions. Hence, they are slow to realize that a given strategy may not be appropriate. See Snyder and Diesing, *Conflict among Nations,* pp. 488ff. This conclusion is not inconsistent with my own argument. But I have a different explanation of where the expectations come from. Whereas Snyder and Diesing argue that these expectations stem from perceptions of the particular adversary, I argue that they derive primarily from an understanding of political conflict developed from domestic politics. One important conclusion that Snyder and Diesing draw that is consistent with my approach is that actors adopt strategies based not on the organizations whence they came but on their personal predilections toward a given strategy. See *Conflict among Nations,* p. 512. In this section the authors were responding to the bureaucratic-politics model, which suggests that "where you stand depends on where you sit."

TWO / *Domestic Bargaining Styles*

1. Volkogonov, *Triumf i Tragediia*, bk. 1, pt. 2, p. 43.

2. One result of this behavior was that the Soviet people referred to the harshest periods of Stalin's rule by naming them after the subordinates who carried out his policies. The purges were known as the *Yezhovshchina*, named for secret police chief Nikolai Yezhov, and the cultural repressions of the late 1940s were called the *Zhdanovshchina*, referring to Stalin's aide, Andrei Zhdanov. In his novel *Children of the Arbat* Anatoly Rybakov has written of Stalin, "The great ruler is the one who can inspire love through fear. Such love can come when all the harshness of his rule is attributed by the people and history not to him personally, but to his executives." Rybakov, *Children of the Arbat* (Boston: Little, Brown, 1988), p. 345.

3. See Cohen, *Bukharin and the Bolshevik Revolution*, pp. 266–67.

4. Trotsky, *Stalin*, p. 400.

5. For a discussion of this concept, see Leites, *Operational Code of the Politburo;* Leites, *Study of Bolshevism.*

6. Stalin's daughter, Svetlana Alliluyeva, described her father this way: "Once he had cast out of his heart someone he had known a long time, once he had mentally relegated that someone to the ranks of his enemies, it was impossible to talk to him about that person any more. He was constitutionally incapable of the reversal that would turn a fancied enemy back into a friend." Alliluyeva, *Twenty Letters to a Friend* (New York: Harper & Row, 1967), p. 59.

7. My emphasis. Stalin wrote this in *Sotsial-Demokrat* 12 (January 1913). Quoted in Leites, *Study of Bolshevism*, p. 325.

8. Deutscher, *Stalin*, pp. 254, 264.

9. Bazhanov, *Vospominaniia Byvshego Sekretarya Stalina*, p. 63.

10. Trotsky, in his "Lessons of October," wrote unfavorably about the role of Kamenev and Zinoviev during the revolution. See discussion in Volkogonov, *Triumf i Tragediia*, bk. 1, pt. 1, pp. 122–23.

11. Ibid., p. 123.

12. Ibid., pp. 121–22.

13. Souvarine, *Stalin*, pp. 402–7.

14. Throughout *Triumf i Tragediia* Volkogonov documents Stalin's efforts in these years to paint himself as the true Leninist and his rivals as betrayers of the cause. See also discussion in Bullock, *Hitler and Stalin*, chap. 4.

15. Deutscher, *Stalin*, p. 168.

16. See Trotsky, *Stalin.*

17. N. Vakar, "Stalin po Vospominaniiam N. N. Zhordania," *Poslednii Novosti* (December 16, 1936): 2. Soviet historian Dmitri Volkogonov has said, "Whenever Stalin pursued some major goal, he took a long time and proceeded with cautious, small steps. But he was also exceptionally persistent and consistent, stopping at nothing. Especially in the struggle for power, for the implementation of some idea of his." *Foreign Broadcast Information Service*, Soviet Union (hereafter referred to as FBIS), June 22, 1988, p. 57.

18. Volkogonov has argued that the Civil War shaped Stalin as a politician by

showing him that applying pressure at critical moments was the key to success. See Volkogonov, *Triumf i Tragediia*, bk. 1, pt. 1, p. 104.

19. Bazhanov, *Vospominaniia Byvshego Sekretarya Stalina*, pp. 146–47.

20. Tucker, *Stalin as Revolutionary*, pp. 373–78. On Bukharin's role in developing the theory of socialism in one country, see also Cohen, *Bukharin and the Bolshevik Revolution*, pp. 147–48, 187.

21. Deutscher, *Stalin*, pp. 282, 285.

22. Carr, *Russian Revolution*, p. 74.

23. Volkogonov, *Triumf i Tragediia*, bk. 1, pt. 1, p. 207.

24. Tucker, *Stalin as Revolutionary*, pp. 377–89. On the Trotsky-Stalin debate, see Volkogonov, *Triumf i Tragediia*, bk. 1, pt. 1, pp. 194ff.; Bullock, *Hitler and Stalin*, chap. 4.

25. As Walter Laqueur noted, Trotsky had, "not for the first time, . . . maneuvered himself into an unpopular position largely because of his ideological rigidity, his lack of pragmatic instinct, and his inability to understand what was and what was not possible in a given situation." See Laqueur, *Stalin*, p. 47.

26. N. Barsukov, "Eshe Vperedi XX S'ezd," *Pravda*, November 17, 1989, p. 3. This article followed two others by the same author in *Pravda*, October 27 and November 10, 1989, on Khrushchev and Malenkov.

27. Tatu, *Power in the Kremlin*, p. 20.

28. Breslauer, *Khrushchev and Brezhnev as Leaders*, p. 12. On Khrushchev's use of social and public pressure, see also pp. 55–56.

29. Agricultural policy was Khrushchev's main project. Edward Crankshaw writes that Khrushchev in his rise to power made more speeches on agriculture (and to agricultural interests) than on everything else combined. Crankshaw, *Khrushchev*, p. 176. Robert Conquest describes Khrushchev's use of agriculture as an "offensive weapon." Conquest, *Power and Policy*, pp. 234–35.

30. Ploss, *Conflict and Decision-Making*, p. 67.

31. On Malenkov taking the Stalinist line, see Medvedev, "Khrushchev: Politicheskaia Biografiia," p. 143; also Adzhubei, *Te Desyat' Let*, p. 89.

32. Ploss, *Conflict and Decision-Making*, pp. 70, 75.

33. G. A. E. Smith, "Agriculture," in *Khrushchev and Khrushchevism*, ed. McCauley, p. 96.

34. Ploss, *Conflict and Decision-Making*, pp. 78–80.

35. Breslauer, *Khrushchev and Brezhnev as Leaders*, p. 35.

36. Frankland, *Khrushchev*, p. 104.

37. Smith, "Agriculture," p. 100.

38. Medvedev and Medvedev, *Khrushchev: The Years in Power*, p. 60.

39. Breslauer, *Khrushchev and Brezhnev as Leaders*, p. 45.

40. Ploss, *Conflict and Decision-Making*, p. 109.

41. Smith, "Agriculture," pp. 106–7.

42. There has been much debate in the past about whether this speech was Khrushchev's initiative, as Carl Linden and Robert Conquest argued, or whether it was forced on him, as Myron Rush suggested. See Linden, *Khrushchev and the Soviet Leadership*, pp. 33–34; Conquest, *Power and Policy*, p. 282; Rush, *Khrushchev and the Stalin Succession*, pp. 1–7.

43. Medvedev, "Khrushchev: Politicheskaia Biografiia," pp. 149–51; also Medvedev, "33 Goda Spustia," pp. 10–11. Another comparable discussion is Yu. V. Aksyutin, "N. S. Khrushchev: My Dolzhny Skazat' Pravdu o Kul'te Lichnosti," in *Nikita Sergeevich Khrushchev*, ed. Aksyutin, pp. 34–35. Khrushchev himself also suggested that he gave his colleagues this ultimatum; see Khrushchev, *Khrushchev Remembers: The Glasnost Tapes*, p. 43. G. I. Voronov, a Central Committee member at the time, has written that the Presidium session prior to the speech was so contentious that someone proposed to remove Khrushchev from that body and make him minister of agriculture. See Voronov, "Nemnogo Vospominanii."

44. My emphasis. Breslauer, *Khrushchev and Brezhnev as Leaders*, p. 33.

45. In July 1954 Khrushchev had stated that by the 1970s, the USSR would have a higher level of consumer goods than the United States. Ibid., p. 36.

46. Frankland, *Khrushchev*, p. 136; Medvedev, "Khrushchev: Politicheskaia Biografiia," p. 168; Anatoly Strelianyi, "Poslednii Romantik," p. 192.

47. Breslauer, *Khrushchev and Brezhnev as Leaders*, p. 37. When Khrushchev was overthrown, the members of the Presidium accused him of disrespect and of having contempt for their opinions. See account by Sergei Khrushchev, "Pensioner Soiuznogo Znachenia," *Ogonyok* 43 (October 1988): 27; also Medvedev, *Khrushchev*, p. 237.

48. For the link between the May speech and the June meeting of the Presidium, see Frankland, *Khrushchev*, p. 136; Medvedev and Medvedev, *Khrushchev*, pp. 75ff.; Medvedev, "Khrushchev: Politicheskaia Biografiia," p. 168. Roy Medvedev reports that Khrushchev was told by specialists that his goals were impossible, but the Soviet leader rejected this view as cautious. The Presidium objected to his proposed increases in production, but "he brushed their objections aside." Medvedev, *Khrushchev*, pp. 115–16.

49. Breslauer, *Khrushchev and Brezhnev as Leaders*, p. 138.

50. After Khrushchev's ouster the new leadership passed a law forbidding one person to hold the positions of both head of the party and chairman of the Council of Ministers (head of government), in order to try to prevent a single leader from rising above the others.

51. Established in November 1962, this body was renamed the Committee of People's Control in 1965. Archie Brown, "Political Developments: Some Conclusions and an Interpretation," in *Soviet Union since the Fall of Khrushchev*, ed. Brown and Kaser, p. 219.

52. Murphy, *Brezhnev*, pp. 251–52.

53. Robert H. McNeal argues that this renaming was simply a return to tradition and should not be taken as a sign of Brezhnev's primacy. He does argue, however, that Brezhnev was predominant by 1970. McNeal, *Bolshevik Tradition*, pp. 180–81.

54. Hough, "Brezhnev Era," p. 2.

55. Valerie Bunce and John M. Echols III, "Soviet Politics in the Brezhnev Era: 'Pluralism' or 'Corporatism,'" in *Soviet Politics in the Brezhnev Era*, ed. Kelley, p. 8; Dornberg, *Brezhnev*, p. 19. Roy Medvedev writes that "Brezhnev resented complications and conflicts in politics and personal relations." Medvedev, "Advantages of Mediocrity," *Moscow News*, no. 37 (1988): 8–9.

56. Brown, "Political Developments," p. 244; Fedor Burlatsky, "End of the Thaw: Reflections on the Nature of Political Leadership," *Literary Gazette International,* July 1990, pp. 9–11; Breslauer, *Khrushchev and Brezhnev as Leaders,* pp. 11–12.

57. Murphy, *Brezhnev,* p. 254.

58. While admitting that Stalin made mistakes, the new line praised Stalin for such things as his leadership during the war. See McNeal, *Bolshevik Tradition,* p. 171.

59. Brown, "Political Developments," pp. 219, 220. Khrushchev had split the party organs into two branches, which upset the regional secretaries since their power was now halved in one stroke.

60. Breslauer, *Khrushchev and Brezhnev as Leaders,* p. 154.

61. Egorychev, "Napravlen Poslom." See also Burlatsky, "Brezhnev i Krushenie Ottepeli."

62. These prices were increased further in 1970. Because prices paid to the peasants increased while retail prices for consumers were kept artificially low, government subsidies had to increase to cover the difference and the overall deficit ballooned, as Mikhail Gorbachev learned.

63. Gelman, *Brezhnev Politburo,* p. 79.

64. Ibid., pp. 82, 79–82.

65. Egorychev makes this argument in "Napravlen Poslom." Brezhnev's foreign minister, Andrei Gromyko, made similar comments in an interview with Donald Trelford. See Trelford, "Walk in the Woods."

66. Dornberg, *Brezhnev,* p. 187.

67. Roy D. Laird, "The Political Economy of Soviet Agriculture under Brezhnev," in *Soviet Politics in the Brezhnev Era,* ed. Kelley, p. 59.

68. Breslauer, *Khrushchev and Brezhnev as Leaders,* pp. 148–49.

69. Ibid., p. 142.

70. See Doder and Branson, *Gorbachev,* chap. 5.

71. See, for example, Hazan, *Gorbachev and His Enemies,* pp. 200ff.

72. Chebrikov lost his position as head of the KGB; Ligachev lost his position as second secretary in charge of ideology; and longtime Politburo member Andrei Gromyko was finally retired. On the destruction of the Secretariat, see "Speeches of Ligachev," p. 8; also Hazan, *Gorbachev and His Enemies,* pp. 72–73; Doder and Branson, *Gorbachev,* pp. 344ff.

73. For a discussion, see Teague and Mann, "Gorbachev's Dual Rule." The Politburo steadily declined in importance. It met only thirty-four times in 1989 and only once each month in the first part of 1990. By then Ligachev was complaining that the Politburo was no longer being consulted. See Alexander Rahr, "From Politburo to Presidential Council," Radio Free Europe/Radio Liberty, *Report on the USSR* 2, no. 22 (June 1, 1990): 2. On Gorbachev's ability to control the Congress of People's Deputies during its first year, see Hahn, "Boss Gorbachev." For a disturbing discussion of the narrowing circle of advisers over time, see Paul Quinn-Judge, "Gorbachev Adopts Siege Mentality," *Boston Globe,* April 14, 1991, pp. 1, 24.

74. As Thane Gustafson and Dawn Mann noted after Gorbachev's first year in power, "Gorbachev's approach has the populism, the zest for change and experi-

mentation, and even some of the confrontational manner of Khrushchev. Like him, Gorbachev plays to popular expectations, and he leans heavily on the party apparatus (in both senses of the word)." Gustafson and Mann, "Gorbachev's First Year: Building Power and Authority," *Problems of Communism* 35 (May–June 1986): 18. Peter Reddaway also wrote of Gorbachev and Khrushchev, "While there are many differences between the two men, the similarities in their temperaments, in the circumstances in which each assumed the helm, and the broad strategies they adopted to break through the inertia they inherited are indeed striking." Reddaway, "Gorbachev the Bold," p. 22.

75. *FBIS*, May 22, 1985, pp. R2, R10. Doder and Branson argue that the address was televised three days after Gorbachev delivered it because television executives were unsure about how to deal with such impromptu behavior. See Doder and Branson, *Gorbachev*, pp. 88–89. On Romanov as the subject of the speech, see Zhores Medvedev, *Gorbachev*, pp. 175–76.

76. *FBIS*, May 22, 1985, pp. R11–12.

77. See ibid., June 12, 1985, pp. R2–19; June 26, 1985, p. R2.

78. Doder and Branson, *Gorbachev*, pp. 190–91.

79. Gorbachev, *Perestroika*, p. 65.

80. *FBIS*, February 25, 1986, p. O13. Doder and Branson wrote of Gorbachev's tactics at the Twenty-seventh Party Congress that his "generalities were designed to camouflage his real intentions. . . . [He] sought to avoid alarming the opposition unnecessarily especially since the drafting of reform would take another year." Doder and Branson, *Gorbachev*, pp. 117–18.

81. For Ligachev's views of these resignation threats, see "Speeches of Ligachev," p. 13.

82. Doder and Branson, *Gorbachev*, p. 194; Medvedev and Chiesa, *Time of Change*, p. 79.

83. Medvedev and Chiesa, *Time of Change*, p. 193. See also Doder and Branson, *Gorbachev*, pp. 309–10.

84. Those within the system and without who criticize him for moving too slowly have lost their perspective; the speed with which he changed the entire nature of politics inside the country (and globally) cannot be dismissed as the work of a plodder.

85. Breslauer makes this point with respect to Khrushchev in *Khrushchev and Brezhnev as Leaders*, p. 11.

86. Certainly the ultimate winner also used the levers of power skillfully in promoting his supporters.

THREE / *Stalin and the Berlin Blockade Crisis*

1. Brzezinski, *Soviet Bloc*, pp. 4–5.

2. For a more thorough discussion of this period, see Shlaim, *United States and the Berlin Blockade*, chap. 2.

3. See Adomeit, *Soviet Risk-Taking*, pp. 78–80.

4. For a good discussion of the implications of currency reform, see ibid., p. 90.

5. Millis, *Forrestal Diaries,* p. 452.

6. Bohlen, *Witness to History,* p. 276.

7. Clay's political assistant, Robert Murphy, describes these early restrictions: "A wooden pole had been put across the road at Helmstedt, the point where the highway from West to East Germany met, and that wooden pole, guarded by only two Mongolian soldiers, represented at that time the Berlin blockade." Murphy, *Diplomat,* p. 314.

8. See George and Smoke, *Deterrence in American Foreign Policy,* pp. 118–19.

9. See Murphy, *Diplomat,* p. 315.

10. See Adomeit, *Soviet Risk-Taking,* p. 83. The British briefly suggested retaliating by impeding Soviet shipping in the Suez and Panama Canal Zones but considered it too provocative. See *Foreign Relations of the United States* (hereafter *FRUS*) (1948) 2:890.

11. *FRUS* (1948) 2:890.

12. Adomeit, *Soviet Risk-Taking,* p. 85.

13. See, for example, *FRUS* (1948) 2:910.

14. After these moves, Western and Eastern currency were both valid in the Western zones of Berlin. After the splitting in two of city administrations in late November and early December, the Western powers prepared to make Western currency sole legal tender, and they did so on March 20, 1949. See, for example, Howley, *Berlin Command,* p. 254.

15. Adomeit, *Soviet Risk-Taking,* p. 93.

16. According to General Clay, Marshal Sokolovsky walked out as rudely as possible. See Clay, *Decision in Germany,* p. 356.

17. Adomeit, *Soviet Risk-Taking,* p. 81.

18. See Soviet notes of February 13 and March 6, 1948, *FRUS* (1948) 2:338, 345–54; also Murphy telegram to secretary of state, March 20, 1948, *FRUS* (1948) 2:883–84.

19. Adomeit, *Soviet Risk-Taking,* p. 84.

20. British Foreign Office, Russia Correspondence, 1948, F.O. 371, "Daily Review of the Soviet Press," April 8, 1948, reel 7, document N4353.

21. *Vneshniaia Politika 1948* 1:229–33.

22. Snyder and Diesing describe the Berlin blockade as an example of an irrevocable commitment. But Stalin framed the blockade so that it was not. Snyder and Diesing acknowledge that the blockade was carried out gradually, and Stalin left himself a loophole. Irrevocable commitments do not leave loopholes. See Snyder and Diesing, *Conflict among Nations,* pp. 227–28, 230–31.

23. On these exchanges, see Adomeit, *Soviet Risk-Taking,* p. 87.

24. In late July the secretary of defense reported to the National Security Council, "Minimum Berlin supply requirements can be met by air transport for at least a considerable, though probably not an indefinite, period." See "U.S. Military Courses of Action with Respect to the Situation in Berlin," July 28, 1948, NSC 24, Top Secret (since declassified), National Archives.

25. See Jean Smith, interview with General Clay, March 9, 1971, Oral History Research Project, Columbia University, p. 743.

26. Davison, *Berlin Blockade*, pp. 110, 117, 155.

27. My emphasis. *Vneshniaia Politika 1948* 1:234. An internal Soviet justice administration directive of this period also treated Berlin as part of the Soviet zone in its discussion of judicial measures that needed to be taken in conjunction with currency reform. See Central Intelligence Agency memorandum, June 30, 1948, *Declassified Documents Reference System* (hereafter *DDRS*) (1977), microfiche 259C.

28. *Vneshniaia Politika 1948* 1:235–36. The head of the Soviet finance administration was even more threatening in the four-power currency discussions of June 22: "We warn both you and the German population that we will use economic and administrative sanctions which will enforce the transition to a single currency in Berlin and the currency of the Soviet zone." See Adomeit, *Soviet Risk-Taking*, p. 92.

29. My emphasis. *Vneshniaia Politika 1948* 2:24–25.

30. *FRUS* (1948) 2:1000.

31. Smith, *My Three Years in Moscow*, pp. 243–44.

32. *FRUS* (1948) 2:1001–3.

33. Smith, *My Three Years in Moscow*, p. 245. For an interesting discussion of the Soviet position, see memo from Charles E. Bohlen to secretary of state, August 4, 1948, Top Secret (since declassified), National Archives, 740.00119 Control (Germany)/8-448.

34. Smith to secretary of state, NIACT 1507, August 3, 1948, Top Secret (since declassified), National Archives, 740.00119 Control (Germany)/8-348.

35. Smith to secretary of state, NIACT 1509, August 3, 1948, Top Secret (since declassified), National Archives, 740.00119 Control (Germany)/8-348.

36. In fact, Secretary of State George Marshall demonstrated how well Stalin was doing so far when he wrote to Smith, "Based on past experience, it is probable that at next meeting Stalin will be very much tougher, having touched base with the Politburo." Marshall to Smith, August 4, 1948, Top Secret (since declassified), National Archives, 740.00119 Control (Germany)/8-448.

37. Smith, *My Three Years in Moscow*, p. 246.

38. Smith to secretary of state, NIACT 1558, August 7, 1948, Top Secret (since declassified), National Archives, 740.00119 Control (Germany)/8-748.

39. Smith to secretary of state, Dispatch #610, August 13, 1948, Top Secret (since declassified), National Archives, 740.00119 Control (Germany)/8-1348.

40. Smith to secretary of state, NIACT 1728, August 24, 1948, Top Secret (since declassified), 740.00119 Control (Germany)/8-2448.

41. Ibid. The British representative may have given the Soviets the wrong impression of Western concerns earlier in the negotiations when he said that "he had received the impression that Molotov possibly had in mind that we intended to exercise some sort of control over this bank. Of course this was not the case." Smith repeated during those same negotiations, "It was not the intention to contest the authority of the Soviet Government in issuing this currency." Molotov made his position clear when he said, "And just as in the Western zone it was the Western Powers who controlled the currency so in the Eastern zone the currency should

be controlled by the Soviet authorities." Smith to secretary of state, NIACT 1558, August 7, 1948, sections 6, 8, National Archives, 740.00119 Control (Germany)/8-748.

42. Smith to secretary of state, NIACT 1728, August 24, 1948, Top Secret (since declassified), National Archives, 740.00119 Control (Germany)/8-2448, p. 4.

43. *FRUS* (1948) 2:1090.

44. For a full discussion of the proposals and counterproposals leading up to and including the directive, see ibid., pp. 1061–91. Note that nowhere did the directive mention the legal rights of the Western powers to stay in Berlin. Secretary of Defense James Forrestal wrote, "The State Department and Clay . . . are very much disturbed about the apparent failure of Bedell Smith to insist upon inclusion in the communiqué announcing the results of the discussions of any reference to the juridical rights of the United States in the Berlin area." He then noted that Smith had been "somewhat captious in arguing with the Department on the line that they are being unnecessarily meticulous." See Millis, *Forrestal Diaries*, pp. 479–80.

45. Some officials in the United States realized that ambiguities in the directive would lead to problems. Charles Bohlen, for example, wrote on September 2 that while Stalin and Molotov had orally "confirmed" the role of the financial commission on currency issues and circulation in Berlin, Sokolovsky "professes ignorance of any such confirmation by Stalin and Molotov and contends that the directive does not expressly state this power of the financial commission." Bohlen noted that the United States sought a direct reference to the power of the financial commission vis-à-vis the German bank of emission, but the British and French had felt that "the definite statements of interpretation by Molotov and Stalin were adequate." See Bohlen memo to the president, September 2, 1948, Top Secret (since declassified) National Archives, 740.00119 Control (Germany)/9-248.

46. Truman, *Years of Trial and Hope*, p. 127.

47. Smith, *My Three Years in Moscow*, p. 252.

48. In a post mortem written on August 17 covering the negotiations to that date, Ambassador Smith wrote that by the beginning of August the Soviets had already given up on suspending the London decisions and simply tried to achieve control of Berlin through agreements with the West. See *FRUS* (1948) 2:1047.

49. See Davison, *Berlin Blockade*, pp. 243–53.

50. "Voprosi Korrespondenta 'Pravdy' i Otvety Tovarishcha I. V. Stalina," *Pravda*, October 29, 1948. Reprinted in *Vneshniaia Politika 1948* 1:32–34.

51. Later, of course, some questioned whether Kingsbury-Smith had submitted these questions on his own initiative; according to the U.S. embassy in Paris, he did. See *FRUS* (1949) 5:563. Kingsbury-Smith has also said that he formulated them on his own. He recounts that he met Bedell Smith in January in Paris. The latter said that he believed Stalin wanted to end the blockade but needed a way to save face. Kingsbury-Smith wrote up his questions and sent them to the Hearst stringer in Moscow, who dropped them in the Kremlin mailbox. Stalin responded almost immediately. Kingsbury-Smith, interview with author, September 12, 1989.

52. Bohlen, *Witness to History*, p. 283. See also Jessup, "Park Avenue Diplomacy," p. 378; Dean Acheson Princeton Seminars, July 2, 1953–May 16, 1954, Acheson Papers, Truman Library, Independence, Mo., pp. 2ff. When asked if he

worded the third question so as not to mention the currency issue, Kingsbury-Smith said that it was an accident; it was simply something he had not thought about. Kingsbury-Smith, interview with author, September 12, 1989.

53. Jessup, "Park Avenue Diplomacy," pp. 379–80.

54. Ibid., pp. 380–81.

55. Acheson, *Present at the Creation*, p. 270.

56. Truman, *Years of Trial and Hope*, p. 130.

57. *FRUS* (1943), Conferences at Cairo and Tehran, pp. 509ff.

58. Ibid., pp. 594ff.

59. On the Königsberg discussion, see ibid., p. 604.

60. Harriman and Abel, *Special Envoy*, pp. 408–9.

61. *FRUS* (1945), Conferences at Malta and Yalta, pp. 669–70.

62. Ibid., pp. 720–21; Harriman and Abel, *Special Envoy*, p. 410.

63. *FRUS* (1945), Malta and Yalta, pp. 802ff., 867ff.

64. Nadeau, *Stalin, Churchill, and Roosevelt*, pp. 192–94.

65. Churchill, *Triumph and Tragedy*, p. 424.

66. *FRUS* (1945) 5:180ff.

67. Ibid., p. 196.

68. Ibid., pp. 202, 203, 204.

69. Ibid., pp. 263–64.

70. Ibid., p. 293.

71. Ibid., pp. 320–21.

72. Nadeau, *Stalin, Churchill, and Roosevelt*, p. 199.

FOUR / *Khrushchev and the Cuban Missile Crisis*

1. The MRBMs had a range of eleven hundred nautical miles; the reach of the IRBMs extended twenty-two hundred nautical miles.

2. Roger Hilsman, then head of intelligence and research in the State Department, says that Gilpatric was chosen to reveal what the United States knew in order to be convincing but not threatening. Hilsman, *To Move a Nation*, pp. 163–64. On Khrushchev's bluffing about Soviet capabilities, see Horelick and Rush, *Strategic Power*, chap. 5. They also discuss the Gilpatric speech and the Soviet response to it, pp. 83ff. For more on the Gilpatric speech, see Beschloss, *Crisis Years*, pp. 329–31.

3. The American nuclear advantage may have been greater than estimated at the time. Russian military historian General Dmitri Volkogonov said in January 1989 that the Soviets had only twenty intercontinental ballistic missiles directed at the United States from the USSR, which means that the projected forty warheads being sent to Cuba would have tripled Soviet capabilities to strike the U.S. homeland. See Bill Keller, "Atom Warheads Deployed in Cuba in '62, Soviets Say," *New York Times*, January 29, 1989. A Central Intelligence Agency estimate in October 1962 put the number at sixty to sixty-five operational ICBMs in the USSR. See SNIE 11-18-62, "Soviet Reactions to Certain U.S. Courses of Action on Cuba," October 19, 1962, *DDRS* (1975), microfiche 48D.

4. Khrushchev, *Khrushchev Remembers*, p. 494. Arnold Horelick persuasively

argues that the strategic balance was the primary motivating force behind the deployment. As he points out, "It is difficult to conceive of any other measure that promised to produce so large an improvement in the Soviet strategic position as quickly or as cheaply." Horelick, "Cuban Missile Crisis," p. 376. This article remains one of the best analyses of why Khrushchev did what he did.

5. The Soviets did not apparently install the missiles as a bargaining chip to make a deal on getting rid of the missiles in Turkey. As discussed below, the desire to link the two for purposes of a swap was apparently an ad hoc decision made during the crisis. On this point, see Raymond Garthoff's comments in Welch, *Hawk's Cay Conference*, pp. 27–28. At this conference William Taubman added a fourth reason for placing the missiles that has been emphasized elsewhere: he argued that Khrushchev's behavior reflected the erosion of his authority at home and said that the first secretary needed a big victory to save his position. Welch, *Hawk's Cay Conference*, p. 24.

6. Garthoff, *Reflections*, p. 12; Garthoff, "Cuban Missile Crisis," p. 64.

7. Chang, *Cuban Missile Crisis, 1962*, 1:43–44. Gromyko says that Khrushchev told him about the plan on the plane ride back from Bulgaria. Gromyko says that he told his boss, "It will cause a political explosion in the USA." Khrushchev reportedly replied, "I still intend to put this question to the Politburo very soon." A. A. Gromyko, "Karibskii Krizis: O Glasnosti Teper' i Skrytnosti Togda," *Izvestiia*, April 15, 1989; Trelford, "Walk in the Woods."

8. Alekseyev, "Karibskii Krizis: Kak Eto Bylo," pp. 27–28.

9. Mikoyan, "Karibskii Krizis," p. 71.

10. Stanislav Kondrashov, "Eshe o Karibskom Krizise," *Izvestiia*, February 28, 1989, p. 5; also Garthoff, "Cuban Missile Crisis," p. 66. In addition to Mikoyan's misgivings, Gromyko also apparently expressed his doubts to Khrushchev. See interview with former ambassador Alekseyev in *Argumenty i Fakty* 10 (1989).

11. Alekseyev interview, *Argumenty i Fakty* 10; also Alekseyev, "Karibskii, Kubinskii, Oktyabr'skii," p. 16.

12. Garthoff, *Reflections*, pp. 20, 39–40. U.S. intelligence reported a "tenuous" and "possible" detection of nuclear material on two of the ships that returned missiles from Cuba to the Soviet Union at the end of the crisis. *The Soviet Bloc Armed Forces and the Cuban Crisis: A Chronology, July–November 1962* (Washington, D.C.: National Indications Center, 1963), p. 97. At a 1992 meeting in Havana General Anatoly Gribkov, who oversaw planning of the operation in 1962, said that thirty-six nuclear warheads for the SS-4s reached Cuba; he also said that Soviet ground troops there had several tactical rocket launchers with nine tactical nuclear warheads. See discussion by Raymond L. Garthoff, "The Havana Conference on the Cuban Missile Crisis," *Cold War International History Project Bulletin*, spring 1992, pp. 2–4. For a view that no nuclear warheads reached the island, see Cline, "Commentary."

13. See, for example, Brugioni, *Eyeball to Eyeball*, pp. 114–15.

14. Of course, as Michael Beschloss has noted, Kennedy's commitments to do something in the event of Soviet deployment of ground-to-ground missiles came months after the Soviet decision to send these missiles to Cuba. Beschloss, *Crisis Years*, p. 6.

15. *Cuban Missile Crisis, 1962,* documents 00363, 03130. In a memo to the president, Carl Kaysen referred to the meeting with Pitterman as producing "more rude noises from Khrushchev" (document 00440).

16. *Vneshniaia Politika 1962,* pp. 352–56.

17. Ibid., p. 358.

18. Ibid., p. 363. A reminder of Khrushchev's position on the issue of defending Cuba was also printed in *Pravda,* September 13, 1962, p. 1.

19. Garthoff, "Cuban Missile Crisis," pp. 69–70.

20. In fact, Robert Kennedy claimed that Bolshakov was instrumental in defusing the tank confrontation in Berlin in 1961. Arthur M. Schlesinger, Jr., *Robert Kennedy and His Times* (New York: Ballantine, 1978), pp. 537–38. For more on the Bolshakov-RFK connection, see Beschloss, *Crisis Years,* chap. 7.

21. This use of Bolshakov to deceive was not the first, and as Beschloss argues, perhaps Khrushchev's earlier use of this channel to deceive Kennedy (e.g., prior to the Vienna summit) without incident emboldened him to do it again. See Beschloss, *Crisis Years,* p. 181. Bolshakov describes his relationship with Robert Kennedy, his recollections of the details of meetings with Khrushchev in September 1962, and his reports to RFK in early October. See Bolshakov, "Hot Line," especially no. 5, pp. 41–42. Bolshakov left the United States within a few months after the crisis. He had been exposed publicly by Joseph Alsop in early November. See Alsop, "The Soviet Deception Plan," *Washington Post,* November 5, 1962.

22. Garthoff, *Reflections,* p. 47.

23. He referred to Berlin and Southeast Asia. When RFK mentioned Cuba, Dobrynin told him not to worry. Apparently Cuba was not part of his original message. Abel, *Missile Crisis,* p. 19.

24. Garthoff, *Reflections,* p. 29; Kennedy, *Thirteen Days,* pp. 2–4. Kennedy also refers to the same message being brought at about the same time by "an important official" returning from Moscow. Presumably he meant Bolshakov. Kennedy, *Thirteen Days,* p. 5.

25. Garthoff, *Reflections,* p. 28; Sorensen, *Kennedy,* p. 691. Apparently Khrushchev was also planning to visit Cuba to sign a five-year mutual defense treaty with Castro. Alekseyev interview, *Argumenty i Fakty* 10.

26. Gromyko, "Karibskii Krizis." He also made the same point in his memoirs. See Gromyko, *Pamyatnoe,* vol. 1, p. 393. Khrushchev, however, suggested in his memoirs that he would not hesitate to lie: "Our position was neither to confirm nor to deny the presence of missiles. In answer to a direct question, we would deny." See Khrushchev, *Khrushchev Remembers: The Glasnost Tapes,* p. 174.

27. The fact that the missiles were becoming operational added to the time constraints the Kennedy administration was working under in deciding whether or not to strike. U.S. defense secretary Robert McNamara has since argued that operability was not important, but as Marc Trachtenberg has pointed out, McNamara was stressing the opposite on October 16 in the Executive Committee. See discussion in Welch, *Hawk's Cay Conference,* pp. 42–45.

28. Pope, *Soviet Views,* pp. 30–31.

29. My emphasis. *Vneshniaia Politika 1962,* pp. 400, 401.

30. Pope, *Soviet Views,* pp. 32–35.

31. Ibid., p. 36.

32. As Beschloss notes, Khrushchev typically had these long meetings with people (*Crisis Years*, p. 199), but it is hard to believe that the Soviet leader had that much time to spare during the crisis.

33. He would reiterate this assurance in his October 27 letter to Kennedy. See below.

34. W. E. Knox, "Close-up of Khrushchev during a Crisis," *New York Times Magazine*, November 18, 1962, pp. 32, 129; Roger Hilsman to secretary of state, October 26, 1962, *DDRS* (1983), microfiche 254.

35. *Vneshniaia Politika 1962*, pp. 407–9.

36. On this latter point, see Beschloss, *Crisis Years*, p. 497.

37. *Cuban Missile Crisis, 1962*, document 02180. For U Thant's proposal, see documents 01109–01111.

38. The second letter was not received until October 27 because of the time difference between Moscow and Washington. For a discussion of the letters, see Beschloss, *Crisis Years*, pp. 516–27.

39. Pope, *Soviet Views*, p. 42.

40. Ibid., pp. 47–48.

41. Ibid., pp. 48–49.

42. Ibid., p. 51.

43. Ibid., p. 54.

44. A member of the U.S. team at the National Photographic Interpretation Center has written that on the morning of October 27 there had been a major reorganization of the Cuban air defense system: "It became obvious that the Russians had taken complete control of the command network. Broadcast channels and the loose communications linkage with the SA-2 sites were now tightly integrated. Russian control of the defense system was also apparent in the introduction of Russian call signs, codes, and procedures now being heard by U.S. monitoring centers." See Brugioni, *Eyeball to Eyeball*, p. 460.

45. Pope, *Soviet Views*, p. 54.

46. *Cuban Missile Crisis Meetings*, October 27, 1962, p. 62.

47. Walter Lippmann, "Blockade Proclaimed," *Washington Post*, October 25, 1962. Apparently Kennedy had earlier in his presidency worried about Khrushchev's view of Lippmann's columns: "I know Khrushchev reads him and he thinks that Walter Lippmann represents American policy. Now how do I get over that problem?" Quoted in Beschloss, *Crisis Years*, p. 110.

48. *Cuban Missile Crisis Meetings*, October 27, 1962, p. 11.

49. Recent information about the crisis suggests that the first letter was sent in such a hurried fashion because on the night of October 25–26 Soviet intelligence had evidence of an imminent U.S. attack on Cuba. The second letter was then issued when the imminence of such an invasion was downgraded. Garthoff, "Cuban Missile Crisis," p. 74.

50. Abel, *Missile Crisis*, p. 176.

51. Ibid., p. 177.

52. Garthoff, *Reflections*, pp. 80–81.

53. On this point, see Whelan, *Soviet Diplomacy and Negotiating Behavior*,

p. 344. Beschloss writes that Dobrynin knew of these conversations and may have cabled the information back to Moscow as well; he also suggests that by 1989 "Fomin was ailing: time may have distorted his memory." Beschloss, *Crisis Years,* p. 515.

54. Garthoff, *Reflections,* p. 81. Beschloss too says the U Thant proposal came from a KGB official with Gromyko's knowledge. Beschloss, *Crisis Years,* p. 515.

55. Beschloss, *Crisis Years,* p. 516.

56. James G. Blight and David A. Welch claim that Khrushchev's first reaction was to urge the ships to keep going, but Anastas Mikoyan ordered them to stop. They cite as sources Sergo Mikoyan and also Roy Medvedev's *All Stalin's Men.* While Medvedev does state that Khrushchev first ordered the ships to keep going, his chronology of events is fuzzy, and nowhere does he say that Anastas Mikoyan sent out new orders over Khrushchev's head. Medvedev, *All Stalin's Men,* pp. 50–52. Blight and Welch, *On the Brink,* p. 306. Garthoff argues that Khrushchev's first inclination was to run the blockade in order to put the burden of using force on the United States but Mikoyan talked him out of it. Garthoff, "Cuban Missile Crisis," p. 70.

57. Intelligence Memorandum, SC 08179/62, October 25, 1962, JFK Library, NSF, NSC, ExComm Meetings, vol. 1, box 316, *DDRS,* microfiche 19A.

58. Garthoff, *Reflections,* p. 66.

59. CIA memorandum, October 19, 1962, *DDRS* (1978), microfiche 7F; October 24, 1962, *DDRS,* R, microfiche 181; October 25, 1962, *DDRS,* R, microfiche 19A.

60. Intelligence Memorandum, SC 08184/62, October 27, 1962, box 316, *DDRS,* R, microfiche 19C, 19D.

61. *Krasnaia Zvezda,* October 5, 1962; *Soviet Bloc Armed Forces,* p. 17.

62. Sagan, "Nuclear Alerts and Crisis Management," p. 109; Sagan also provides a discussion of the DefCon levels.

63. Office of Current Intelligence Memorandum, TCS no. 13927, October 23, 1962, *DDRS,* R, microfiche 18G.

64. DCSOPS/OPS, telegram no DA920637 to JCS, CNO, CGUS-ARMC, October 24, 1962, *DDRS,* R, microfiche 156C; Chang, *Cuban Missile Crisis, 1962,* p. 64.

65. *Soviet Bloc Armed Forces,* p. 70; CIA Intelligence Memorandum, SC 08181/62, October 26, 1962, *DDRS,* R, microfiche 19B.

66. Trachtenberg, "Influence of Nuclear Weapons," pp. 157–58.

67. Ibid., pp. 158–60; see also Betts, *Nuclear Blackmail,* p. 120.

68. See *Cuban Missile Crisis Meetings,* October 27, 1962, p. 45.

69. Allyn, Blight, and Welch, "Essence of Revision," pp. 160–61. On this series of events, see also Garthoff, *Reflections,* pp. 84–85; Garthoff, "Havana Conference," p. 3. In a letter to Castro on October 28 Khrushchev implied that he had not given the order, saying, "Yesterday you shot one of [the U.S. airplanes] down." See letter from Khrushchev to Castro, reprinted in the *San Francisco Chronicle,* December 5, 1990, Briefing Section, p. 2. On the view that the Cubans fired the missile, see Daniel Ellsberg, "The Day Castro Almost Started World War III," *New York Times,* October 31, 1987, p. 27. Herbert Dinerstein suggested that the Soviet

military, unhappy with Khrushchev's negotiating with Kennedy, ordered the downing of the plane in order to provoke the United States. Dinerstein, *Making of a Missile Crisis*, pp. 228–29.

70. Fyodor Burlatsky has said that the letter was prepared at Khrushchev's dacha. "When the letter was finished, a man was dispatched with it to drive very quickly to the radio station. He was told to have it for transmission before 3:00. They were very nervous." Welch, *Cambridge Conference*, p. 42.

71. Norman Cousins, "The Cuban Missile Crisis: An Anniversary," *Saturday Review* 5 (October 15, 1977): 4. Khrushchev later told the Supreme Soviet in his report on the crisis that he had received intelligence information on the morning of October 27 saying that an attack on Cuba would take place in the next two or three days. Of course, he would have to say something along these lines to justify capitulating so quickly. See Pope, *Soviet Views*, p. 87.

72. Alekseyev, "Karibskii Krizis," p. 32.

73. Pope, *Soviet Views*, p. 58.

74. Ibid., p. 60.

75. Seymour M. Hersh, "Was Castro Out of Control in 1962?" *Washington Post*, October 11, 1987, p. H1.

76. Allyn, Blight, and Welch, "Essence of Revision," p. 160, n. 103.

77. Garthoff, "Cuban Missile Crisis," p. 74.

78. Hilsman, *To Move a Nation*, p. 224.

79. Kennedy, *Thirteen Days*, pp. 85–87.

80. Garthoff, *Reflections*, pp. 86–88.

81. Ibid.

82. In a letter to Kennedy on October 28 Khrushchev went out of his way to reaffirm his willingness to keep the agreement on the missile swap a secret: "I find it necessary to tell you that I realize that considering in public the problem of dismantling the U.S. missile bases in Turkey is a somewhat delicate matter for you. I am aware of the complexity of the problem and see your suggestion that there be no public discussion of it as reasonable." See "Khrushchev-Kennedy Correspondence," p. 55.

83. He might have tried to put the missiles in Cuba publicly. McGeorge Bundy and Robert McNamara have argued that if Khrushchev had placed the missiles publicly, as the United States had done in Turkey, it would have made the choices much more difficult for the United States. Garthoff, "Cuban Missile Crisis," p. 65. Khrushchev's deliberate deception gave Kennedy more of a moral high ground from which to coerce Khrushchev to back down. Paul Nitze, on the other hand, argues that none of these considerations matter. He believes that there was a clear distinction between U.S. missiles in Europe designed to defend against the Soviet threat and Soviet missiles in Cuba that posed a new threat. Nitze, interview with author, September 7, 1989.

84. Adomeit, *Soviet Risk-Taking*, pp. 316ff.

85. Schick, *Berlin Crisis*, pp. 16–17.

86. Adomeit, *Soviet Risk-Taking*, pp. 292–93.

87. *Pravda*, November 28, 1958, p. 2.

88. Ibid., p. 1.

89. George and Smoke, *Deterrence in American Foreign Policy,* p. 391.

90. Harriman, "My Alarming Interview."

91. *Pravda,* May 21, 1960, p. 2.

92. For an excellent discussion of the new ultimatum at Vienna, see Beschloss, *Crisis Years,* pp. 217–36.

93. George and Smoke, *Deterrence in American Foreign Policy,* p. 415.

94. *Pravda,* June 16, 1961; August 8, 1961.

95. On this point, see Beschloss, *Crisis Years,* p. 351.

96. Ibid., p. 268.

F I V E / *Brezhnev and the 1973 Middle East War*

1. See, for example, Paul Jabber and Roman Kolkowicz, "The Arab-Israeli Wars of 1967 and 1973," in *Diplomacy of Power,* ed. Kaplan, pp. 412–67; Bell, "October Middle East War"; Fukuyama, "Nuclear Shadowboxing"; Fukuyama, *Moscow's Post-Brezhnev Reassessment.* In the first piece Fukuyama argues that the Soviets were cautious because of the predominance of American interests, and in the second piece he views this caution as a product of "Moscow's lack of attractive intervention options" (p. 65).

2. See Rubinstein, *Red Star,* pp. 279–80; Abraham S. Becker, "The Super-powers in the Arab-Israeli Conflict, 1970–73," in *Economics and Politics,* ed. Becker, Hansen, and Kerr, p. 117.

3. These agreements were the Anti-Ballistic Missile (ABM) treaty, the SALT I treaty, the Basic Principles Agreement, and the Agreement on the Prevention of Nuclear War.

4. Garthoff, *Detente and Confrontation,* p. 362. Sadat noted that "for the first time, too, shipments started promptly." Sadat, *In Search of Identity,* p. 238. The Soviets did not enhance their commitment to Egypt to the level it had been prior to the 1972 expulsion. Galia Golan, "Soviet Decisionmaking in the Yom Kippur War, 1973," in *Soviet Decisionmaking,* ed. Valenta and Potter, p. 187.

5. Kissinger, *Years of Upheaval,* p. 461.

6. Garthoff, *Detente and Confrontation,* p. 363.

7. Alexander L. George, "The Arab-Israeli War of October 1973: Origins and Impact," in *Managing U.S.-Soviet Rivalry,* ed. George, pp. 145–46.

8. Garthoff, *Detente and Confrontation,* p. 363.

9. Kissinger, *Years of Upheaval,* p. 463.

10. Heikal, *Road to Ramadan,* p. 24.

11. The Agreement on the Prevention of Nuclear War of June 1973 stated that the United States and Soviet Union "agree that they will act in such a manner as to prevent the development of situations capable of causing a dangerous exacerba-tion of their relations, as to avoid military confrontations, and as to exclude the outbreak of nuclear war." The Basic Principles Agreement of 1972 had also stated, "The USA and the USSR attach major importance to preventing the development of situations capable of causing a dangerous exacerbation of their relations. . . . The USA and the USSR have a special responsibility . . . to do everything in their

power so that conflicts or situations will not arise which would serve to increase international tensions." See Garthoff, *Detente and Confrontation*, p. 387.

12. Heikal, *Road to Ramadan*, p. 34; also "October War Counter Claims." Sadat claimed that Brezhnev did not even respond to the Egyptian query about the Soviet attitude. Sadat, *In Search of Identity*, p. 246.

13. See Quandt, *Soviet Policy*, p. 12; Rubinstein, *Red Star*, pp. 260–61.

14. Golan, "Soviet Decisionmaking," p. 198.

15. Garthoff rejects this interpretation, arguing that the evacuation was a precautionary move, not a signal, although he cites no evidence for either view. Garthoff, *Detente and Confrontation*, p. 367. Sadat too saw the evacuation as a sign that the Soviets believed Egypt would lose. Sadat, *In Search of Identity*, pp. 246–47.

16. Heikal, *Road to Ramadan*, p. 209.

17. Karen Dawisha has written that apparently a "tactical suggestion" by Assad before the war became an "urgent request" by Brezhnev after the war began. Dawisha, *Soviet Foreign Policy*, pp. 66–67.

18. Heikal, *Road to Ramadan*, pp. 208–9; Sadat, *In Search of Identity*, pp. 252–53.

19. Kissinger, *Years of Upheaval*, p. 473.

20. Ibid., pp. 474–75.

21. Ibid., p. 481.

22. Golan, *Yom Kippur and After*, pp. 78–80.

23. *Pravda*, October 7, 1973.

24. Kissinger, *Years of Upheaval*, pp. 486–87.

25. *Pravda*, October 9, 1973.

26. Glassman, *Arms for the Arabs*, p. 144.

27. BBC Summary of World Broadcasts, Part 4: Middle East and Africa, October 11, 1973, ME 4421/A/5.

28. Sadat, *In Search of Identity*, p. 254.

29. Kissinger, *Years of Upheaval*, p. 498.

30. *Pravda*, October 13, 1973.

31. Kissinger, *Years of Upheaval*, pp. 509–10.

32. Ibid., p. 522.

33. As late as October 15 the Soviets had pledged "to assist in every way" the Arab goal of regaining the occupied territories. This pledge came after a meeting among Boumedienne and Brezhnev, President Nikolai Podgorny, Kosygin, Gromyko, and Grechko. *New York Times*, October 16, 1973.

34. Kissinger, *Years of Upheaval*, p. 532. Jon Glassman argues that there were in fact Cuban military units in Syria—although not on the battlefield—and he says that twenty North Korean pilots flew passive air defense missions into the interior of Egypt. Glassman dismisses rumors of North Vietnamese involvement. See *Arms for the Arabs*, pp. 134, 136, 227. The *New York Times* reported a clash between the North Korean pilots and Israelis south of Cairo on the 18th. See *New York Times*, October 19, 1973, p. 17; also U.S. House of Representatives, Committee on Foreign Affairs, Subcommittee on the Near East and South Asia, 93d Cong., 1st sess., *The Impact of the October Middle East War* (Washington, D.C.: Government Printing Office, 1973), pp. 65–66, 110.

35. Kissinger, *Years of Upheaval*, pp. 539–40.
36. Ibid., p. 542.
37. Ibid., pp. 550, 553–54.
38. Garthoff, *Detente and Confrontation*, p. 374.
39. Kissinger, *Years of Upheaval*, pp. 570–72.
40. Nixon, *RN*, p. 936.
41. Golan, *Yom Kippur and After*, p. 118.
42. Kissinger, *Years of Upheaval*, p. 572.
43. Soviet suspicions were likely enhanced by the fact that Kissinger had stopped in Israel on his way home from Moscow.
44. Kissinger, *Years of Upheaval*, p. 578.
45. Ibid., pp. 579–80.
46. Ibid., p. 583.
47. Nixon, *RN*, p. 938.
48. Kissinger, *Years of Upheaval*, p. 591; Blechman and Hart, "Political Utility," p. 141.
49. Kissinger, *Years of Upheaval*, pp. 588–91.
50. Ibid., p. 597.
51. Ibid., p. 601.
52. Ibid., p. 608.
53. *Pravda*, October 28, 1973.
54. Porter, *USSR in Third World Conflicts*, pp. 130–31.
55. Golan, "Soviet Decisionmaking," p. 202.
56. Kissinger, *Years of Upheaval*, p. 497.
57. See Golan, "Soviet Decisionmaking," p. 202.
58. Heikal, *Road to Ramadan*, p. 212.
59. Ibid., p. 214; Porter, *USSR in Third World Conflicts*, p. 126.
60. Kissinger, *Years of Upheaval*, p. 497. Kissinger notes that the airlift must have been organized several days ahead of time, given its magnitude.
61. Dawisha, *Soviet Foreign Policy*, pp. 66–67. See also *New York Times*, October 9, 1973. The exchange took place through regular channels on the night of October 7.
62. Alan Dowty argues that by October 9 the Soviets were reacting to Syrian failures, and the United States was responding to Egyptian successes. Dowty, *Middle East Crisis*, p. 231.
63. Heikal, *Road to Ramadan*, p. 215. Sadat reportedly said to Heikal on October 10, "As I told Hafez Assad, territory isn't important; what is important is to exhaust the enemy. I don't want to make the mistake of pushing forward too fast just for the sake of occupying more territory. We must make the enemy bleed" (p. 220).
64. Sadat, *In Search of Identity*, p. 244.
65. Heikal, *Road to Ramadan*, p. 219.
66. Ibid., pp. 218–20; also "October War Counter Claims," pp. 162–64. Drew Middleton reported that the Soviet military was disappointed that the Egyptians did not accomplish more on the ground because of the inflexibility of their command. See *New York Times*, October 25, 1973, p. 18. In his book on local wars

Soviet general I. E. Shavrov wrote that the Egyptian battle plan, worked out in the summer of 1973, called for the crossing of the Suez canal and for the seizing of the Mitla and Giddi passes on the seventh and eighth days of the war. Having accomplished this, the Egyptians could then force Israel to the negotiating table. See Shavrov, *Lokal'nye Voiny*, pp. 152–53. Kissinger wrote in his memoirs that Egyptian prisoners of war told the Israelis that they had "drilled for years to perfect the technique of crossing the Suez Canal; beyond it they had no operational plan except to hang on." Kissinger, *Years of Upheaval*, p. 459.

67. Heikal, *Road to Ramadan*, pp. 218–19.

68. Sadat, *In Search of Identity*, pp. 258–59.

69. Glassman, *Arms for the Arabs*, p. 130; Porter, *USSR and Third World Conflicts*, p. 132.

70. Quandt, *Soviet Policy*, p. 19.

71. Golan, *Yom Kippur and After*, p. 86; Porter, *USSR and Third World Conflicts*, p. 132.

72. Garthoff, *Detente and Confrontation*, p. 377. Garthoff discusses the many confusing accounts of the timing of the alerts of these divisions.

73. Golan, "Soviet Decisionmaking," pp. 203 ff.; Quandt, *Soviet Policy*, p. 21.

74. Garthoff, *Detente and Confrontation*, p. 378.

75. Golan, "Soviet Decisionmaking," p. 209.

76. See Hart, "Soviet Approaches." On October 23 U.S. intelligence detected radioactive material in ships passing through the Bosporus. There has been much speculation about the kind of signal that might have been intended and whether nuclear missiles were being shipped to fit the Egyptian SCUDs. This material may have been on board as a way to demonstrate a stronger Soviet commitment rather than to prepare Egyptian missiles with nuclear warheads. See Golan, "Soviet Decisionmaking," p. 209; Golan, *Yom Kippur and After*, pp. 124–25; Kalb and Kalb, *Kissinger*, p. 488. It may also have been sent to deter *Israeli* use of nuclear weapons. See Shavrov, *Lokal'nye Voiny*, pp. 161–62. Soviet Foreign Ministry official Oleg Grinevsky said that Israel showed its nuclear weapons to Soviet satellites flying overhead in order to remind the USSR of Israeli capabilities. Discussion at Cornell University, November 11, 1991.

77. Kissinger, *Years of Upheaval*, p. 519.

78. See Jabber and Kolkowicz, "Arab-Israeli Wars of 1967 and 1973," p. 463.

79. Kissinger, *Years of Upheaval*, p. 507.

80. See, for example, Spechler, *Domestic Influences*.

81. Golan, "Soviet Decisionmaking," pp. 189–90.

82. Mlynář, *Nightfrost in Prague*.

83. Dawisha, *The Kremlin and the Prague Spring*, p. 256.

84. Ibid., pp. 260–65; Mlynář, *Nightfrost in Prague*, pp. 153–54.

85. Mlynář, *Nightfrost in Prague*, p. 152.

86. Ibid., p. 154; Dawisha, *The Kremlin and the Prague Spring*, pp. 265 ff.

87. Dawisha, *The Kremlin and the Prague Spring*, pp. 299–300.

88. Valenta, *Soviet Intervention in Czechoslovakia*, pp. 81–82, 85, 84.

89. See, for example, Dawisha, *The Kremlin and the Prague Spring*, p. 286; Mlynář, *Nightfrost in Prague*, pp. 155, 168; Valenta, *Soviet Intervention*, p. 85.

SIX / *Gorbachev and German Unification*

1. Philip Zelikow, interview with the author, November 26, 1991. In 1989–90 Zelikow was the director of European security affairs for the National Security Council.

2. Another factor may have been that, as Stephen Szabo has remarked, "Gorbachev was overwhelmed by the demands of managing the Soviet economy and the nationalities disputes and had little time to worry about the Germans. This accounted in part for the sporadic nature of Soviet policy, jerking back and forth as Gorbachev became more or less engaged." Szabo, *Diplomacy of German Unification*, p. 28.

3. See, for example, Adomeit, "Gorbachev and German Unification," p. 5; also Kaiser, "Germany's Unification," p. 182. For good overviews of Soviet–East European relations in the period, see Karen Dawisha, *Eastern Europe, Gorbachev, and Reform: The Great Challenge*, 2d ed. (Cambridge: Cambridge University Press, 1990); also Charles Gati, *The Bloc That Failed: Soviet–East European Relations in Transition* (Bloomington: Indiana University Press, 1990).

4. On Soviet–East European economic relations, see Paul Marer, "The Political Economy of Soviet Relations with Eastern Europe," in *Soviet Policy in Eastern Europe*, ed. Sarah Meiklejohn Terry (New Haven: Yale University Press, 1984), p. 174.

5. *Pravda*, July 8, 1987, p. 2.

6. See, for example, Gorbachev, *Perestroika*, p. 200; *Pravda*, October 25, 1988, p. 2.

7. Oberdorfer, *The Turn*, p. 362; Barbara Donovan, "East Germans in Hungary Allowed to Go West," Radio Free Europe/Radio Liberty, RAD background report/172, September 14, 1989; *New York Times*, September 11, 1989, pp. 1, 12. Szabo argues that the Hungarians sought Soviet approval only after they scrapped the agreement. See *Diplomacy of German Unification*, p. 36.

8. *Pravda*, October 7, 1989.

9. On this decision, see discussion in Pond, *Beyond the Wall*, pp. 119–20.

10. Beschloss and Talbott, *At the Highest Levels*, p. 134.

11. *Pravda*, November 15, 1989, p. 2.

12. *New York Times*, November 15, 1989, p. 14.

13. Kaiser, "Germany's Unification," p. 184; *Washington Post*, November 30, 1989, p. A53; Szabo, *Diplomacy of German Unification*, pp. 38ff.

14. Peter R. Weilemann, "The German Contribution toward Overcoming the Division of Europe—Chancellor Helmut Kohl's 10 Points," *Aussen Politik* 41, no. 1 (1990): 19. Apparently, Kohl was envisioning a five-year process at this time. See Pond, *Beyond the Wall*, pp. 137–38.

15. *Washington Post*, November 30, 1989, pp. A53, A57.

16. Oberdorfer, *The Turn*, pp. 381–85; Adomeit, "Gorbachev and German Unification," p. 8. For more on the concerns conveyed by Gorbachev and Shevardnadze at Malta, see Beschloss and Talbott, *At the Highest Levels*, p. 157.

17. *New York Times*, December 6, 1989, p. A19.

18. This scenario did concern officials in the Bush administration. Zelikow, interview with the author, November 26, 1991.

19. *New York Times,* December 7, 1989, p. A21.

20. *Pravda,* December 10, 1989, p. 2.

21. Adomeit, "Gorbachev and German Unification," p. 9.

22. *New York Times,* January 31, 1990, pp. A1, A11.

23. Ibid., February 1, 1990, pp. A1, A12.

24. A few days after the Modrow meeting, Shevardnadze put forward a strange request: he called for an all-European referendum on German unification that would also include the United States and Canada, or at least full parliamentary discussions in these countries, saying, "It is important that not only politicians but also the people have decided the fate of the future of Europe." See *Pravda,* February 3, 1990, p. 5. If the Soviets were serious about this proposal, they clearly hoped to play on unease in the rest of Europe about a reunified Germany. Gorbachev had used such popular pressure successfully at home in his attack on the old guard. This time the proposal was out of place and an odd gesture.

25. For a similar argument, see Pond, *Beyond the Wall,* pp. 173 ff.

26. *Pravda,* February 7, 1990, p. 6.

27. *New York Times,* February 2, 1990, pp. A1, A11; February 3, 1990, p. A8; *Washington Post,* February 3, 1990, p. A20; February 7, 1990, p. A19; *Wall Street Journal,* February 7, 1990, p. A14; Szabo, *Diplomacy of German Unification,* pp. 56–58.

28. A senior White House official was even quoted at the time as saying that a united Germany could remain neutral as long as it was politically and economically oriented toward the West. *New York Times,* February 10, 1990, pp. 1, 6; *Washington Post,* February 7, 1990, p. A19; February 8, 1990, pp. A29, A30; February 12, 1990, p. A25. Furthermore, a poll taken in West Germany on February 3 showed that nearly 60 percent favored reunification even if Germany had to be neutral. *Christian Science Monitor,* February 6, 1990, p. 2.

29. According to Philip Zelikow, one of the problems for the United States was that Baker was traveling for much of this period while the precise language on Germany's relationship with NATO was being worked out in Washington. Zelikow, interview with the author, November 26, 1991.

30. Pond describes Baker's press conference remarks as a "miscue," but the ambiguity in his terminology continued later, as is discussed below. See Pond, *Beyond the Wall,* p. 179.

31. Transcript, *This Week with David Brinkley,* February 18, 1990, pp. 5, 8.

32. *Washington Post,* February 19, 1990, p. A36. See also *The Economist,* July 21, 1990, p. 47; Pond, *Beyond the Wall,* pp. 182 ff.

33. *Washington Post,* February 26, 1990, p. A16.

34. Beschloss and Talbott, *At the Highest Levels,* pp. 185–86.

35. *New York Times,* February 11, 1990, p. 21.

36. *Los Angeles Times,* February 13, 1990, p. 10. On the *Brinkley* show of February 18 Woerner had noted, "By the way, Gorbachev himself did not commit himself to any kind of solution." Transcript, p. 4.

37. *New York Times,* February 16, 1990, pp. A1, A9. Two-plus-four meant that the two Germanys would first work out the internal details of unification and then the four powers having rights stemming from World War II would come into the process to negotiate with the two Germanys on the external aspects of the problem.

38. Ibid., February 14, 1990, pp. A1, A10; February 15, 1990, p. A18.

39. Ibid., February 16, 1990, p. A8.

40. *Pravda*, February 21, 1990, p. 1.

41. *New York Times*, February 21, 1990, pp. A1, A11.

42. Ibid., March 21, 1990, p. A16.

43. Ibid., March 18, 1990, pp. A1, A14.

44. Ibid. Earlier, the head of the Soviet conventional arms delegation in Vienna, Oleg Grinevsky, had called for reductions in the German armed forces. See *Pravda*, March 16, 1990, p. 1; *New York Times*, March 16, 1990, p. A8. Nikolai Portugalov, the Central Committee's adviser on German issues, had said on March 19 that the Soviet objection to NATO membership was merely "the starting position in the negotiations." *New York Times*, March 21, 1990, p. A16.

45. See, for example, Suzanne Crow, "The Changing Soviet View of German Unification," Radio Free Europe/Radio Liberty, *Report on the USSR*, August 3, 1990, p. 2.

46. Zelikow, interview with the author, November 26, 1991.

47. Oberdorfer, *The Turn*, p. 416; *New York Times*, April 7, 1990, pp. 1, 6.

48. *New York Times*, April 11, 1990, p. A1, A10.

49. As Shevardnadze acknowledged in his memoirs, the talks were really one-plus-five. See Shevardnadze, *The Future Belongs to Freedom*, p. 137.

50. Ibid., p. 138.

51. Baker himself and Manfred Woerner had made the same statement at the North Atlantic Council ministerial meeting in Brussels on May 3. See ibid., p. 139; *Foreign Policy Bulletin* 1 (July–August 1990): 35.

52. Oberdorfer, *The Turn*, pp. 416–17; Kaiser, "Germany's Unification," p. 190. The nine assurances had first been presented by Baker in his February meetings in Moscow. See Szabo, *Diplomacy of German Unification*, p. 61.

53. "Joint News Conference, June 3, 1990," *Foreign Policy Bulletin* 1 (July–August 1990): 14.

54. Oberdorfer, *The Turn*, pp. 417–19, 429. In his press briefing of June 8 after the NATO ministerial meeting in Scotland, Baker would only say, "I did get a sense at least of movement from my meeting with Foreign Minister Shevardnadze in Copenhagen." *Foreign Policy Bulletin* 1 (July–August 1990): 44.

55. *Foreign Policy Bulletin* 1 (July–August 1990): 43–44.

56. Ibid., pp. 49ff.; Crow, "Changing Soviet View of German Unification," p. 3; *Chicago Tribune*, June 24, 1990, pp. 19, 22.

57. *Pravda*, June 26, 1990, p. 3.

58. *FBIS*, July 11, 1990, p. 8.

59. See, for example, Chiesa, "28th Congress," p. 35.

60. *Pravda*, July 18, 1990, pp. 1, 5.

61. *The Economist*, July 21, 1990, p. 47.

62. Gorbachev, *Perestroika*, p. 237. See also Oberdorfer, *The Turn*, pp. 186–87.

63. Oberdorfer, *The Turn*, pp. 190–91; Shultz, *Turmoil and Triumph*, p. 758.

64. Oberdorfer, *The Turn*, p. 196; Shultz, *Turmoil and Triumph*, p. 767.

65. Oberdorfer, *The Turn*, pp. 196–97, 199.

66. Ibid., pp. 202–4.

67. Jonathan Haslam, *The Soviet Union and the Politics of Nuclear Weapons*

in Europe, 1969–87 (Ithaca: Cornell University Press, 1990), p. 166. Reagan later wrote, "I realized that he had brought me to Iceland with one purpose: to kill the Strategic Defense Initiative." Ronald Reagan, *An American Life* (New York: Simon and Schuster, 1990), p. 679.

68. See Shultz, *Turmoil and Triumph*, p. 775.

69. *Pravda*, October 14, 1986, pp. 1–2. See also discussion in Gorbachev, *Perestroika*, p. 238.

70. *Izvestiia*, October 24, 1986.

SEVEN / *Reexamining the Model*

1. On the use of counterfactual arguments, see Fearon, "Counterfactuals and Hypothesis Testing."

2. The discussion about an alternative strategy for Khrushchev in Cuba stems in part from conversations I have had with Steve Weber.

3. Raymond Garthoff agrees that the Soviets lost a great deal by denying the existence of the missiles for several days, and that if they had called for negotiations immediately, the United States would have been in a much weaker position to take military action. Garthoff also suggests that Khrushchev's relations with Castro would have been better, since Cuban interests would have loomed larger sooner. But he also believes that the Turkish missiles would not have been brought up, since they did not appear as a major issue until October 25–26. Garthoff, interview with the author, September 13, 1989.

4. For a discussion of Stalin's failure to understand how his actions in Eastern Europe would affect the West and how easily he might have succeeded in fulfilling his goals without hardening Western resolve against him, see McGeorge Bundy, "The Test of Yalta," *Foreign Affairs* 27 (July 1949): 618–29.

5. Jervis, *Perception and Misperception*, pp. 278, 220.

6. For a discussion of this problem of "cognitive rigidity," see Snyder and Diesing, *Conflict among Nations*, p. 495.

7. George and Smoke, *Deterrence in American Foreign Policy*.

8. In a footnote the authors acknowledge that Khrushchev could have made the deployment in a gradual fashion rather than trying for the *fait accompli* and then justified it publicly by referring to U.S. behavior. See ibid., p. 538.

9. Snyder and Diesing, *Conflict among Nations*, p. 494.

10. George, "Operational Code," p. 179.

11. Hugh Sidey, *A Very Personal Presidency: Lyndon Johnson in the White House* (New York: Atheneum, 1968), p. 221; A. J. P. Taylor, *The Origins of the Second World War*, 2d ed. (New York: Fawcett, 1961), p. 280; William R. Rock, *Neville Chamberlain* (New York: Twayne, 1969), p. 210.

Select Bibliography

Document Collections

British Foreign Office. Russia Correspondence. F.O. 371, 1948.

Chang, Laurence, and Peter Kornbluh, eds. *The Cuban Missile Crisis, 1962: A National Security Archive Documents Reader.* New York: New Press, 1992.

Cuban Missile Crisis Meetings. October 27, 1962. Papers of John F. Kennedy, Presidential Papers, President's Office Files, Presidential Recordings, John F. Kennedy Library, Boston, Mass.

The Cuban Missile Crisis, 1962. Alexandria, Va.: Chadwyck-Healey and National Security Archive, 1990. Microfiche.

Declassified Documents Reference System. Washington, D.C.: Carrolton. Microfiche.

Foreign Relations of the United States. Washington, D.C.: Government Printing Office.

National Archives, United States. 740.00119 Control (Germany).

Royal Institute of International Affairs. *Documents on Germany under Occupation, 1945–54.* London: Oxford University Press, 1955.

Vneshniaia Politika Sovetskogo Soiuza: Dokumenty i Materialy 1948 g. 2 vols. Moscow: Gospolitizdat, 1948.

Vneshniaia Politika Sovetskogo Soiuza i Mezhdunarodnye Otnosheniia, Sbornik Dokumentov, 1962. Moscow: Izdatel'stvo Instituta Mezhdunarodnykh Otnoshenii, 1963.

Books and Articles

Abel, Elie. *The Missile Crisis.* Philadelphia: J. B. Lippincott, 1966.

Abelson, Robert P. "Script Processing in Attitude Formation and Decision Making." In *Cognition and Social Behavior*, edited by John S. Carroll and John W. Payne, pp. 33–45. New York: John Wiley & Sons, 1975.

Acheson, Dean. *Present at the Creation*. New York: W. W. Norton, 1969.

Adomeit, Hannes. "Gorbachev and German Unification: Revision of Thinking, Realignment of Power." *Problems of Communism* 39 (July–August 1990): 1–23.

———. *Soviet Risk-Taking and Crisis Behavior*. London: George Allen & Unwin, 1982.

Adzhubei, Aleksei. *Te Desyat' Let*. Moscow: Sovetskaya Rossiya, 1989.

Aggarwal, Vinod K., and Pierre Allan. "Evolution in Bargaining Theories: Toward an Integrated Approach to Explain Strategies of the Weak." Paper presented at the annual meeting of the American Political Science Association, Chicago, September 1–4, 1983.

Aksyutin, Yu. V., ed. *Nikita Sergeevich Khrushchev: Materialy k Biografii*. Moscow: Politizdat, 1989.

Alekseyev, Aleksandr. "Karibskii Krizis: Kak Eto Bylo." *Ekho Planety*, no. 33 (November 1988): 26–37.

———. "Karibskii, Kubinskii, Oktyabr'skii. . . ." *Ekho Planety*, no. 7 (February 1989): 16–18.

Allyn, Bruce J.; James G. Blight; and David A. Welch. "Essence of Revision: Moscow, Havana, and the Cuban Missile Crisis." *International Security* 14 (winter 1989/90): 136–72.

Anderson, Richard D., Jr. "Competitive Politics and Soviet Foreign Policy: Authority Building and Bargaining in the Brezhnev Politburo." Ph.D. diss., University of California, Berkeley, 1989.

Aspaturian, Vernon V. "Internal Politics and Foreign Policy in the Soviet System." In *Approaches to Comparative and International Politics*, edited by R. Barry Farrell, pp. 212–87. Evanston: Northwestern University Press, 1966.

Axelrod, Robert. "Schema Theory: An Information Processing Model of Perception and Cognition." *American Political Science Review* 67 (1973): 1248–66.

Axelrod, Robert, and William Zimmerman. "The Soviet Press on Soviet Foreign Policy: A Usually Reliable Source." *British Journal of Political Science* 11 (spring 1981): 183–200.

Barber, James David. *The Presidential Character: Predicting Performance in the White House*. 2d ed. Englewood Cliffs, N.J.: Prentice-Hall, 1977.

Bazhanov, Boris. *Vospominaniia Byvshego Sekretarya Stalina*. Paris: Izdatel'stvo Tret'ia Volna, 1980.

Becker, Abraham S.; Bert Hansen; and Malcolm H. Kerr, eds. *The Economics and Politics of the Middle East*. New York: American Elsevier, 1975.

Bell, Coral. *The Conventions of Crisis: A Study in Diplomatic Management*. London: Oxford University Press, 1971.

———. "The October Middle East War: A Case Study in Crisis Management during Detente." *International Affairs* 50 (October 1974): 531–43.

Beschloss, Michael R. *The Crisis Years: Kennedy and Khrushchev, 1960–1963*. New York: Harper Collins, 1991.

Beschloss, Michael R., and Strobe Talbott. *At the Highest Levels: The Inside Story of the End of the Cold War*. Boston: Little, Brown, 1993.

Betts, Richard K. *Nuclear Blackmail and Nuclear Balance.* Washington, D.C.: Brookings Institution, 1987.

Blechman, Barry M., and Douglas M. Hart. "The Political Utility of Nuclear Weapons: The 1973 Middle East Crisis." *International Security* 7 (summer 1982): 132–56.

Blight, James G., and David Welch. *On the Brink.* New York: Hill & Wang, 1989.

Bohlen, Charles E. *Witness to History, 1929–1969.* New York: W. W. Norton, 1973.

Bolshakov, Georgy. "The Hot Line." *New Times,* nos. 4–6 (1989).

Brecher, Michael. *Decisions in Crisis.* Berkeley and Los Angeles: University of California Press, 1980.

Breslauer, George W. *Khrushchev and Brezhnev as Leaders: Building Authority in Soviet Politics.* London: George Allen & Unwin, 1982.

Brown, Archie, and Michael Kaser, eds. *The Soviet Union since the Fall of Khrushchev.* 2d ed. London: Macmillan, 1978.

Brugioni, Dino A. *Eyeball to Eyeball: The Inside Story of the Cuban Missile Crisis.* Edited by Robert F. McCort. New York: Random House, 1990, 1991.

Brzezinski, Zbigniew. *The Soviet Bloc: Unity and Conflict.* Rev. ed. Cambridge: Harvard University Press, 1971.

Bullock, Alan. *Hitler and Stalin: Parallel Lives.* New York: Alfred A. Knopf, 1992.

Burlatsky, Fedor. "Brezhnev i Krushenie Ottepeli." *Literaturnaia Gazeta,* September 14, 1988, p. 14.

Burns, James MacGregor. *Leadership.* New York: Harper & Row, 1978.

Carr, Edward Hallett. *The Russian Revolution from Lenin to Stalin (1917–1929).* London: Macmillan, 1979.

Chang, Laurence, ed. *The Cuban Missile Crisis, 1962.* 2 vols. Alexandria, Va.: Chadwyck-Healey and National Security Archive, 1990.

Chiesa, Giulietto. "The 28th Congress of the CPSU." *Problems of Communism* 39 (July–August 1990): 24–38.

Churchill, Winston S. *Triumph and Tragedy.* Boston: Houghton Mifflin, 1953.

Clay, Lucius D. *Decision in Germany.* New York: Doubleday, 1950.

Cline, Ray S. "Commentary: The Cuban Missile Crisis." *Foreign Affairs* 68 (fall 1989): 190–96.

Cohen, Stephen F. *Bukharin and the Bolshevik Revolution: A Political Biography, 1888–1938.* New York: Vintage Books, 1975.

Conquest, Robert. *Power and Policy in the USSR.* London: Macmillan, 1961.

Crankshaw, Edward. *Khrushchev: A Career.* New York: Viking, 1966.

Dallin, Alexander. "The Domestic Sources of Soviet Foreign Policy." In *The Domestic Context of Soviet Foreign Policy,* edited by Seweryn Bialer, pp. 335–408. Boulder, Colo.: Westview, 1981.

———. "Soviet Foreign Policy and Domestic Politics: A Framework for Analysis." *Journal of International Affairs* 23 (1966): 250–65.

Dallin, Alexander, and Alan F. Westin, eds. *Politics in the Soviet Union.* New York: Harcourt, Brace & World, 1966.

Davison, W. Phillips. *The Berlin Blockade: A Study in Cold War Politics.* Princeton: Princeton University Press, 1958.

Dawisha, Karen. *The Kremlin and the Prague Spring*. Berkeley and Los Angeles: University of California Press, 1984.

————. *Soviet Foreign Policy towards Egypt*. London: Macmillan, 1979.

Dawson, Paul A. "The Formation and Structure of Political Belief Systems." *Political Behavior* 1 (summer 1979): 99–122.

Deutscher, Isaac. *Stalin: A Political Biography*. New York: Oxford University Press, 1949.

Dinerstein, Herbert. *The Making of a Missile Crisis*. Baltimore: Johns Hopkins University Press, 1976.

Doder, Dusko, and Louise Branson. *Gorbachev: Heretic in the Kremlin*. New York: Viking, 1990.

Dornberg, John. *Brezhnev: The Masks of Power*. London: Vikas, 1974.

Dowty, Alan. *Middle East Crisis*. Berkeley and Los Angeles: University of California Press, 1984.

Egorychev, Nikolai. "Napravlen Poslom." *Ogonyok* 6 (February 1986): 30.

Etheridge, Lloyd S. "Personality Effects on American Foreign Policy, 1898–1968: A Test of Interpersonal Generalization Theory." *American Political Science Review* 72 (June 1978): 434–51.

Falkowski, Lawrence S., ed. *Psychological Models in International Politics*. Boulder, Colo.: Westview, 1979.

Fearon, James D. "Counterfactuals and Hypothesis Testing in Political Science." *World Politics* 43 (January 1991): 169–95.

Fiske, Susan T., and Shelley E. Taylor. *Social Cognition*. Reading, Mass.: Addison-Wesley, 1984.

————. *Social Cognition*. 2d ed. New York: McGraw-Hill, 1991.

Frankland, Mark. *Khrushchev*. Middlesex: Penguin, 1966.

Fukuyama, Francis. *Moscow's Post-Brezhnev Reassessment of the Third World*. R-3337-USDP. Santa Monica: RAND, 1986.

————. "Nuclear Shadowboxing: Soviet Intervention in the Middle East." *Orbis* 25 (fall 1981): 579–605.

Garthoff, Raymond. "Cuban Missile Crisis: The Soviet Story." *Foreign Policy* 72 (fall 1988): 61–80.

————. *Detente and Confrontation*. Washington, D.C.: Brookings Institution, 1985.

————. *Reflections on the Cuban Missile Crisis*. Rev. ed. Washington, D.C.: Brookings Institution, 1989.

Gelman, Harry. *The Brezhnev Politburo and the Decline of Detente*. Ithaca: Cornell University Press, 1984.

George, Alexander L. "Case Studies and Theory Development." Paper presented at the Second Annual Symposium on Information Processing in Organizations, Carnegie-Mellon University, Pittsburgh, Pa., October 15–16, 1982.

————. "Crisis Management: The Interaction of Political and Military Considerations." *Survival* 26 (September–October 1984): 223–34.

————. "The Operational Code: A Neglected Approach to the Study of Political Leaders and Decision-Making." In *The Conduct of Soviet Foreign Policy*, edited by Erik P. Hoffmann and Frederic J. Fleron, Jr., pp. 165–90. New York: Aldine, 1980.

————, ed. *Managing U.S.-Soviet Rivalry: Problems of Crisis Prevention.* Boulder, Colo.: Westview, 1983.

George, Alexander L., and Juliette L. George. *Woodrow Wilson and Colonel House.* New York: Dover, 1964.

George, Alexander L.; David K. Hall; and William R. Simons. *The Limits of Coercive Diplomacy.* Boston: Little, Brown, 1971.

George, Alexander L., and Richard Smoke. *Deterrence in American Foreign Policy: Theory and Practice.* New York: Columbia University Press, 1974.

Glad, Betty. *Charles Evans Hughes and the Illusions of Innocence.* Urbana: University of Illinois Press, 1966.

Glass, Arnold Lewis, and Keith James Holyoak. *Cognition.* 2d ed. New York: Random House, 1986.

Glassman, Jon D. *Arms for the Arabs: The Soviet Union and War in the Middle East.* Baltimore: Johns Hopkins University Press, 1975.

Golan, Galia. *Yom Kippur and After.* Cambridge: Cambridge University Press, 1977.

Goldgeier, James Marc. "Soviet Leaders and International Crises: The Influence of Domestic Political Experiences on Foreign Policy Strategies." Ph.D. diss., University of California, Berkeley, 1990.

Gorbachev, Mikhail. *Perestroika: New Thinking for Our Country and the World.* New York: Harper & Row, 1987.

Gromyko, A. A. *Pamyatnoe.* Moscow: Izdatel'stvo Politicheskoi Literatury, 1988.

Hahn, Jeffrey W. "Boss Gorbachev Confronts His New Congress." *Orbis* 34 (spring 1984): 163–78.

Harriman, W. Averell. "My Alarming Interview with Khrushchev." *Life,* July 13, 1959, pp. 33–35.

Harriman, W. Averell, and Elie Abel. *Special Envoy to Churchill and Stalin, 1941–1946.* New York: Random House, 1975.

Hart, Douglas M. "Soviet Approaches to Crisis Management: The Military Dimension." *Survival* 26 (September–October 1984): 214–22.

Hazan, Baruch. *Gorbachev and His Enemies: The Struggle for Perestroika.* Boulder, Colo.: Westview, 1990.

Heikal, Mohammed. *The Road to Ramadan.* New York: Quadrangle, 1975.

Hermann, Charles F., ed. *International Crises: Insights from Behavioral Research.* New York: Free Press, 1972.

Herrmann, Richard. "The Empirical Challenge of the Cognitive Revolution: A Strategy for Drawing Inferences about Perception." *International Studies Quarterly* 32 (June 1988): 175–203.

Hilsman, Roger. *To Move a Nation.* New York: Dell, 1967.

Holsti, Ole R. "The Belief System and National Images: A Case Study." *Journal of Conflict Resolution* 6 (September 1962): 244–52.

————. "Foreign Policy Decisionmakers Viewed Psychologically: 'Cognitive Process' Approaches." In *In Search of Global Patterns,* edited by James N. Rosenau, pp. 120–44. New York: Free Press, 1976.

Horelick, Arnold L. "The Cuban Missile Crisis: An Analysis of Soviet Calculations and Behavior." *World Politics* 16 (April 1964): 363–89.

Horelick, Arnold L., and Myron Rush. *Strategic Power and Soviet Foreign Policy.* Chicago: University of Chicago Press, 1966.

Hough, Jerry. "The Brezhnev Era." *Problems of Communism* 25 (March–April 1976): 1–17.

Howley, Frank. *Berlin Command.* New York: G. P. Putnam's Sons, 1950.

Janis, Irving L. *Victims of Groupthink.* Boston: Houghton Mifflin, 1972.

Jervis, Robert. "Bargaining and Bargaining Tactics." In *Coercion,* edited by J. Roland Pennock and John W. Chapman, pp. 272–88. Chicago: Atherton, 1972.

———. *The Logic of Images in International Relations.* Princeton: Princeton University Press, 1970.

———. *Perception and Misperception in International Politics.* Princeton: Princeton University Press, 1976.

Jessup, Philip C. "The Berlin Blockade and the Use of the United Nations." *Foreign Affairs* 50 (October 1971): 163–73.

———. "Park Avenue Diplomacy: Ending the Berlin Blockade." *Political Science Quarterly* 87 (September 1972): 377–400.

Jones, W. M. *Soviet Leadership Politics and Leadership Views on the Use of Military Force.* N-1210-AF. Santa Monica: RAND, 1979.

Kahneman, Daniel; Paul Slovic; and Amos Tversky. *Judgment under Uncertainty: Heuristics and Biases.* Cambridge: Cambridge University Press, 1982.

Kaiser, Karl. "Germany's Unification." *Foreign Affairs* 70 (winter 1990/91): 179–205.

Kalb, Marvin, and Bernard Kalb. *Kissinger.* Boston: Little, Brown, 1974.

———. "Twenty Days in October." *New York Times Magazine,* June 23, 1974.

Kaplan, Stephen S. *Diplomacy of Power.* Washington, D.C.: Brookings Institution, 1981.

Kelley, Donald R. *Soviet Politics in the Brezhnev Era.* New York: Praeger, 1980.

Kelman, Herbert C. "The Role of the Individual in International Relations: Some Conceptual and Methodological Considerations." *Journal of International Affairs* 24 (1970): 1–17.

Kennan, George. *Memoirs, 1925–1950.* Boston: Little, Brown, 1967.

Kennedy, Robert F. *Thirteen Days.* New York: W. W. Norton, 1971.

Khong, Yuen Foong. *Analogies at War: Korea, Munich, Dien Bien Phu, and the Vietnam Decisions of 1965.* Princeton: Princeton University Press, 1992.

Khrushchev, Nikita S. *Khrushchev Remembers.* Translated and edited by Strobe Talbott. Boston: Little, Brown, 1970.

———. *Khrushchev Remembers: The Glasnost Tapes.* Translated and edited by Jerrold L. Schecter with Vyacheslav V. Luchkov. Boston: Little, Brown, 1990.

———. *Khrushchev Remembers: The Last Testament.* Translated and edited by Strobe Talbott. Boston: Little, Brown, 1974.

Khrushchev, Sergei. "Pensioner Soiuznogo Znachenia." *Ogonyok* 40–43 (October 1988): 26–30, 26–29, 26–29, 25–28.

"Khrushchev-Kennedy Correspondence during the Caribbean Crisis." *International Affairs* (1992): 9–143.

Kissinger, Henry. *Years of Upheaval.* Boston: Little, Brown, 1982.

Laqueur, Walter. *Stalin: The Glasnost Revelations.* New York: Charles Scribner's Sons, 1991.

Larson, Deborah Welch. *Origins of Containment.* Princeton: Princeton University Press, 1985.

Lau, Richard R., and David O. Sears, eds. *Political Cognition.* Hillsdale, N.J.: Lawrence Erlbaum Associates, 1986.

Lebow, Richard Ned. *Between Peace and War: The Nature of International Crisis.* Baltimore: Johns Hopkins University Press, 1981.

Leites, Nathan. *Kremlin Moods.* RM-3535-ISA. Santa Monica: RAND, 1964.

————. *The Operational Code of the Politburo.* R-206. Santa Monica: RAND, 1951.

————. *A Study of Bolshevism.* Glencoe, Ill.: Free Press, 1953.

Linden, Carl. *Khrushchev and the Soviet Leadership, 1957–1964.* Baltimore: Johns Hopkins Press, 1966.

Mackintosh, J. M. *Strategy and Tactics of Soviet Foreign Policy.* London: Oxford University Press, 1962.

Maoz, Zeev. "Power, Capabilities, and Paradoxical Conflict Outcomes." *World Politics* 41 (January 1989): 239–66.

McCauley, Martin, ed. *Khrushchev and Khrushchevism.* London: Macmillan, 1987.

McNeal, Robert H. *The Bolshevik Tradition.* 2d ed. Englewood Cliffs, N.J.: Prentice-Hall, 1975.

Medvedev, Roy A. *All Stalin's Men.* Garden City, N.Y.: Anchor, 1985.

————. *Khrushchev.* Garden City, N.Y.: Anchor, 1983.

————. "N. S. Khrushchev: Politicheskaia Biografiia." *Druzhba Narodov* 7–9 (1989): 118–57, 162–207, 196–217.

————. "33 Goda Spustia." *Nedelia* 17 (1989): 10–11.

Medvedev, Roy A., and Giulietto Chiesa. *Time of Change: An Insider's View of Russia's Transformation.* New York: Pantheon, 1989.

Medvedev, Roy A., and Zhores A. Medvedev. *Khrushchev: The Years in Power.* New York: W. W. Norton, 1978.

Medvedev, Zhores A. *Gorbachev.* New York: W. W. Norton, 1986, 1987.

Medvedko, L. I. *K Vostoku i Zapadu ot Suetsa.* Moscow: Politizdat, 1980.

Mikoyan, S. A. "Karibskii Krizis, Kakim On Viditsia na Rasstoyanii." *Latinskaia Amerika* (January 1988): 67–80, 143–44.

Millis, Walter, ed. *The Forrestal Diaries.* New York: Viking, 1951.

Mlynář, Zdeněk. *Nightfrost in Prague.* Translated by Paul Wilson. New York: Karz, 1980.

Murphy, Paul J. *Brezhnev, Soviet Politician.* Jefferson, N.C.: McFarland, 1981.

Murphy, Robert. *Diplomat among Warriors.* New York: Doubleday, 1964.

Nadeau, Remi. *Stalin, Churchill, and Roosevelt Divide Europe.* New York: Praeger, 1990.

Nisbett, Richard, and Lee Ross. *Human Inference: Strategies and Shortcomings of Social Judgment.* Englewood Cliffs, N.J.: Prentice-Hall, 1980.

Nixon, Richard. *RN: The Memoirs of Richard Nixon.* New York: Grosset and Dunlap, 1978.

Oberdorfer, Don. *The Turn: From the Cold War to a New Era.* New York: Poseidon, 1991.
"October War Counter Claims." *Journal of Palestine Studies* 3 (summer 1974): 161–64.
Ploss, Sidney I. *Conflict and Decision-Making in Soviet Russia: A Case Study of Agricultural Policy, 1953–63.* Princeton: Princeton University Press, 1965.
Pond, Elizabeth. *Beyond the Wall: Germany's Road to Unification.* Washington, D.C.: Brookings Institution, 1993.
Pope, Ronald. *Soviet Views on the Cuban Missile Crisis.* Washington, D.C.: University Press of America, 1982.
Porter, Bruce D. *The USSR in Third World Conflicts: Soviet Arms and Diplomacy in Local Wars, 1945–1980.* Cambridge: Cambridge University Press, 1984.
Pruitt, Dean G. "Indirect Communication and the Search for Agreement in Negotiation." *Journal of Applied Social Psychology* 1 (July–September 1971): 205–39.
Putnam, Robert D. "Diplomacy and Domestic Politics: The Logic of Two-Level Games." *International Organization* 42 (summer 1988): 427–60.
Quandt, William B. *Soviet Policy in the October 1973 War.* R-1864 ISA. Santa Monica: RAND, 1976.
Read, Stephen J. "Once Is Enough: Causal Reasoning from a Single Instance." *Journal of Personality and Social Psychology* 45 (1983): 323–34.
Reddaway, Peter. "Gorbachev the Bold." *New York Review of Books,* May 28, 1987, p. 22.
Richter, James. "Action and Reaction in Khrushchev's Foreign Policy: Leadership Politics and Soviet Responses to the International Environment." Ph.D. diss., University of California, Berkeley, 1988.
Ross, Dennis. "Coalition Maintenance in the Soviet Union." *World Politics* 32 (January 1980): 258–80.
———. "Risk Aversion in Soviet Decisionmaking." In *Soviet Decisionmaking for National Security,* edited by Jiří Valenta and William Potter, pp. 237–51. London: George Allen & Unwin, 1984.
Rothbart, Myron; Mark Evans; and Solomon Fulero. "Recall for Confirming Events: Memory Processes and the Maintenance of Social Stereotypes." *Journal of Experimental Social Psychology* 15 (1979): 343–55.
Rubinstein, Alvin. *Red Star on the Nile.* Princeton: Princeton University Press, 1977.
Rush, Myron. *Khrushchev and the Stalin Succession: A Study of Political Communication in the USSR.* RM-1883. Santa Monica: RAND, 1957.
Sadat, Anwar. *In Search of Identity.* New York: Harper & Row, 1978.
Sagan, Scott D. "Nuclear Alerts and Crisis Management." *International Security* 9 (spring 1985): 99–139.
Schelling, Thomas C. *Arms and Influence.* New Haven: Yale University Press, 1966.
———. *The Strategy of Conflict.* Cambridge: Harvard University Press, 1960.
Schick, Jack M. *The Berlin Crisis, 1958–1962.* Philadelphia: University of Pennsylvania Press, 1971.
Shavrov, I. E. *Lokal'nye Voiny: Istoriia i Sovremennost.* Moscow: Voenizdat, 1981.

Shepard, Graham H. "Personality Effects on American Foreign Policy, 1969–84: A Second Test of Interpersonal Generalization Theory." *International Studies Quarterly* 32 (March 1988): 91–123.

Shevardnadze, Eduard. *The Future Belongs to Freedom.* Translated by Catherine A. Fitzpatrick. New York: Free Press, 1991.

Shlaim, Avi. *The United States and the Berlin Blockade, 1948–49.* Berkeley and Los Angeles: University of California Press, 1983.

Shultz, George P. *Turmoil and Triumph: My Years as Secretary of State.* New York: Charles Scribner's Sons, 1993.

Simon, Herbert A. *Models of Thought.* New Haven: Yale University Press, 1979.

Singer, J. David. "The Level-of-Analysis Problem in International Relations." *World Politics* 14 (October 1961): 77–92.

Smith, Jean Edward, ed. *The Papers of General Lucius D. Clay.* 2 vols. Bloomington: Indiana University Press, 1974.

Smith, Walter Bedell. *My Three Years in Moscow.* Philadelphia: J. B. Lippincott, 1949.

Snyder, Glenn, and Paul Diesing. *Conflict among Nations.* Princeton: Princeton University Press, 1977.

Snyder, Jack. "The Gorbachev Revolution: A Waning of Soviet Expansionism?" *International Security* 12 (winter 1987/88): 93–131.

———. *Myths of Empire: Domestic Politics and International Ambition.* Ithaca: Cornell University Press, 1991.

Sorensen, Theodore C. *Kennedy.* New York: Harper & Row, 1965.

Souvarine, Boris. *Stalin: A Critical Survey of Bolshevism.* New York: Alliance, 1939.

Spechler, Dina Rome. *Domestic Influences on Soviet Foreign Policy.* Washington, D.C.: University Press of America, 1978.

"Speeches of Egor Kuz'mich Ligachev at the Kennan Institute, Fall 1991." Occasional Paper no. 247. Washington, D.C.: Kennan Institute, 1992.

Strelianyi, Anatoly. "Poslednii Romantik." *Druzhba Narodov* 11 (1988): 190–228.

Szabo, Stephen F. *The Diplomacy of German Unification.* New York: St. Martin's, 1992.

Tatu, Michel. *Power in the Kremlin: From Khrushchev to Kosygin.* New York: Viking, 1969.

Teague, Elizabeth, and Dawn Mann. "Gorbachev's Dual Rule." *Problems of Communism* 39 (January–February 1990): 1–14.

Telhami, Shibley. *Power and Leadership in International Bargaining: The Path to the Camp David Accords.* New York: Columbia University Press, 1990.

Tetlock, Philip E. "Policy-Makers' Images of International Conflict." *Journal of Social Issues* 39 (1983): 67–86.

Tetlock, Philip E.; Faye Crosby; and Travis L. Crosby. "Political Psychobiography." *Micropolitics* 1 (1981): 191–213.

Thompson, Robert Smith. *The Missiles of October: The Declassified Story of John F. Kennedy and the Cuban Missile Crisis.* New York: Simon & Schuster, 1992.

Thucydides. *History of the Peloponnesian War*. Rpt. ed. New York: Penguin, 1972.

Trachtenberg, Marc. "The Influence of Nuclear Weapons in the Cuban Missile Crisis." *International Security* 10 (summer 1985): 137–63.

Trelford, Donald. "A Walk in the Woods with Gromyko." *London Observer*, April 2, 1989, p. 23.

Trotsky, Leon. *Stalin: An Appraisal of the Man and His Influence*. New York: Harper & Brothers, 1941.

Truman, Harry S. *Memoirs: Years of Trial and Hope*. Vol 2. New York: Doubleday, 1956.

Tucker, Robert C. *The Soviet Political Mind: Stalinism and Post Stalin Change*. Rev. ed. New York: W. W. Norton, 1971.

———. *Stalin as Revolutionary, 1879–1929*. New York: W. W. Norton, 1973.

Tversky, Amos, and Daniel Kahneman. "The Framing of Decisions and the Psychology of Choice." *Science* 211 (January 30, 1981): 453–58.

United States Department of State. Office of Public Affairs. *The Berlin Crisis: A Report on the Moscow Discussions, 1948*. Washington, D.C.: Government Printing Office, 1948.

Valenta, Jiří. "The Bureaucratic Politics Paradigm and the Soviet Invasion of Czechoslovakia." *Political Science Quarterly* 94 (spring 1979): 55–76.

———. *Soviet Intervention in Czechoslovakia, 1968: Anatomy of a Decision*. Baltimore: Johns Hopkins University Press, 1979.

Valenta, Jiří, and William Potter, eds. *Soviet Decisionmaking for National Security*. London: George Allen & Unwin, 1984.

Vertzberger, Yaacov Y. I. "Foreign Policy Decisionmakers as Practical-Intuitive Historians: Applied History and Its Shortcomings." *International Studies Quarterly* 30 (1986): 223–47.

Volkogonov, Dmitri. *Triumf i Tragediia*. Moscow: Novosti, 1989.

Voronov, G. I. "Nemnogo Vospominanii." *Druzhba Narodov* 1 (1989): 192–201.

Waltz, Kenneth N. *Man, the State, and War: A Theoretical Analysis*. New York: Columbia University Press, 1954, 1959.

———. *Theory of International Politics*. Reading, Mass.: Addison-Wesley, 1979.

Welch, David A., ed. *Proceedings of the Cambridge Conference on the Cuban Missile Crisis*. Harvard University. Center for Science and International Affairs. Working Paper no. 89-2, 1989.

———. *Proceedings of the Hawk's Cay Conference on the Cuban Missile Crisis*. Harvard University. Center for Science and International Affairs. Working Paper no. 89-1, 1989.

Whelan, Joseph G. *Soviet Diplomacy and Negotiating Behavior: The Emerging New Context for US Diplomacy*. Boulder, Colo.: Westview, 1983.

Windsor, Philip. *City on Leave: A History of Berlin, 1945–62*. New York: Praeger, 1963.

Wohlstetter, Albert, and Roberta Wohlstetter. *Controlling the Risks in Cuba*. Adelphi Paper no. 17. London: IISS, 1965.

Young, Oran. *The Politics of Force: Bargaining during International Crises*. Princeton: Princeton University Press, 1968.

Index

Library of Congress Cataloging-in-Publication Data

Goldgeier, James M.
　　Leadership style and Soviet foreign policy : Stalin,
Khrushchev, Brezhnev, Gorbachev / James M. Goldgeier.
　　　　p.　　cm. — (Perspectives on security)
　　Includes bibliographical references and index.
　　ISBN 0-8018-4866-0 (alk. paper)
　　　1. Soviet Union—Foreign relations—1945–1991.
　　2. Soviet Union—Politics and government—1945–1991.
　　I. Title.　II. Series.
　　DK266.45.G65　1994
　　327.47—dc20　　　　　　　　　　　　　94-330

DATE DUE